THE FRENCH IN CENTRAL AMERICA

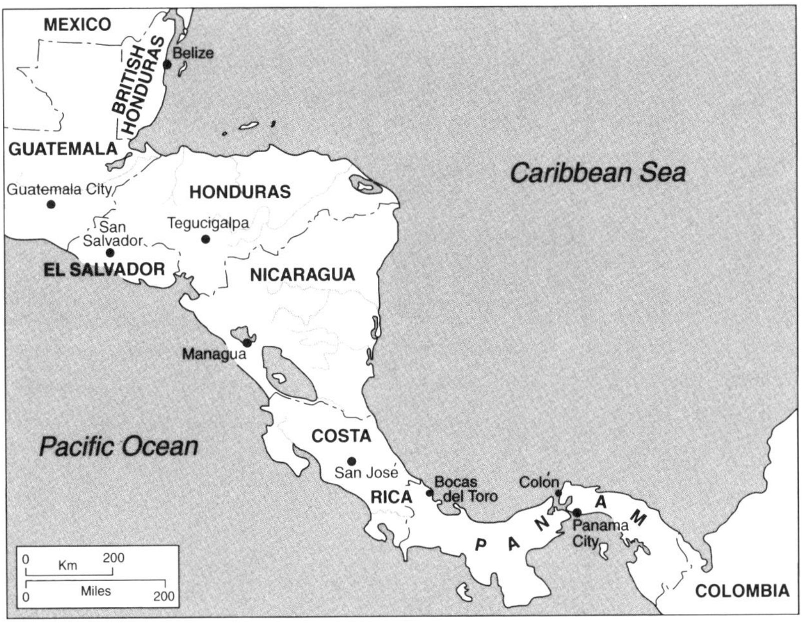

From Lester Langley and Thomas Schoonover, *The Banana Men* (Lexington: University Press of Kentucky, 1994). © 1994 by the University Press of Kentucky. Reprinted by permission of the University Press of Kentucky.

THE FRENCH IN CENTRAL AMERICA

CULTURE AND COMMERCE, 1820-1930

THOMAS D. SCHOONOVER

SR BOOKS

A Scholarly Resources Inc. Imprint
Wilmington, Delaware

First published 2000
Printed and bound in the United States of America

Scholarly Resources Inc.
104 Greenhill Avenue
Wilmington, DE 19805-1897
www.scholarly.com

Library of Congress Cataloging-in-Publication Data

Schoonover, Thomas David, 1936–
The French in Central America : culture and commerce, 1820–1930 / Thomas D. Schoonover
p. cm. — (Latin American silhouettes : studies in history and culture)
Includes bibliographical references (p. –) and index.
ISBN 0-8420-2792-0 (cloth : alk. paper)
1. Central America—Relations—France. 2. France—Relations—Central America. 3. Central America—History—1821–1951. 4. Central America—Commerce—France—History. 5. France—Commerce—Central America—History. I. Title. II. Series: Latin American silhouettes.
F1436.8.F8S37 1999 99-29226
CIP

∞ The paper used in this publication meets the minimum requirements of the American National Standard for permanence of paper for printed library materials, Z39.48, 1984.

Dedicated to the encouragements in my life

Ebba, Paco, Crystal, and Shane

Contents

Preface

This study of French relations with Central America from 1823 to 1930 traces its lineage back to my fascination with the mix of the U.S. Civil War (a liberal war to preserve a unified state), the Mexican liberal *reforma,* and the French Intervention in Mexico (a conservative counterrevolution to unseat liberal power). Maximilian and Napoleon III expected to acquire influence in the isthmian and Caribbean areas as a consequence of their Mexican empire. Their goal was to deny the United States expansion southward while dominating the isthmian transit routes that linked the Atlantic and Pacific half-worlds. The study of liberalism and conservatism in Mexican-U.S.-French relations in the 1860s revealed imperial competitiveness and led me to the examination of imperialism, ideology, and social change in Central America during the age of liberalism (and positivism in Latin America) and industrial revolutions in the north Atlantic.

The study of Central America's relations with the world in the nineteenth and early twentieth centuries has focused upon Britain and the United States and overlooked important relationships between Central America and Germany, Mexico, France, Holland, Spain, Italy, Belgium, Norway, Sweden, Japan, and various South American states, such as in their competitive striving for transit routes, trade, and investment opportunities. A multiplicity of interested states, private enterprises or groups, and later multinational bodies participated in isthmian events and social processes. Whereas bilateral diplomatic relations remain a useful vehicle for sorting out great-power relations with isthmian societies, they need to be supplemented with the role of transnational institutions and organizations to illuminate this complicated history. National history has been an inefficient vehicle for writing the history of the nineteenth and twentieth centuries. Historians need to place national history within an international framework. I hope that this book will encourage traditional historians to reexamine their research designs and suggest the explanatory power of international history to students of French and of Central American history.

The materials for this study were gathered over two decades of work in archives and research centers in France, Spain, both Germanies, the United States, Central America, Mexico, Switzerland, and Austria. The British Foreign Office records on microfilm were also consulted. There was, however, an imbalance in data collection between the isthmian states and the imperial powers. Only in Costa Rican (and rarely in Honduran and Guatemalan) archives could materials be obtained about the decision-making processes of Central American governments approximating those available in metropole states. U.S. and European archives hold records of private individuals, associations, or firms that are seldom available in Central American depositories. I found it as easy to locate private archival material relative to Central American individuals and organizations in the metropole archives as on the isthmus. Unfortunately, earthquakes and fires have destroyed much Nicaraguan and Salvadoran archival material. So many foreign ministry, naval, and other governmental officials, as well as businessmen and travelers who commented on their experiences, interacted with Central American affairs that it was not always possible to identify them or their roles in the region satisfactorily. Perhaps the greatest challenge of this project has been to achieve brevity and yet maintain balance between the monographic nature of the archival research and a desire to analyze Franco-Central American relations broadly within a world context.

During my research, I acquired personal and institutional debts on a scale commensurate with world system theory. Three people have helped continuously over the years—Ebba Schoonover, Ralph Lee Woodward, and Walter LaFeber. Lee Woodward, the 1995 Humanist of the Year in Louisiana, guided an NEH Summer Seminar that I attended, and he has encouraged me to continue in a never-ending task. Walt LaFeber readily volunteered to critique my work over the years. His friendship (and scholarship) assist me to this day. Ebba Schoonover, my wife, has helped me with the research and editorial tasks necessary to convert ideas and outlines into text.

Several colleagues have read one or more chapters of this book and contributed to its improvement. Hoping I have not forgotten anyone, I gratefully and warmly again thank James Dormon, Frédéric Mauro, John O'Connor, William Schneider,

Richard Salisbury, and Mathé Allain. Dormon and Gloria Fiero have encouraged and sustained me as colleagues and dear friends in ways beyond words. Gene Tanke helped me search for a better organized and more explicit way to present my research. The photo of the Torre del Reformador appears thanks to the history department of the Universidad del Valle of Guatemala and Jorge Luján Muñoz. Student aides EkJuana Fruge, Mayra Rodríguez, Ron West, and Shawna Swilley helped with the word processing through several early revisions.

Without the support of the National Endowment for the Humanities, the German Academic Exchange Service (DAAD), the Fritz Thyssen Foundation (Germany), the American Philosophical Society, the Southern Regional Education Board, Tulane University's Mellon Travel grants, and the American Historical Association's Albert Beveridge Fund, the multicultural and multilingual research for these studies would have been inconceivable. I thank my former department head at the University of Louisiana at Lafayette, James Dormon, and Academic Vice President Gary Marotta of the same institution for their confidence in me and support of my research and writing. This manuscript and I benefited from a summer semester as a visiting professor at Cornell in 1990 and a year, 1981–82, as a Fulbright Senior Lecturer at the University of Bielefeld. Colleagues in the history departments at both universities strove to aid my scholarship in a most impressive manner. I am grateful for both experiences.

Abbreviations Used in Notes

AA	Auswärtiges Amt
AAM	Archive de l'armée de la mer, Paris
AAT	Archive de l'armée de la terre, Paris
AGCA	Archivo General de Centro América, Guatemala City
AMAE	Archive du ministère des affaires étrangères, Paris
AMAE, Madrid	Archivo del Ministerio de Asuntos Extranjeros, Madrid
AMEF	Archive du ministère de l'économie et des finances, Paris
AN	Archives nationales, Paris
AN, CR	Archivos Nacionales, Costa Rica, San José
BAM	Bundesarchiv, Merseburg
C.A.	Central America
CCC	Correspondance Commerciale et Consulaire
CD	Consular Despatches
CP	Correspondance Politique
FO	Foreign Office
IHK, Dortmund	Industrie- und Handelskammer, Dortmund
MAE	Ministère des affaires étrangères
MID	Military Intelligence Division
MRE	Ministerio de Relaciones Exteriores
NA	National Archives, Washington, DC
N.S.	New Series
PAAA	Politisches Archiv des Auswärtigen Amts, Bonn
PRO	Public Record Office, London
RG	Record Group

Introduction

As I have grappled with the impact of ideology, industrialization, and an expansive *Weltanschauung* on relations between the United States and Central America, I constantly have been forced to consider the ways in which bilateral exchange has been shaped by the actions of other nations—chiefly the nations of Western Europe. French scholars have produced little of what Braudelians (followers of the modern French historian Fernand Braudel) disparagingly referred to as *histoire événementielle* (history of events, or narrative history) on French involvement on the Central American isthmus and not much more of what they approvingly labeled *histoire totale*, the analysis of structure and change.

This lack of scholarly interest has seemed odd. The leaders of the industrial states commonly understood that bilateral relationships were affected by competitors. They used liberal capitalist tools in the world system to overcome domestic weaknesses. Their need to expand their spheres of activity derived from many pressing problems—large and persistent unemployment, maldistribution of goods and services, the weakening of national prestige and patriotism, the uncertainty of preserving elite and class privileges, the desire for more rapid accumulation of wealth and power, the unreliability of progress under laissez-faire, the restricted national markets, and a lack of safe and productive investment opportunities. Economic malfunction and subsequent frustration and fear drove domestic businesses to organize as corporations and then to try pools, trusts, cartels, and holding companies on the national scene and finally transnational corporations on the international level. The desire of these combinations to dominate business opportunities encouraged political action to assure them access to the world economy. Thus, France and other European metropoles (roughly, centers of expansive industrial production, long-distance trade, and finance and accumulation, but defined more extensively below) claimed access to the commercial and investment opportunities presented by the isthmus. The U.S. government, recognizing that foreign competition would undermine its capacity to use Latin America to ease its own social and economic crises, responded by asserting a privileged position in the New World—the Monroe Doctrine and its corollaries.[1]

This book points to the broad, multistate dimension of international affairs. It was organized under the influence of a world systems approach and on the assumption that theories of social imperialism and dependency are useful tools for analyzing the impact of metropole rivalry upon the domestic and international history of Central America in the nineteenth and twentieth centuries.

World systems theory (which owes much to Fernand Braudel and other Annales historians as well as to the American sociologist Immanuel Wallerstein) describes the relationships among metropole (or core), semiperiphery, and periphery states or areas. A metropole is defined, in part, by its urge to incorporate distant areas into its political economy in order to enlarge the pool of land, labor, and capital from which its entrepreneurs can accumulate value. A metropole not only controls the factors of domestic production and distribution but also acquires the political power and technology to control factors of production—land, labor, and capital—and distribution on the periphery (states that lack control over all or most of the factors of production and distribution) and semiperiphery (states that control one or two, but not all, of the factors of production). A semiperiphery state is both exploited in and an exploiter of the world economy. Metropoles preserved domestic political stability and improved the life-styles and capital accumulation of their entrepreneurial and working classes in part by manipulating the periphery. Moreover, metropoles competed with each other to control the factors of production on the periphery as they strained to obtain hegemony within the world economy.

The world economy, of course, has always been a dynamic, changing system. Since ancient times, producers and distributors have recognized that the exchange of commodities over long distances involved large quantities of goods and generated a large accumulation of value. By raising popular expectations and redefining the notion of well-being, the variety of products received from distant interchange became a motor for economic growth. As European technology introduced mass-produced goods and new products, the need for raw materials and food expanded. Pressure grew to incorporate more areas into Europe's accumulation process—that is, into its production and distribution network. When the statesmen, entrepreneurs, and military leaders of the maritime nations realized that only a narrow strip of land separated the Atlantic and Pacific oceans at Panama, they contemplated a distribution system encompassing the whole world.[2] This interest in world trade routes explains much of the urgency and determination shown by metropole and Central American geopoliticians, entrepreneurs, and intellectuals in the nineteenth and early twentieth centuries.

French involvement in the New World and in the Caribbean region dated from early in the sixteenth century. Between 1504 and the 1820s, France established trading colonies, sugar plantations, and settlements from the Río de la Plata area to Canada. French traders and colonists operated off the coast of Brazil in 1504 and maintained stations there until 1615. The trading relationship was significant, and about five hundred French vessels visited Brazil between 1560 and 1610. In 1624, Rouen merchants established a trading post in what became French Guiana. Two decades later, the town of Cayenne was founded there. But by the seventeenth century, the most important French possessions in the New World were located in the Caribbean. French buccaneers settled in Saint Christophe in 1625. In 1635 the French conquered the islands of Martinique and Guadeloupe, and in 1641, French buccaneers settled on the northwestern shores of Hispañola (later Saint Domingue, then Haiti). In 1664, Louis XIV claimed these settlements for France, giving control of them to the French West Indies Company. France reaped great wealth from the sugar of Martinique, Guadeloupe, and Saint Domingue before Haiti's independence struggle began in 1791. France recognized Haiti's independence in 1824. Indeed, the French language and French commercial ties, military influence, and artistic and cultural influences touched Latin America well before Central America achieved independence. These influences continued, in different forms, throughout the first century of Central American independence.[3]

Nineteenth-century France was a metropole society able to exercise control over the factors of production—land, labor, capital—and distribution in its quest for security and well-being. In the mid-nineteenth century, it pursued social imperialist policies to exploit the transit, market, and investment opportunities in the Central American and Caribbean region. In social imperialism, the metropole ameliorates domestic social woes and preserves its prosperity and national defense through exploitation of opportunities abroad. In essence, social imperialism exported or obscured the problems, burdens, and injustices of a national political economy. The shock waves of the world economic crisis of 1873 to 1898 fueled the nationalism of liberalism and persuaded the leaders in metropole nations to expand through formal colonialism and informal imperialism. France sought preeminent roles for its nation's technology and capital at Suez and Panama. At various times, they targeted the Central American isthmus as a place to relieve domestic unemployment through colonization, as a communications center to facilitate the distribution of French production, and as a desirable location for some surplus investment capital.[4]

By the late nineteenth century, the leaders in France needed to implement social imperialism while simultaneously moderating the internal discord arising from domestic competition during a period of comparatively unrestricted laissez-faire industrial capitalism. The mediating order was organized (or corporate) capitalism, which employed a varied body of economic, political, social, and cultural organizations. Entrepreneurs and politicians established centralized bureaucratic corporate agencies (in the words of historian Robert Wiebe) that sought to preserve the image of a laissez-faire system to justify privatization of profit, yet that also sought to institutionalize cartel or oligapolistic arrangements linking government officials, businessmen, and leaders of labor, social, and cultural movements in cooperative situations. France implemented social imperialism in various ways, but the most common forms were through multinational corporations (for example, Compagnie foncière et agricole de l'Amérique centrale), nonbusiness transnational organizations (International Congress of Americanists), governmental or quasi-governmental agencies (Alliance française), and private social and cultural bodies (francophone or francophile cultural associations and religious orders). The French government provided social overhead capital in the form of diplomatic and consular services, naval forces to maintain order, special commissions, experts, subsidies, and tariff and tax advantages; all of these were indirect aid to firms and other private organizations. And the much lower expectations and standard of living in the periphery allowed organized capitalism to pursue policies abroad with smaller sums.[5]

Social imperialism flourished in an era of intense competition between metropole states. The Central American nations—which had limited resource bases, smaller and less educated populations, and less development of capital, communications, and technology—were made to bear part of the burden of metropole unemployment and social disorder in addition to their own problems. Thus some disorder in Central American societies derived from their ties to the metropole states. Social imperialism was implemented through metropole financial, business, political, and military groups in alliance with members of the bourgeoisie on the periphery—called compradors. Central American compradors had two chief functions: They facilitated the entrance into the region of foreign corporations and political influence, and they managed the domestic order favorably for foreign business enterprises. Whereas the United States, Germany, and Britain established comprador groups chiefly within the political and economic sectors of Central American states, France created compradors in the cultural, educational, and intellectual areas also, in the expectation that cultural leadership would produce economic and political benefits.

Social imperialism frequently brought dependent status to the societies on the periphery. *Dependencia* theory pointed out that metropole development required the underdevelopment of the periphery: If the periphery were ever to become developed, the exploitation and extraction of value would have to cease. After 150 years of "development," Central America is full of signs of metropole presence, but the common standard of living is even further from the norm of the metropole populations than it was in the early nineteenth century. Dependency theory focuses on the international structure as opposed to the bilateral ties of the metropole-periphery relationship. I use social imperialism to explain the goals and policies of specific factions that expected external conduct to relieve domestic political, social, and economic failures within the metropole states, and dependency theory to show the international consequences of metropole intrusions into the states on the isthmus.[6]

Central America's relationship to the North Atlantic nations was tenuous during the colonial era and the first half-century of independence. Central America had a marginal role in the Spanish economy; it exported cocoa, tobacco, gold, silver, hides and skins, indigo, cochineal, and hardwoods, but the total value of these was modest by Spanish trading standards with the New World. And illegal British operations on the Atlantic coast of the isthmus—an area that Spain never controlled effectively during its colonial rule—frequently removed the gold and hardwoods from Central America.[7]

European and North American governments had only limited contact with the isthmian region during both the Spanish colonial years and the era of the Central American Federation (1823 to ca. 1843) because Central America produced little for the world market, and the metropole states had not yet begun serious competition for interoceanic transit. In the early nineteenth century, French merchants and the French navy regularly visited the isthmus. In the mid-nineteenth century, the expanding metropole economies initiated the competition for land, colonization opportunities, and transit rights that blossomed into acquisition and political intervention in the later decades of the nineteenth century. Some foreign penetration was welcome, some was not.[8]

Central America opened up reluctantly to the liberal, industrializing states of the North Atlantic. First, coffee developed into a major export crop in Costa Rica around 1840. Then, between 1847 and 1858, French, U.S., and British entrepreneurs pursued five interoceanic transit projects in Nicaragua and Panama. U.S. entrepreneurs built a railroad in Panama and operated the Accessory Transit Company in Nicaragua. French promoters and geopoliticians were unable either to establish colonies of French or to implement transit concessions in the Chiriquí region of the Panamanian-Costa Rican border or, in a separate scheme, to build a canal in Nicaragua. British investors funded an interoceanic railroad in Honduras. These routes did not satisfy the metropoles, but merely whetted their appetite for more transit routes. Appeals for a canal or a railroad increased over the next half-century. The French initiated a canal project at Panama in 1879; U.S. and British investors undertook transisthmian railroad projects in 1857, 1869, and 1871 in Honduras and Costa Rica; U.S. investors formed two Nicaraguan canal companies; and various schemes proposed transit at the Tehuantepec isthmus. The French Panama canal, the Honduran railroad, and the Nicaraguan canal projects all failed, but the Costa Rican railroad was completed, although it was not extended to the Pacific until the early twentieth century. A railroad was also built across the Tehuantepec isthmus. These projects corresponded with the worldwide surge of metropole activity to use technological developments to incorporate Africa, Asia, and Latin America more effectively into the world system. French geopoliticians expected to connect their Pacific and Caribbean possessions with an isthmian canal to strengthen national well-being and security.[9]

In the 1880s two capital-intensive, export-oriented activities—banana cultivation on plantations and mining (capital and technology having revived this old economic activity)—supplemented coffee production. Coffee, bananas, and minerals formed the heart of Central American export activity until after World War II. Other export products—cotton, forest products, meat, hides, live cattle, and sugar—proved distinctly secondary in producing exchange or attracting foreign capital. The French were major players in Salvadoran coffee but minor participants in bananas, mining, and coffee production elsewhere, and Central American governments increasingly called upon them to supply capital and technology in the late nineteenth and early twentieth centuries.[10]

As social imperialism intensified metropole competition, it also stimulated Central American societies to resist exploitation. And as this resistance grew, the metropoles needed to restrict the sovereignty and increase the dependency of the Central American states. From the beginning, the Central American states tried to create breathing space by playing the metropole powers off against each other. In the early nineteenth century, when the British were pervasive in the region, Central American governments sought aid from France and the United States. Later, when U.S. interests became more aggressive, the Central Americans called upon France, Austria, Prussia, Italy, Mexico, and even Britain to support their resistance. Seduced by the competitive world system and the preponderant power of the industrializing states, Central Americans replaced subsistence agriculture with a plantation, export-oriented crop system in the expectation of material progress, often called development. Only after being incorporated more completely into the world economy did these states discover the severe limitations that had been placed upon their sovereignty, their capacity for self-government, and their ability to feed their own populations. Since disorder in the periphery reduced the ability of the metropole to accumulate wealth, the metropoles cultivated comprador groups that would establish order and allow foreign interests maximum access to the wealth of the Central American societies.[11]

This book describes the relationship between French and Central American societies from the 1820s to 1930. French scholars have usually concerned themselves with inter-European affairs, with the building and preservation of the French empires, and with contemporary U.S.-French (European) relations, particularly since World War II. Moreover, students of France's international relations have slighted the various forms of informal empire, preferring to study French colonialism. Therefore, the small body of writing on French involvement in Central America consists of some theoretical or macro-level conjectures, a few contemporary analyses, a modest amount of narrative or biography of specific events or people, and some broad interpretative observations on Franco-Latin American relations. I recognized that important initial tasks in this study would be to establish the chronology of events; to identify the personalities and structural forces that defined the relations of French society with those of the isthmus; to outline the areas of conflict between metropole and periphery; to sketch the aspects of world capital, labor, or distribution that were evident in French interests on the isthmus; and to compile the statistical series needed to understand foreign penetration of the isthmian states. Some statistical tables on French settlers, businesses, trade, and investment are appended to this volume. The evaluations and reports of diplomats, private entrepreneurs, and publicists—which describe and interpret the events and trends of a specific time—supply the largest body of material we have regarding motive and purpose.[12] Since this volume covers a 110-year period and cites major figures in foreign and domestic affairs for at least eleven countries, I have opted to avoid naming persons who are not major players in the story or significant figures in their own right, although many of these individuals are mentioned by name in the notes. Even after exercising care along this line, I expect several hundred names to appear in the text, more than enough for a small book. A brief evaluation of the principal archival collections precedes a complete listing of printed primary sources and a selective listing of secondary materials. Items cited only once or twice in the notes are not repeated in the bibliography.

My conception of international history requires me to determine how the domestic social, economic, political, cultural, and security concerns of France and the Central American states interacted on the transnational level. And I needed to understand the role of third parties, such as the United States, Britain, and Germany, upon "bilateral" Franco-Central American relations. Paris, Washington, London, and Berlin, as well as Central America are the physical settings for this story because the intrusions of Europeans and North Americans on the isthmus established the parameters of this episode of international history.[13]

Notes

1. Immanuel Wallerstein, *Historical Capitalism* (London, 1983); Immanuel Wallerstein, "The Rise and Future Demise of the World Capitalist System: Concepts for Comparative Analysis," *Comparative Studies in Society and History* 16 (Sept. 1974): 387–415; essays by Nicole Bousquet, James C. Cronin, Albert Bergesen, Cynthia H. Enloe, and Suzanne Jonas and Marlene Dixon in Terence K. Hopkins and Immanuel Wallerstein, eds., *Processes of the World-System* (Beverly Hills, CA, 1980); Christopher Chase-Dunn, "Core-Periphery Relations: The Effects of Core Competition," in Barbara Hockey Kaplan, ed., *Social Change in the Capitalist World Economy* (Beverly Hills, CA, 1977), 159–76; Peter B. Evans, Dietrich Rueschemeyer, and Theda Skocpol, eds., *Bringing the State Back In* (Cambridge, Eng., 1985); Immanuel Wallerstein, *The Politics of the World-Economy* (Cambridge, Eng., 1984); Michael Beaud, *Histoire du capitalisme de 1500 à nos jours* (Paris, 1981); Paul M. Kennedy, *The Rise and Fall of the Great Powers: Economic Change and Military Conflict from 1500 to 2000* (New York, 1987).

2. On the world system or world economy theories of international relations, see Fernand Braudel, *Civilisation matérielle, économie et capitalisme, xve–xviiie siècle* (3 vols.; Paris, 1979), translated as *The Structures of Everyday Life, The Wheels of Commerce*, and *The Perspective of the World* (New York, 1984); Fernand Braudel, *Afterthoughts on Material Civilization and Capitalism* (Baltimore, 1977); Immanuel Wallerstein, *The Modern World System* (3 vols.; Orlando, FL, 1974–1988); Terence K. Hopkins and Immanuel Wallerstein, eds., *World-Systems Analysis: Theory and Methodology* (Beverly Hills, 1982); Theda Skocpol, ed., *Vision and Method in Historical Sociology* (Cambridge, Eng., 1984), esp. chapters 1, 5, 9, 10, and 11; Charles Tilly, *Big Structures, Large Processes, Huge Comparisons* (New York, 1984).

3. "French Colonization in Brazil," "French Guiana," and "French West Indies," *Encyclopedia of Latin American History and Culture*, edited by Barbara Tenenbaum (5 vols.; New York, 1996), 2: 615–17, 620–21; Robert Aldrich, *Greater France: A History of French Overseas Expansion* (New York, 1996), 13–14.

4. Sanford Elwitt, *The Making of the Third Republic: Class and Politics in France, 1868–1884* (Baton Rouge, 1975), 273–314; Thomas McCormick, *China Market: America's Quest for Informal Empire, 1893–1901* (Chicago, 1967), 17–52; Bernard Semmel, *Imperialism and Social Reform, 1885–1914* (Cambridge, Eng., 1960); Hans-Ulrich Wehler, *Der Aufstieg des amerikanischen Imperialismus* (Göttingen, 1974), esp. 7–73. For a critique, see Geoff Eley, "Defining Social Imperialism: Use and Abuse of an Idea," *Social History* 1 (1976): 265–90. While Thomas Richard Shannon, *An Introduction to the World-System Perspective* (Boulder, CO, 1989) is generally sympathetic, he does analyze the theory and is occasionally critical. Two readers focusing upon the Latin American political economy offer alternatives to dependency, world-system, or social-imperialism perspectives. They are Peter F. Klaren and Thomas J. Bossert, eds., *Promises of Development: Theories of Change in Latin America* (Boulder, CO, 1986) and Jonathan Hartlyn and Samuel A. Morley, eds., *Latin American Political Economy: Financial Crisis and Political Change* (Boulder, CO, 1986). Another pair of readers examine theories of imperialism and expansion on a world scale and thus offer a less parochial view: Edward Weisband, ed., *Poverty Amidst Plenty: World Political*

Economy and Distributive Justice (Boulder, CO, 1989), and George T. Crane and Abla Amawi, eds., *The Theoretical Evolution of International Political Economy* (New York, 1991).

5. Rudolph Hilferding, *Finance Capitalism* (New York, 1985); Jean-Charles Asselain, *Histoire économique de la France du xviii*[e] *siècle à nos jours* (2 vols.; Paris, 1984), 1: 152–221; Roger Magraw, *France, 1815–1914: The Bourgeois Century* (New York, 1983), 207–54; Anthony Rowley, *Evolution économique de la France du milieu du xix*[e] *siècle à 1914* (Paris, 1982), 369–433; Jürgen Kocka, "Organisierter Kapitalismus oder staatsmonopolistischer Kapitalismus? Begriffliche Vorbemerkungen," in Heinrich A. Winkler, ed., *Organisierter Kapitalismus: Voraussetzungen und Ansätze* (Göttingen, 1974), 19–35; Samir Amin, Giovanni Arrighi, André Gunder Frank, and Immanuel Wallerstein, *Transforming the Revolution: Social Movements and the World-System* (New York, 1990), 13–52; Wallerstein, *Historical Capitalism*, 39.

6. Fernando H. Cardoso and Enzo Faletto, *Dependency and Development in Latin America* (Berkeley, 1979); André Gunder Frank, *Capitalism and Underdevelopment in Latin America* (New York, 1967); Samir Amin, *Unequal Development* (New York, 1976); James Petras, "Dependency and World System Theory: A Critique and New Directions," *Latin American Perspectives* 30–31 (Summer–Fall 1981): 148–55.

7. Ciro Cardoso and Héctor Pérez Brignoli, *Centro América y la economía occidental (1520–1930)* (San José, CR, 1977), 87–135; Ralph Lee Woodward, Jr., *Central America: A Nation Divided* (2d ed.; New York, 1985), 25–148; Héctor Pérez Brignoli, *Breve historia de Centro América* (Madrid, 1985).

8. Cardoso and Pérez Brignoli, *Centro América y la economía occidental*, 135–79; Ralph Lee Woodward, Jr., "Central America from Independence to c. 1870," in Leslie Bethell, ed., *The Cambridge History of Latin America* (8 vols.; Cambridge, Eng., 1982–93), 3: 471–506; Pérez Brignoli, *Breve historia de Centro América*; Thomas Schoonover, "Germany in Central America, 1820s to 1929: An Overview," *Jahrbuch für Geschichte von Staat, Wirtschaft und Gesellschaft Lateinamerikas* 25 (1988): 33–59; Thomas Schoonover, "Prussia and the Protection of German Transit through Middle America and Trade with the Pacific Basin, 1848–1851," *Jahrbuch für Geschichte von Staat, Wirtschaft und Gesellschaft Lateinamerikas* 22 (1985): 393–422; Thomas Schoonover, "Costa Rican Trade and Navigation Ties with the United States, Germany, and Europe, 1840–1885," *Jahrbuch für Geschichte von Staat, Wirtschaft und Gesellschaft Lateinamerikas* 14 (1977): 269–309.

9. Thomas Schoonover, "Metropole Rivalry in Central America, 1820s to 1929: An Overview," in Ralph Lee Woodward, Jr., ed., *Central America: Historical Perspectives on the Contemporary Crises* (Westport, CT, 1988), 21–46; David McCullough, *The Path between the Seas: The Creation of the Panama Canal, 1870–1914* (New York, 1977), 17–40; James W. Skinner, *France and Panama: The Unknown Years, 1894–1908* (New York, 1989); Charles Stansifer, "E. George Squier and the Honduran Interoceanic Railroad Project," *Hispanic American Historical Review* 46 (Feb. 1966): 1–27.

10. Ciro Cardoso, "Central America: The Liberal Era, c. 1870–1930," in Leslie Bethell, ed., *The Cambridge History of Latin America*, 5: 197–227; Cardoso and Pérez Brignoli, *Centro América y la economía occidental*, 181–320; Walter LaFeber, *Inevitable Revolutions: The United States in Central America* (New York, 1983), 31–39; Pablo González Casanova, *América Latina: historia de medio siglo. 2. Centroamérica, México y el Caribe* (Mexico, 1981).

11. Pablo González Casanova, *Imperialismo y liberación: Una introducción a la historia contemporánea de América Latina* (4th ed.; Mexico, 1983); Woodward, *Central America,* 177–269; Cardoso, "Central America: The Liberal Era," 5: 197–227; E. Bradford Burns, *Progress and Poverty: Latin America in the Nineteenth Century* (Berkeley, 1980), 132–54; Frédéric Mauro, "Tensions and the Transmission of Tensions in the European Expansion to America (1500–1900)," *Plantation Society* 1 (June 1979): 149–59; Ali Mazrui, "From Social Darwinism to Current Theories of Modernization," *World Politics* 21 (Oct. 1968): 69–83; Eric R. Wolf, *Europe and the People without History* (Berkeley, 1982), 3–23, 263–383; Aristides Isaac Gomez de León, "Le Commerce international et le sous-développement de l'Amérique centrale" (Ph.D. diss., 3e cycle, Université Pasteur de Strasbourg, 1978).

12. Pierre Léon, *Economies et sociétés de l'Amérique latine. Essais sur les problèmes du développement à l'époque contemporaine, 1815–1967* (Paris, 1969); Pierre Rénouvin, *Histoire des relations internationales* (reprint; 8 vols.; Paris, 1970); Charles V. Aubrun, *L'Amérique centrale* (Paris, 1968); Guy Lasserre, *Les Amériques du centre* (Paris, 1974); Georges LaFond, *L'Effort français en Amérique latine* (Paris, 1917); Georges LaFond, *La France en Amérique latine* (Paris, 1922); Max Sorre, *Mexique. Amérique centrale* (Paris, 1928); Frédéric Mauro, *L'Amérique espagnole et portugaise de 1920 à nos jours* (Paris, 1975); Jacques Lambert, *Amérique latine: Structures sociales et institutions politiques* (Paris, 1963); Carlos Roses-Alvarado, "Les Echanges commerciaux entre la France et l'Amérique centrale: 1850–1930" (Ph.D. diss., Université de Paris III, 1979).

13. Schoonover, "Metropole Rivalry in Central America"; Thomas Schoonover, "Imperialism in Middle America: United States Competition with Britain, Germany, and France in Middle America, 1820s–1920s," in Rhodri Jeffreys-Jones, ed., *Eagle against Empire: American Opposition to European Imperialism, 1914–1982* (Aix-en-Provence, France, 1983), 41–58; Claude Fohlen, "L'Expérience américaine. Un cas unique?" *Conjoncture économique, structures sociales: Hommage à Ernest Labrousse* (Paris, 1974), 105–17.

1

Early French Interests in Central America, 1820–1848

The social, political, and economic changes in France between 1789 and 1815 were traumatic. This disarray endured until midcentury. After 1815 the domestic economy recovered steadily except in the area of internal communications and transportation, which developed more slowly. French shippers and merchants had been major participants in the commercial life of Central America's Pacific coast ports. However, French merchant and shipping ties deteriorated throughout Latin America after the 1820s. France's weakened domestic economy limited the capacity of its industry and commerce to compete in Central America. Though French ideas, language, and culture were highly valued in Central America, France's slowness in recognizing the independence of the new republics, its small merchant marine, its cautious bankers, its preference for producing luxury goods—and Britain's quickness in obtaining favorable commercial treaties with Latin America and the effectiveness of British consuls—explain the decline in France's trading position in Latin America.[1]

From the mid-eighteenth to the mid-nineteenth centuries, France and the other metropole economies industrialized as they slowly adopted liberalism. Liberal theory held that political economies that did not grow would stagnate, decay, and collapse. This growth hypothesis shaped the *Weltanschauung* of and sharpened the competition between metropole states. French society entered industrial capitalism under laissez-faire shortly after Great Britain, but it adapted less smoothly. Between 1820 and 1850 the French economy was unable to integrate the domestic factors of production—land, labor, and capital—as effectively as Great Britain. In France, goods still moved chiefly by water and cart. French entrepreneurs invested heavily in transportation that served either foreign trade or the smallest domestic communities rather than in railroads to integrate the regions of France more closely or to incorporate the regions of France, such as the Midi, into the world economy. The distribution of prestige, well-being, and security in post-Napoleonic France remained uncertain until after 1848. This instability hindered the capacity of French merchants or capitalists to preserve their commerce and investment abroad, let alone to expand rapidly in the face of the competition from other metropole states.[2]

Data on demographics and capital investment indicate an expanding economy from the end of the Napoleonic period until the ascendency of Napoleon III. The population grew modestly from 1816 to 1846, about 0.55 percent annually, before declining sharply to 0.27 percent for the two decades after 1846. The labor force grew at a steadily decreasing annual number in a pattern that suggested stagnation. Historian François Caron cited the mean annual increases in working-age population as 125,000 in the period from 1816 to 1846, and 80,000 in the period from 1846 to 1871. The leaders of a political economy experiencing such a phenomenon looked for ways to compensate for the weakness. The decline in the workforce was offset in part through doubling the value of industrial investment between 1840 and 1869. But French leaders also looked abroad to employ cheap labor to preserve and expand France's material well-being.[3]

The agricultural sector played a major role in the French economy. Wine and flour were exported in large quantities to Central America. The industrial and financial sectors reduced agriculture's role in France's foreign exchange only in the last decades of the nineteenth century. But from the 1820s to the 1860s, agricultural production grew steadily.[4]

The French economy met the capital needs of domestic firms, banks, and agriculture. Yet French industrial progress and capital accumulation during the nineteenth century was less spectacular than that of Britain, the United States, or Germany. French firms generated as much as 80 percent of the capital they required for expansion through self-financing. French banks financed public borrowing and commerce until 1840 but did not establish industrial and development roles until the 1850s and 1860s. A propensity to invest surplus capital in foreign (mostly European) state bonds created a slowly increasing credit entry (interest payments) in France's international balance sheet. But

French investors and financiers generally shied away from loans outside of Europe until the late nineteenth century.[5]

The empirical data on commerce and colonization for the nineteenth century needs to be read with some caution. Indirect routes, corrupt individuals, and the difficulty of gathering data and keeping records make the figures suggestive rather than precise. The sparse data on French-Central American trade and shipping ties in the 1830s and 1840s suggest that France supplied between 4 and 20 percent of Guatemalan imports and purchased perhaps about 5 percent of Guatemalan exports. In 1836 and 1837, French vessels made up 10 percent of the ships and 19 percent of the tonnage in Corinto, a chief Pacific coast port for Nicaraguan commerce. French shippers supplied 25 percent of the vessels and 11 percent of the tonnage used in Salvadoran commerce in 1846. In the 1840s the French merchant marine supplied about 11 percent of the vessels and 8 percent of the tonnage in Costa Rica's carrying trade.[6] For the early decades of the nineteenth century, the limited data on French residents suggests a moderate to large number of colonists or businessmen in Panama and Guatemala (Table 1).

French migrants entered a Central America where the individual states were physically isolated from each other. The major cities, agricultural areas, and populated regions on the isthmus were poorly interconnected, and movement of people and goods was difficult except by water. The social and political leadership was divided over the best course to pursue. The conservatives, called *serviles* in Central America, wished to keep authority in the hands of traditional isthmian institutions—the creoles, the church, and the landowning classes. In their view, political, economic, and social life required few adjustments. The liberals wanted to open up Central American political life, society, and economy to the educated and advantaged persons of European stock. They wished to reshape isthmian society according to ideas borrowed from the U.S. and French revolutionary experiences and from European liberal thinkers.[7]

Guatemala, El Salvador, Honduras, Nicaragua, and Costa Rica united in the Central American Federation in 1824. Neither the liberals nor the conservatives could govern effectively through the Federation, however. The modest success of the liberals in the 1820s and 1830s was eroded through inexperience in governing, a miscalculation of the power of tradition (especially among the Indian peasants), the failure of many social, economic, and political reforms, and isthmian society's reaction to foreign intrusion into its political economy and culture. Internal division between liberals and conservatives, encouraged by some foreign diplomats and promoters, contributed to the disintegration of the Federation into five sovereign states between 1837 and 1843.

During the Federation, however, authorities were peppered with foreign appeals for concessions. Commonly these requests aimed to develop communications to exploit an area. Successful projects—U.S. and European steamship lines, the Panama railroad, a variety of roads and ports—and a multitude of failed schemes for interoceanic canals, railroads, river clearances, and road construction dot the chronology beginning in the 1820s. Although the majority of such schemes originated with U.S. or European promoters, the Central American elites occasionally appointed agents to attract metropole technology, capital, and entrepreneurial skills to their favored projects. The competition often turned dangerous when an interoceanic scheme appeared a realistic possibility.[8]

After 1823 the Central American societies slowly modified their colonial export production cycles. They continued to produce the products of the Spanish colonial period—cochineal (*grana*) in Guatemala, indigo (*añil*) in El Salvador, minerals, cattle, hides, and hardwoods in Honduras, and cattle and hides in Nicaragua—and added new ones. Costa Rican farmers experimented with coffee trees in the early decades of the nineteenth century and began to export coffee in the late 1830s. Both isthmian liberals and foreign promoters and entrepreneurs urged the development of export products from agriculture and mining.[9] The Central American societies remained agricultural and mineral producers, they merely expanded the list of commodities.

The French government hoped that the Latin American wars for independence would lead to commercial opportunities. However, a lack of agents to protect its interests weakened France's position in the Latin New World. French naval officers, foreign ministry officials, and businessmen inherited a significant presence in Central America, but they regularly complained of France's deteriorating position in trade and shipping. French manufacturers did not adjust well to Central American consumers. For example, the French textile industry, which traditionally produced high quality, luxury products, demonstrated little inclination to learn native preferences or to compete with inexpensive British textiles. Thus the inexpensive Breton linens received an unfortunate reputation for shoddiness that made

French merchants reluctant to offer them in the Latin American markets.[10] These merchants struggled to compete effectively in world commerce.

The French navy played an important role in sustaining French interests, prestige, and status in Latin America. Naval officials suggested that French settlers in Latin America would provide a balance against Britain and the United States and would consume French manufactures. The necessary resources were not always available. A naval commander lamented his inability with only two vessels to protect a national commerce valued at 25 million francs and spread over 1,500 leagues and 20 harbors on the Pacific coast of Latin America. The 1 million francs of trade with Central America did not earn that region a high priority from France, even though the isthmus supported one of the highest per capita consumptions of French exports in the world. The navy could not protect all the areas in Latin America that lacked diplomatic or consular representation.[11] Still, from the 1830s through the 1850s, French naval vessels were the most frequent war vessels in Central American harbors on the Pacific coast.

The French navy was expected to encourage colonists as well as support commercial activity and secure transit rights. In 1827, F. L. Voidet de Beaufort, then living in Guatemala, suggested that French settlers be established near the likely route of the Nicaragua canal. To boost French influence and increase the security of the settlers, he expected local officials to name a few French instructors to train the soldiers charged with maintaining order among the indigenous population. Voidet argued that a colony in Central America could be acquired without expense, while its value would skyrocket when the Nicaragua canal was completed. He anticipated preferential treatment for the colonists because the French and Central American populations were both of the Catholic religion. The minister of the navy and colonies shared Voidet's fears that if France hesitated, Britain would dominate the market and destroy the existing preference for French products. But the minister was less convinced that Voidet's proposal offered the best prospect for achieving France's objectives.[12]

The French government recognized that if it secured a strategically valuable transit point (preferably a canal) on the American continent, the route would benefit France's exchange with the west coast of America and with Polynesia, China, Japan, Java, and India. The inhabitants of the French colonies Martinique and Guadeloupe, one report presumed, would find employment during construction of the canal, and the economy of those two islands would service the trade passing through the canal. France and Europe would gain access to tropical products and would benefit from the investment of European capital in the construction work. This study projected a wide range of benefits to the French empire from an interoceanic canal.[13]

French emigrants, merchants, and officials kept the government alerted to problems in relations with Central America. As early as 1827, an estimated one hundred French residents in Guatemala impatiently awaited a consul who would pursue agreements favorable to France. One French resident, Vinchon de Quémont, argued that the large number of French citizens living in Central America made protection perhaps more necessary in that region than elsewhere in Latin America. He pointed out that Britain, Holland, the United States, Colombia, and Peru had diplomatic agents in Guatemala, whereas France did not despite a trade valued at 600,000 francs and second only to that of the British. In late 1827, Quémont solicited the post of consular agent in Central America.[14]

In the late 1820s, Quémont described commercial and political opportunities for Frenchmen arising from the burdens of competing foreign powers. Although the French suffered from a lack of consular representation, the British, North Americans, and the Dutch all bore the stigma of the Protestant religion, and Spain the passion to reconquer "its" colonies. In early 1829 a French merchant complained when Guatemalan officials removed his goods from a French vessel. An inquiry revealed that the merchant had not paid 300 pesos in taxes and what the merchandise removed was possibly illegal arms. While a consul would not reduce all friction, Quémont argued that French commercial interests required permanent representation. In addition, the French minister in Mexico, A. O. Cochelet, blamed the decline in French commerce on the lack of a consular agent to assure the minimum necessary protection. He appealed for the appointment of a chargé and five vice-consuls, lest important matters of transit and commerce be settled without French participation.[15]

In 1830 the French government charged Cochelet with reporting periodically on Middle America. The minister lamented that France was without a proper representative in Guatemala while the Dutch were negotiating to build a canal in Nicaragua that might favor French vessels because many British East Indies vessels were too large to pass through it. A Dutch group received a canal concession but encountered difficulty in raising capital, and Quémont and Cochelet inquired whether French capital might undertake the project, either alone or in combination with other European countries. Cochelet hoped that the French would not abandon the project to the British.[16]

Initially, Cochelet expected Central America to develop into a fruitful area for French commercial expansion. In late 1831 he argued for a policy that would facilitate French activity there, but several months later he decided that constant internal strife and disorder reduced Central America's market potential and made the construction of a canal unlikely. In the unsettled conditions, French trade with Central America continued to decline.[17]

On July 20, 1832, the French government finally responded to persistent admonitions and named Bernard-Bienvenu de Clairambault vice-consul for Central America with residence in Guatemala. Clairambault, a career consul with prior experience in Alexandria and Tripoli in North Africa, served in Guatemala for twelve years. Near the end of his career, he was made a chevalier de la Légion d'honneur. He found that Central America's favorable geographic position, rich soil, and abundant products could make it an "entrepôt of the two worlds," provided the constant disorder ended. Aware that the British sent a naval vessel to the isthmus every month (normally to Belize and Greytown on the sparsely settled Atlantic coast), Clairambault recommended regular visits from a French vessel. The French government soon decided that one consul could not adequately serve a large and poorly interconnected area. It hoped to halt the deterioration of France's commercial position and influence with vice-consuls at Omoa and Truxillo in Honduras, at Granada in Nicaragua, at San José in Costa Rica, and at Sonsonate in El Salvador.[18]

French officials negotiated a trade treaty with Central America in 1832 to promote the sale of French silks and other products. The Guatemalan government was willing to barter commercial advantages for a loan. Guatemalan diplomat Próspero Herrera linked a 5 million-franc loan to a 5 percent reduction of the duty on French wines and brandies. He argued that Guatemala could become an attractive distribution center where the wealthy from neighboring countries would purchase French wines and alcoholic beverages. Although the French commerce minister viewed the loan with caution, his enthusiasm for the potential trade benefits and for achieving France's geopolitical objectives overcame his reservations. He wrote:

> French commerce should use all practical means to attract the interests of a new state which searches for friendship in Europe and which has already defied Britain because it views the colony of Belize as a menace. [Central America] appears very inclined to establish almost exclusive relations with France. The French firm Dumartray . . . already established in Nicaragua and Costa Rica, has prepared the way for the influence which France seems called upon to exercise in Central America's very alluring and rich future.

The location of the Central American republics between two oceans, he said, could serve "the destiny of our commerce."[19]

Ultimately, Herrera and French officials negotiated a commercial treaty, which disturbed some Guatemalan politicians because it granted France exclusive commercial concessions. The Guatemalan lower house reluctantly voted approval, but the senate rejected the pact. Guatemalan officials contended that because Central American governments received a significant share of their revenue from the tax on aguardiente (an alcoholic drink derived from sugarcane), the privileges conceded French wines and brandies threatened their financial stability. The French foreign minister concluded that Guatemala's failure to ratify the treaty greatly reduced Central America's meaning for France. Clairambault conceded that without the stabilizing influence of a treaty and with continued strife between liberals and *serviles*, it would be difficult to develop profitable relations with Middle America.[20]

Colonel Mercher, a former imperial artillery officer with many friends in the French press, lamented that England, Switzerland, and Germany had built markets for their manufactured goods in Central America while French trade lagged. He charged that the absence of war vessels and the insufficient number of agents had reduced France's influence. He advised sending a war vessel and taking other steps to return French influence to its earlier level.[21] He expected the nation's political economy to benefit from French participation in the development of Central America.

Officials from France and the Central American states noted the need for more effective maritime freight services. In the mid-1830s, Herrera requested that the French government establish regular ship service from Bordeaux to Vera Cruz, with a stop at

Omoa to encourage trade. The French government suggested that such a project needed to be undertaken by a private French shipping line. In 1840 a group of French businessmen solicited approval for ship service between Central America and Marseilles. This proposal moved forward slowly. Others encouraged the French merchant fleet interests. Admiral Ludovic Joseph Alfred de Moges, commanding the French naval forces in the Caribbean and an able spokesman for a dynamic French role in Central America, observed that the British monopoly of mail-steamer service in the Caribbean and Gulf of Mexico aided British domination of regional commerce and generated considerable political influence. A natural response, he insisted, would be the introduction of French mail service to the Antilles. In the mid-1840s a French promoter contracted for a regular mail-steamer service between France and Aspinwall-Colón and the Antilles. Despite initial political success and support from people like Moges, the project failed.[22]

French officials expected the navy to play some role in halting British efforts to dominate the area's commerce. The British seizure of San Juan del Norte and extension of the Miskito kingdom on Nicaragua's Atlantic coast exposed British expansionism. A French diplomat wanted France to offer to arbitrate between Britain and Nicaragua, but a British-inspired anti-French propaganda campaign hindered the effort. Admiral Arnons recommended opening a consulate in Panama to protect French interests from British pretensions. In 1843, Moges proposed combining Martinique and Guadeloupe, the Belgian settlement of Santo Tomás and Río Dulce in Guatemala, and the Franco-Granadian Company to form a solid bloc of French geographic, military, and economic power to resist British encroachment.[23] In the 1840s, French officials perceived the British as the chief challengers to their country's interests.

Moges warned that "only France . . . can stop this unrelenting British acquisition of power." In Guatemala, Consul Albert Huet described the disadvantage of not having a war vessel at hand. In 1842, British vessels had successfully demanded repayment of a loan, but Huet could make no demand on behalf of French creditors because he wished to avoid the embarrassment and loss of prestige that would follow a rebuff by Central American authorities.[24]

French businessmen, officials, and transients did not hesitate to call for French war vessels or landing parties when affairs in Central America threatened their perception of order.

Their views often impressed the French government. Beginning in 1840, its vessels visited Central American waters regularly for a few years. Occasionally, the sparse information about Central American geography inhibited the naval role. For example, the captain of a vessel ordered to contact the consul at Izabal, Guatemala, had no chart that located Izabal. Admiral Moges asserted that the Antilles squadron could not assign one vessel to make the rounds of Central America and Panama unless it was reinforced. However, no extra vessel was forthcoming in the 1840s, although the French squadron in the Pacific visited Central America more regularly.[25]

French officials recognized the need to preserve France's commercial position in Central America. About 1840 the French finance minister supported Oscar de Theil's petition to become a consular agent at Santo Tomás because that port regularly received large numbers of French and Belgian colonists and was visited by some two hundred small merchant ships every year. In 1841, France's minister of foreign affairs sent an economic expert, Léon Lecomte, on a special mission to the Caribbean. Lecomte expected the establishment of transatlantic shipping lines and an interoceanic communications enterprise to be "for the glory of France, for the prosperity of America, and to increase French political, naval, industrial, and commercial influence in Central America." He saw a dynamic stage in the world economy.[26]

In the early 1840s attaché Duflot de Mofías of the French legation in Mexico recognized that many French emigrated from France because the economy there was unable to offer them suitable work opportunities. He planned to utilize these French emigrants to curtail U.S. expansionism in the northern half of the New World. He wanted France to seize the Hawaiian Islands and to purchase the Californian port of de la Bodega prior to acquiring San Francisco, "the key to the Pacific." He expected the resident French and Spanish Catholics in California to attract additional French settlers who would form the basis for a "New French America."[27] His scheme would preserve the economic, political, and cultural force generated by French migrants and prevent the United States from solidifying its position as a Pacific power.

French businessmen recognized the role of metropole competition in resolving geopolitical questions related to uses of the isthmus. "The increasing march of industry in all European states," the Isthmus of Panama Company wrote, "which introduced a feared competition among the established producers, awoke the desire . . . to multiply commercial relations by facilitating access to new markets." When the Guatemalan government announced its readiness to conclude commercial treaties, the French consul suggested that "it might be advantageous for France to be the first to conclude such a treaty." French officials searched for an edge against other metropole or semiperiphery nations.[28]

The competition for transit and commerce flared in the 1840s with treaties (Bidlack Treaty, 1846; Hise-Selva pact, 1847), concessions (two Mexican concessions at Tehuantepec; the Cornelius Vanderbilt transit concession in Nicaragua, 1849), filibustering (Britain protects the Miskito King, 1843, and occupies San Juan del Norte, 1848; several Cuban expeditions, 1849), and wars (Mexican, 1847) dotting the international landscape. In 1841, Moges considered it an appropriate time for France to negotiate a canal concession in Central America, which he believed was of the greatest long-term importance for French commerce. He judged that U.S. industry and technology were not sufficiently advanced to undertake such a project, and he wanted to create a counterweight to British influence in the Gulf of Mexico and the Antilles and to establish a French monopoly of the isthmian canal. He cautioned, however, that Europeans generally overlooked the need to build strategic power to resist the growing strength and involvement of the United States, which intended to capture the commercial riches of the former Spanish areas.[29]

In the early 1840s the Franco-Granadian Company, affiliated with the French commercial house Salomon et Compagnie in New Granada, acquired a concession to build an interoceanic transit route at Panama. In 1843 its privilege was canceled for nonfulfillment of contractual obligations. The French minister in New Granada found no reason to protest. The French minister of foreign affairs, however, concerned with the consequences of the cancellation upon France's commercial role in the world economy, sent a special mission to evaluate interoceanic transit possibilities. Moges stationed a naval vessel on the Caribbean coast to support the special mission's surveying party. The survey located coal sites and found there was local sympathy for France. Although the activity of Salomon and its agent reeked of speculation and illicit dealings, Moges was captivated by the promises of the schemers. He praised the courageous efforts of the Franco-Granadian Company and the Salomon firm and expressed hope that the Salomon project would be pushed toward completion.[30]

French special agent Napoléon Garella was instructed to evaluate all isthmian transit routes, not just the Salomon project. The French minister in New Granada disliked Garella's conduct, but he commended Garella's secretary, J. de Courtines. In late 1844 the Salomon firm hinted that it was ready to initiate work on a railroad and then on a canal, but first it wished to know the position of the French government with regard to its claims against New Granada. The Foreign Ministry offered no support until the firm supplied sufficient information to permit an investigation of its protest against cancellation. A committee of French engineers concluded that Garella's canal was viable if the Great Powers, or a private company, supported it with subventions and guarantees. The minister of public works recommended the study of competitive transit systems, however, and the Nicaraguan government wanted its routes to be examined.[31]

In 1844 the French promoter Adolphe Denain acknowledged that French "trade with Asia was modest," but he contended that it would become considerable within a decade or two. Contrary to the views of most Frenchmen, Denain warned that either a railroad or a canal at Panama would strengthen France's commercial competitors, especially the United States and Britain. He advocated instead cart roads between the isthmian rivers that flowed into the Atlantic and the Pacific. Roads offered a comparative advantage for French commerce. They would tip the scales toward French merchants because their luxury exports could bear expensive land communications better than the cheaper U.S. and British staple products. The French consul in Panama and agents of the French companies interested in constructing either a railroad or a canal there rejected Denain's arguments. Moreover, the consul objected that Denain's proposal exposed the lack of unity among Frenchmen regarding the isthmus. Denain also argued that a canal would not serve Panamanian interests well and might subordinate New Granada's self-government to a foreign power. The diplomat P. de Vallet disagreed. He called for a canal and expressed the hope that France could build it alone if France, Britain, and the United States could not agree to a joint project.[32]

Denain recognized that the major European powers needed to supply funds for the canal project because Latin American capital was inadequate, but he also perceived that cooperation between the Europeans would require an unlikely division of benefits. He was particularly concerned when a British steamship company sent two agents to New Granada to negate the mission of Garella and Courtines. He warned that Britain was waiting for France to join its capital to the ill-considered Franco-Granadian Company transit project and advised that French interests acquire only "a military base and a way station for the region [in the Pacific] which it commands." Short-term, Denain expected a canal would fall under British or U.S. control and, long-term, that the United States, for geopolitical reasons, would dominate any isthmian canal.[33]

Many French Foreign Ministry officials were not convinced that an isthmian canal project was practical. Mofías (and apparently Napoleon III) preferred Nicaragua for an interoceanic canal because its harbors could best support large vessels. He considered Tehuantepec the least desirable location. The Foreign Ministry official E. Guy lamented that the Franco-Granadian Company was encountering much disfavor because its project greatly favored future French commerce in the Pacific. He expected that the company's defeat in the canal project would entail a loss of French influence, prestige, and commerce in Latin America to whoever built the canal.[34]

In 1847, Guy's hopes were revived. He was enthusiastic about the Compagnie de Panama's concession to build a railroad across Panama, which would create significant commercial advantages for French trade on the Pacific coast of South America. The railroad would elevate France's status and influence and thus enable it to compete more effectively with Britain. His optimism soon faded. A year later, he was distressed when private U.S. interests acquired the right to construct a railroad across the isthmus.[35] U.S. entrepreneur William Aspinwall oversaw the construction of the Panama Railroad.

Regardless of who built the transit, French officials studied the possibility of acquiring a naval base to protect French interests in the region of potential interoceanic transit. Captain Comte Louis Henri de Gueydon reported that the Cocos Islands—a small group that lay southwest of Panama and belonged to Costa Rica—had excellent anchorage, offered good opportunities for colonists in lumbering and agriculture, and seemed to have a healthy climate, if very rainy. Moges underscored the need to secure naval stations to aid the fleet's strategic mission and to fulfill the demands of French industry and commerce for new markets. By the mid-1840s the French government's pursuit of commercial and transit opportunities had fostered a modest increase in the number of French merchants on the isthmus.[36]

A French Foreign Ministry memorandum of 1843 warned that a British monopoly of the isthmus threatened to destabilize the balanced access to world commerce with consequent profound geopolitical significance for France. In 1844 the Nicaraguan agent in Paris claimed that Britain "used its war vessels merely as a pretext to resolve in a self-interested manner" matters of transit and commerce. He hoped for French action to stymie English aggressiveness. French diplomat Jean-Marie Raimond Baradère argued that Britain had seized San Juan del Norte and sought naval bases to grasp the lead in world commerce. British interest in the Belgian colony at Santo Tomás and its domination of the Atlantic coast of Nicaragua disturbed the Foreign Ministry, which authorized its consul at Realejo, Nicaragua, to protect French interests.[37]

Metropoles sought to manipulate land, labor, and capital as well as distribution options on the periphery to serve their ends. French agents tried to mold Central American areas to serve the French political economy. Baradère hoped to convert Guatemalan tobacco production from a domestic to an international crop by appealing to the Guatemalan government to remove the national tobacco tax. He also petitioned for permission to export the tobacco grown on the Atlantic coast near Zacapa and Gualan to France. But the government rejected the appeal and his petition. Another French agent, E. Perrin, was convinced that a treaty could develop a market in Honduras for French products and that some of France's unemployed might migrate there. An alliance with France, he proclaimed, would bring stability and riches to Honduras and allow it to escape the fate of becoming a British colony.[38]

As metropole entrepreneurs, colonists, and officials penetrated Central American societies in search of fortune and security, xenophobic reactions multiplied. A Guatemalan decree in 1844 threatened foreign citizens with loss of citizenship or loss of protection for their property. Baradère claimed that most of the thirty French residents were respected traders and that if the Guatemalan government did not protect French residents, he presumed that French high society would demand attention to the complaints of the imperial officer, Colonel Mercher.[39]

The French found Central Americans confused in their understanding of foreign countries and in their conduct toward foreigners. For example, a French agent noted that Central

Americans often called foreigners they disliked "Spanish" (español), a term expressing rejection of the legacy of colonial subjugation. Later, when English conduct had earned an undesirable reputation, many foreigners, including Frenchmen, were labeled "English" (inglés). In 1840 the French consul attempted to correct this popular confusion by proclaiming the preeminence of the French nation as a conveyer of culture, civilization, and Christianity.[40]

Several French naval officers recognized the disadvantages of using force in dealing with the isthmian states. In late 1845 the French government decided to use naval vessels to assist Baradère in collecting debts due Frenchmen. The admiral commanding the fleet objected. "Instead of employing force against these weak states," he warned France that it would be better to "protect them from Britain, which seeks through its colony in Belize and its Mosquito protectorate constantly to expand its territory and its authority at the expense of these states." Later, Gueydon persuaded the Central American countries to liquidate the old Mercher claims (about $100,000, dating back to the late 1820s) through a repayment plan spread over twenty years. He was proud that the French, unlike the British, had not used force against the small isthmian nations and was pleased to observe "how good are the relations which we have established with the Central American states, how large the influence which we have acquired today, and finally how satisfying the results which we have obtained without recourse to force." He expected a considerate policy to create a long-term advantage for French interests.[41]

When a Central American state felt pressure from one metropole government, it frequently sought counterpressure from other metropole states. Thus the French consul in Panama appended statistics on Costa Rican and Nicaraguan trade and an estimate of their commercial potential for the French economy when he forwarded a Costa Rican request for aid to resist British pressure over a loan repayment. Later, Costa Rican diplomat Nazario Toledo solicited French protectorate status in an attempt to salvage his nation's canal rights in a power struggle with Nicaragua. The French government was reluctant, but the Costa Rican government threatened to turn to England or the United States if France refused.[42]

Captain Gueydon recognized that the Central American countries did not really want to become protectorates. They often solicited foreign aid only to preserve their independence when threatened by metropole states. He doubted that many Central Americans would welcome the return of monarchy. If a protectorate appeared necessary to preserve independence, he believed that most Central Americans favored a multinational protectorate because it offered the best chance of preserving sovereignty.[43] In an area of great strategic and economic interest such as the isthmus, the metropoles were unlikely to offer meaningful single guarantees. While the leaders in the metropoles might well dream of such advantages, the guarantees were normally multistate or open for others to join. The metropoles commonly avoided the risk of unnecessary conflict over something of great universal value for all.

In the late 1840s, the struggle for influence in Mexico, Central America, and Colombia became especially acute. British and North American competition on the isthmus threatened to gobble up the available transit opportunities. Most European nations sent agents to prevent any power from acquiring exclusive access to the Pacific basin trading area. In 1850 the British and U.S. governments defined their shared transit rights on the isthmus in the Clayton-Bulwer pact, but it was open for others to join. France contemplated using naval bases, colonies, trade treaties, protectorates, and cultural ties to secure its influence in Central America. Gueydon believed that the small states of Central America, which generally favored France over England, would offer "all of the advantages of a colony without any of the inconveniences."[44]

From the 1820s through the 1840s, when British activity was dynamic, many French politicians, diplomats, businessmen, and military officers lamented the relative decline of French influence and commerce. They sought to persuade their government to reverse the trend. French leaders often claimed that their country's liberal and civilizing reputation would incline Central American leaders to prefer French influence in major transit and commercial projects. In fact, with Central American conservatives often sympathetic to Britain, both France and the United States found the Central American liberal factions to be friendly. The Clayton-Bulwer pact may have eased U.S.-British tensions on the isthmus, but it also stimulated increased activity from the French and Prussian governments in the 1850s. These two states sought to assure that they would not be excluded from this major world transit spot.

Metropole geopolitics linked competition in the world economy with access to the transit routes at Suez and the Central American isthmus. With the widespread assumptions that European industry would continue to expand and that the European markets would not expand fast enough to consume the surplus production, the more industrialized countries looked abroad for markets to "preserve" their domestic growth and create opportunities for investment. On the other side of the Suez and Panama isthmuses loomed the teeming masses and rich resources of South and East Asia, Oceania, and the west coast of two American continents. French officials and businessmen believed that cheap, speedy, and dependable communication routes would allow exchange with these markets, and the future would appear less forbidding. They recognized that for France to retain a competitive position in Europe's balance of power, investment capital and technology had to be placed in Central America to open up the Pacific basin half-world.

Notes

1. François Caron, *An Economic History of Modern France* (New York, 1979), 27–33, 67–74; Jean-Charles Asselain, *Histoire économique de la France* (2 vols.; Paris, 1984), 1: 113–32; André Jardin and André-Jean Tudesq, *La France des notables: 1815–1848* (2 vols.; Paris, 1973); Alfred Cobban, *A History of Modern France* (2 vols.; Harmondsworth, Eng., 1961); J. P. T. Bury, *France, 1814–1940* (New York, 1962); Jacques Houdaille, "Les Français et les afrancesados en Amérique centrale, 1700–1810," *Revista de historia de América* 44 (Dec. 1957): 305–30; Roger Price, *The Modernization of Rural France: Communications Networks and Agricultural Market Structures in Nineteenth Century France* (New York, 1983); Michel Barak, "Intérêts régionaux haute banque parisienne et pouvoir d'état: (à propos d'un projet marseillais de navigation à vapeur transatlantique en 1840)," *Revue historique* 251 (April–June 1974): 331–72; François Crouzet, "Encore la croissance économique française au xixe siècle," *Revue du nord* 54 (July–Sept. 1972): 3–20; Roger Price, *An Economic History of Modern France, 1730–1914* (New York, 1981), 35–37, 131–37; Joaquín Pérez, "El comercio francés en la época de la restauración y el proceso de la independencia americana," *Investigaciones y ensayos* 26 (Jan.–June 1979): 259–69; Iwan Morgan, "French Policy in Spanish America: 1830–1848," *Journal of Latin American Studies* 10 (Nov. 1978): 309–28; Jean Bouvier, "Les Traits majeurs de l'impérialisme français avant 1914," *Le Mouvement social* 86 (1974): 3–24.

2. Caron, *An Economic History of Modern France*, 38–39; Arthur Lewis Dunham, *The Industrial Revolution in France, 1815–1848* (New York, 1955); Cecil O. Smith, Jr., "The Longest Run: Public Engineers and Planning in France," *American Historical Review* 95 (June 1990): 657–80; Rondo E. Cameron, "Economic Growth and Stagnation in France, 1815–1914," *Journal of Modern History* 30 (March 1958): 1–13; Rondo E. Cameron, "Die französische Wirtschaft—Vergangenheit, Gegenwart, Zukunft," in Gilbert Ziebura, ed., *Wirtschaft und Gesellschaft in Frankreich seit 1789* (Cologne,

1975), 149–65; Louis Bergeron, *Les Capitalistes en France (1780–1914)* (Paris, 1978); N. F. R. Crafts, "Economic Growth in France and Britain, 1830–1910: A Review of the Evidence," *Journal of Economic History* 44 (March 1984): 49–67; Tom Kemp, *Historical Patterns of Industrialization* (London, 1971); Jan Marczewski, "Le Produit physique de l'économie française de 1789 à 1913, comparaison avec la Grande Bretagne," *Cahiers de l'Institut de science économique appliquée* 148 (July 1965): vii-cliv; Jan Marczewski, "Some Aspects of the Economic Growth of France, 1660–1958," *Economic Development and Cultural Change* 9 (1961): 369–86; Jean-Pierre Rioux, *La Révolution industrielle, 1780–1880* (Paris, 1971).

3. Caron, *An Economic History of Modern France*, 8–11, 13–21, 38–39, 76, 138; Alfred Sauvy, "Le Revenu des français au xixe siècle," *Population* 20 (May 1965): 517–18. Lévy-Leboyer computed a more favorable annual growth of the working population: from 1800/04 to 1825/29 it was 0.5 percent; from 1825/29 to 1845/49 it was 0.6 percent, in "La Décélération de l'économie française dans la seconde moitié du xixe siècle," *Revue d'histoire économique et sociale* 49 (1971): 485–504.

4. Caron, *An Economic History of Modern France*, 104–15; Adeline Daumard, "L'Évolution des structures sociales en France à l'époque de l'industrialisation (1815–1914)," *Revue historique* 247 (April–June 1972): 325–46.

5. Caron, *An Economic History of Modern France*, 24–25, 78–85; Rondo E. Cameron, *Banking in the Early Stages of Industrialization: A Study in Comparative Economic History* (New York, 1967); Rondo E. Cameron, *France and the Economic Development of Europe, 1800–1914* (Princeton, 1961); Maurice Lévy-Leboyer, *Les Banques européennes et l'industrialisation internationale dans la première moitié du xixe siècle* (Paris, 1964); David Landes, "The Old Bank and the New: The Financial Revolution of the Nineteenth Century," in François Crouzet, W. H. Chaloner, W. M. Stern, eds., *Essays in European Economic History, 1789–1914* (London, 1969), 112–27; William H. Newell, "The Agricultural Revolution in Nineteenth-Century France," *Journal of Economic History* 33 (Dec. 1973): 697–730; Price, *An Economic History of Modern France*, 137–42; J.-J. Carré, P. Dubois, and E. Malinvaud, *French Economic Growth* (Stanford, 1975), 11–15.

6. Thomas Schoonover and Ebba Schoonover, "Statistics for the Understanding of the Foreign Intrusion into Central America from the 1820s to 1930, Part 3," *Revista anuario de estudios centroamericanos* 17:2 (1991): 77–119.

7. Woodward, *Central America*, 92–148; Ralph Lee Woodward, Jr., "Economic Development and Dependency in Nineteenth-Century Guatemala," in Richard Tardanico, ed., *Crises in the Caribbean Basin* (Newbury Park, CA, 1987), 59–78; Ralph Lee Woodward, Jr., *Central America: Historical Perspectives on Revolution and Reaction* (Greenville, NC, 1986); Henri Enjalbert, "Les Capitales de l'Amérique centrale, sites anciens et essor récent," *Caravelle* 3 (1964): 303–19.

8. Cardoso and Pérez Brignoli, *Centro América y la economía occidental*; Schoonover, "Metropole Rivalry in Central America"; Woodward, "Central America from Independence to c. 1870"; Frédéric Mauro, "Conjoncture économique et structure sociale en Amérique latine depuis l'époque coloniale," in *Conjoncture économique, structures sociales: Hommage à Ernest Labrousse* (Paris, 1974), 237–51; Carlos Meléndez Chaverri, "Intereses

extranjeros en Centro América durante la primera mitad del siglo XIX," in *Memoria del primer congreso de historia Centro-América-Panamá* (San José, CR, 1956); Edelberto Torres-Rivas, ed., *Financiamiento extranjero en América Central* (San José, CR, 1974), 15–42; Edelberto Torres-Rivas and Julio César Pinto, *Problemas en la formación del estado nacional en Centroamérica* (San José, CR, 1983).

9. Woodward, "Central America from Independence to c. 1870"; Pérez Brignoli, *Breve historia de Centro América*; Edelberto Torres-Rivas, *Elementos para la caracterización de la estructura agraria en Costa Rica* (San José, CR, 1978).

10. Instruction to Admiral Jacob, March 22, 1821, Marine BB^4 vol. 418, Archives nationales, Paris (hereafter cited as Marine BB^4 418, AN); Jürgen Schneider, *Frankreich und die Unabhängigkeit Spanisch-Amerikas* (2 vols.; Stuttgart, 1981).

11. Cornette de Venancourt, "Projet de colonisation sur la côte des Patagons, Amérique Méridionale," July 4, 1829, Marine BB^4 519, AN; Captain de Camprès to Admiral, Dec. 3, 1830, Marine BB^4 526, AN; Admiral Baron Duperre to Captain Melay, March 2, 1826, Marine BB^4 424, AN.

12. F. L. Voidet de Beaufort to Ministère des affaires étrangères (hereafter cited as MAE), June 20, 1827, Min. marine et colonies to MAE, June 30, 1827, Correspondence politique à 1871, Amérique centrale, tome 1, Archive du ministère des affaires étrangères, Paris (hereafter cited as CP 1871, Amér. cent., v. 1, AMAE).

13. Colonel Mercher, "Avantages politiques, commerciaux, coloniaux, et financiers de la communication océanique par l'isthme de Nicaragua," April 2, 1835, Mémoires et documents, Amér., v. 6f (Panama 5), pp. 30–37, AMAE (copy in F^{12} 6326, AN); Mercher, "Communications de l'Europe avec l'Asie de préférence par l'isthme de Nicaragua à tout autre point du continent américain," Nov. 25, 1834, F^{12} 6326, AN (copy in CP 1871, Amér. cent., v. 8, pp. 252–57, AMAE); Mercher, "Mémoire de M. Mercher sur les républiques américaines," July 4, 1835, BB^7 11, Archive de l' armée de la mer (hereafter cited as AAM).

14. Voidet de Beaufort to MAE, June 20, 1827, Vinchon de Quémont to MAE, Oct. 16, 1827, Jan. 24, Feb. 21, 1828, CP 1871, Amér. cent., v. 1, AMAE; Quémont to MAE, Oct. 16, Dec. 16, 1827, Correspondence consulaire et commerciale, Guatemala, v. 1, AMAE (hereafter cited as CCC, Guat., v. 1, AMAE).

15. Quémont to MAE, Oct. 10, 1828, CP 1871, Amér. cent., v. 1, AMAE; Aquée (?) to Captain Le Coupe, Feb. 19, 1829, Le Coupe to Min. marine, June 4, 1829, Marine, BB^4 515, AN.

16. A. O. Cochelet to MAE, April 16, May 8, 1830, Vinchon de Quémont to MAE, Nov. 18, 1830, CP 1871, Amér. cent., v. 1, AMAE; Cochelet to MAE, June 1830, Feb. 10, Nov. 2, 1831, Quémont to MAE, [May–June, 1831], CCC, Guat., v. 1, AMAE.

17. Cochelet to MAE, Nov. 24, 1831, July 10, 1832, CCC, Guat., v. 1, AMAE; Cochelet to MAE, Jan. 20, Feb. 11, 1832, CP 1871, Amér. cent., v. 2, AMAE.

18. Bernard-Bienvenu de Clairambault to MAE, March 17, Sept. 3, 1833, CCC, Guat., v. 1, AMAE; MAE to Auguste Mahélin, Oct. 31, 1835, Mahélin to MAE, Sept. 30, 1838, May 1839, and other correspondence, pp. 53–78, 356–63 in particular, CCC, San Salv., unnumbered, AMAE; Monique de

Nomazy (AMAE) to author, Feb. 4, 1991, and attachment on Clairambault's career.

19. Próspero Herrera to MAE, Sept. 15, 1832, MAE to Herrera, Nov. 15, 1832, Ministère du commerce et des travaux publics to MAE, Feb. 28, 1833, MAE to Clairambault, April 9, 1833, CP 1871, Amér. cent., v. 2, AMAE; note, n. d. [late 1831], "Observaciones del gobierno sobre el tratado concluido entre los Señores Deffandis y David plenipotenciarios de S. M. el Rey de los Franceses y el Cno. Próspero Herrera por parte de esta República," June 7, 1833, Négociations commerciales, Centre-Amérique, v. 1, AMAE.

20. "Observaciones del gobierno sobre el tratado concluido entre los Señores Deffandis y David y el Cno. Próspero Herrera," June 7, 1833, Négociations commerciales, Centre-Amérique, v. 1, AMAE; Clairambault to MAE, July 18, 1833; MAE to Clairambault, May 29, 1834, CCC, Guat., v. 1, AMAE.

21. Mercher, "Avantages politiques, commerciaux, coloniaux, et financiers de la communication océanique par l'isthme de Nicaragua," April 2, 1835, Mémoires et documents, Amér., v. 6f (Panama 5), pp. 30–37, AMAE; Mercher, "Communications de l'Europe avec l'Asie de préférence par l'isthme de Nicaragua à tout autre point du continent américain," Nov. 25, 1834, F^{12} 6326, AN; Mercher, "Mémoire de M. Mercher sur les républiques américaines," July 4, 1835, BB^7 11, AAM.

22. See correspondence between Herrera and MAE, CCC, San Salv., unnumbered, pp. 1–6, AMAE; Barak, "Intérêts régionaux: Un projet marseillais de navigation à vapeur transatlantique en 1840," Affaires divers commerciales, carton 135, Paquebots et services postaux, Nouvelle Grenade, 1842–1846, AMAE; Admiral Ludovic Joseph Alfred de Moges to Min. marine, Sept. 29, 1841, Marine BB^4 609, AN.

23. "Etat politique du Centre Amérique, Juillet et Août, 1841," Admiral Arnons to Min. marine, Dec. 12, 1841, Marine BB^4 609, AN; Moges to Min. marine, Aug. 21, 1843, CP 1871, Amér. cent., v. 6, AMAE; Adolphe Denain, *Considérations sur les intérêts politiques et commerciaux qui se rattachent à l'isthme de Panama et aux différents isthmes de l'Amérique centrale; relation directe de ces isthmes avec celui de Suez* (Paris, 1845), 18–21, 66–69, 190–99, 211; F. Jacquemont to MAE, July 1, 1844, CCC, Pan., v. 1, AMAE; Nicolas Leysbeth, *Historique de la colonisation Belge à Santo Tomás de Guatemala* (Bruxelles, 1938).

24. Moges to Min. marine, Aug. 21, 1843, CP 1871, Amér. cent., v. 6 (copy in v. 6 bis) AMAE; Huet to MAE, June 7, 1842, CCC, Guat., v. 1, AMAE.

25. Captain Le Nouvel to Min. marine, Aug. 30, 1840, MAE to Min. marine, Aug. 30, Sept. 30, 1840, Min. marine to MAE, June 19, 1841, CP 1871, Amér. cent., v. 3, AMAE; Arnons to Min. marine, Dec. 15, 1840, Marine BB^4 601, AN; Moges to Min. marine, April 10, June 25, Oct. 24, Dec. 7, 1842, Marine, BB^4 613, AN; Moges to Min. marine, Oct. 12, 1843, Marine BB^4 619, AN.

26. Petition of Oscar de Theil, [ca. 1840], exp. Guat., dossier 3, Berryer Papiers, 223 AP 15, AN; MAE to Léon Lecomte, Dec. 15, 1841, Min. marine to MAE, Dec. 11, 1841, Mémoires et documents, Amér., v. 47, AMAE; William J. Griffith, *Empires in the Wilderness: Foreign Colonization and Development in Guatemala, 1834–1844* (Chapel Hill, 1965).

27. Duflot de Mofías, "Mémoire sur l'Oregon ou territoire du Río Columbia en litige entre l'Angleterre et les Etats-Unis, considérations sur l'Amérique, Russe, Résumé des mémoires précedents et coup d'oeil général sur l'avenir des provinces de l'Amérique situées au nord de l'equateur sur l'océan pacifique," [1843?], Mémoires et documents Amér., v. 44, AMAE; René Gonnard, *L'Emigration européenne au xix*[e] *siècle* (Paris, 1906).

28. Albert Huet to MAE, Nov. 28, 1843, CCC, Guat., v. 1, AMAE; Compagnie de l'isthme de Panama, *Jonction des deux océans chemin de fer. Canal maritime* (Paris, [1844]), 2.

29. Moges to Min. marine, Sept. 29, 1841, Marine BB[4] 609, AN; Léon Lecomte, "Mémoire sur la navigation transatlantique," March 26, 1841, Mémoires et documents, Amér., v. 47, AMAE; Moges to Guizot, May 15, 1842, Mémoires et documents, Amér., v. 4, AMAE.

30. C. de Liet to MAE, Nov. 20, 1843, MAE to Napoléon Garella, Jan. 29, 1844, MAE to Min. marine, Feb. 20, 1844, Jacquemont to MAE, March 5, July 9, 1844, "Note sur une demande de M. M. Salomon," Dec. 9, 1844, Mémoires et documents, Amér., v. 4, AMAE; Omar Jaen Suárez, "La presencia francesa en Panamá durante el siglo XIX," *Lotería* 330–31 (Sept.–Oct. 1983): 175–76; Moges to Min. marine, April 17, 1844, Marine BB[4] 628, AN; Michel Chevalier, "L'Isthme de Panama; l'isthme de Suez," *Revue des deux mondes* 14 (Jan. 1, 1844): 5–74.

31. Liet to MAE, Nov. 20, 1843, MAE to Garella, Jan. 29, 1844, MAE to Min. marine, Feb. 20, 1844, Jacquemont to MAE, March 5, July 9, 1844, "Note sur une demande de M. M. Salomon," Dec. 9, 1844, Mémoires et documents, Amér., v. 4, AMAE; Jaen Suárez, "La presencia francesa en Panamá durante el siglo XIX," 175–76; Min. travaux publics to MAE, Dec. 17, 1845, Mémoires et documents, Amér., v. 48, AMAE; Philadelphia Benavent to MAE, Nov. 7, 1846, MAE to Benavent, March 20, 1847, CP 1871, Amér. cent., v. 6 bis, AMAE.

32. Moges to Min. marine, Aug. 21, 1843, CP 1871, Amér. cent., v. 6; Denain, *Considérations sur . . . l'isthme de Panama*, 18–21, 66–69, 190–99, 211; Jacquemont to MAE, July 1, 1844, CCC, Pan., v. 1, AMAE; P. de Vallet to Guizot, Oct. 17, 1845, Mémoires et documents, Amér., v. 48, AMAE; Adolphe Denain, *Ensayo sobre los intereses políticos y comerciales del istmo de Panamá considerándoles bajo el punto de vista de la Nueva Grenada* (Panama, 1844); Joachim Kühn, "Napoleon III. und der Nikaraguakanal," *Historische Zeitschrift* 208 (1969): 296–306.

33. Denain, *Considérations sur . . . l'isthme de Panama*, esp. 18–21, 66–69, 190–99, 210; Vallet to Guizot, Feb. 22, 1845, Mémoires et documents, Amér., v. 48, AMAE; Morgan, "French Policy in Spanish America, 1830–1848," 309–13.

34. Duflot de Mofías "Mémoires sur l'état politique et commercial du Méxique et sur la communication de l'océan Atlantique avec l'Amérique du Sud à travers l'isthme de Tehuantepec," [1840–1843], Mémoires et documents, Amér., v. 44, AMAE; E. Guy to Guizot, Dec. 17, 1847, Mémoires et documents, Amér., v. 48, AMAE.

35. Guy to MAE, Aug. 10, 1847, April 5, 1848, CCC, Pan., v. 1, AMAE.

36. Commander Louis Henri de Gueydon to Admiral Ferdinand Alphonse Hamelin, Nov. 1, 1846, Marine BB[4] 1023, AN; Moges to Min. marine, April 10, June 25, Oct. 24, Dec. 7, 1842, Marine BB[4] 613, AN; Moges

to Min. marine, Oct. 12, 1843, Marine BB[4] 619, AN; Baradère to MAE, May 26, 1845, Perrin to MAE, Oct. 1, 1845, CCC, Guat., v. 2, AMAE.

37. Baradère to MAE, July 29, 1844, Feb. 26, March 31, 1845, MAE to Perrin, April 27, 1845, MAE to Baradère, Nov. 25, 1845, CCC, Guat., v. 2, AMAE; J. Hartmann Liebach, "Notes sur le commerce d'exportations," March 8, 1843, Affaires divers commerciales, carton 670, Missions divers, Mémoires de particuliers, AMAE; Francisco Castellón to king of France, Jan. 26, 1844, CP 1871, Amér. cent., v. 6 bis, AMAE.

38. Baradère to Ministerio de Relaciones Exteriores (hereafter cited as MRE), July 14, 1845, Feb. 7, April 6, 18, May 9, 29, 1846, B99-5-6/4315/93220, MRE, Archivo General de Centro América (hereafter cited as AGCA); Perrin to MAE, Sept. 15, 1845, CP 1871, Amér., cent., v. 6 bis, AMAE.

39. Baradère to MAE, Feb. 20, March 30, 1844, CP 1871, Amér. cent., v. 4, AMAE (copy in CCC, Guat., v. 2, AMAE).

40. Auguste to MAE, Feb. 6, 1840, CP 1871, Amér. cent., v. 3, AMAE.

41. Hamelin to Min. marine, July 10, 1846, CP 1871, Amér. cent., v. 5, AMAE; Gueydon to Baradère, March 5, 26, 1848, BB[4] 1597, AAM (copies in CP 1871, Amér. cent., v. 7, AMAE).

42. Guy to MAE, Dec. 15, 1847, Mémoires et documents, Amér., v. 48, AMAE; Baradère to MAE, Jan. 3, 1848, CP 1871, Amér. cent., v. 7, AMAE.

43. Gueydon to Min. marine, April 3, 1848, CP 1871, Amér. cent., v. 7, AMAE (copy in Marine BB[4] 663, AN).

44. Gueydon to Admiral Le Goarant de Tromelin, April 29, 1848, BB[4] 1596, AAM; Edward W. Richards "Louis Napoleon and Central America," *Journal of Modern History* 34 (June 1962): 178–884; Schoonover, "Imperialism in Middle America."

2

Napoleon III's New Empire

Colonies, Trade, and Military Bases, 1848–1871

The competition on the isthmus between the United States and Great Britain focused the attention of all maritime states on control of transit routes from Tehuantepec to Panama. As the gateway to commerce in the vast Pacific area, the Central American isthmus attracted heightened interest in the Second Empire. With long-term prestige, security, markets, and investment opportunities in the balance, not only the British, French, and North Americans, but also Prussia, the Hansa cities, Belgium, Holland, Spain, and Savoy (Italy) sent agents to prevent any one power from dominating access to the Pacific basin. The French government pursued naval bases, access for colonists, trade, and protectorates. It encouraged cultural ties that would mature into friendly relationships and subsequent diplomatic negotiations to establish political and military security.[1] Leaders throughout Europe recognized that a canal had become a necessity for expanding world commerce.

After the coups of 1848 established inner stability in France, Napoleon III's government sought to reconstruct the French empire in order to regain international prestige and to increase the nation's access to raw materials, markets, and investment opportunities. The agricultural sector contributed to stabilization of the French economy by growing at approximately 1.1 percent annually, from about 1820 to the mid-1870s. However, French society underwent demographic and economic downturns after the mid-nineteenth century. The annual population growth rate declined from a feeble 0.27 percent during the years 1846 to 1866 to 0.19 percent in the 1866 to 1886 period. The domestic labor force grew, but at a steadily decreasing annual number. François Caron estimated the mean annual increase in working-age population to be 100,000 in the period from 1846 to 1866, and then 70,000 yearly until 1886. He calculated that the working population only grew from 16,240,000 in 1852 to 17,430,000 in 1882. Confronted by a stagnating labor force, the leaders of the French political economy looked for alternative means to rectify the maladjustment. Since liberal ideology considered growth fundamental for a healthy society, some searched abroad for means to expand the economy.[2]

The impact of the decline in working population upon production was offset in part through investment, which just about doubled between 1840 and 1844 and 1865 and 1869. Only a few French banks, especially the Crédit Mobilier, a large merchant bank founded in 1852 and favored by Napoleon III, and the Banque de Paris et des Pays-Bas, established industrial and developmental roles in the 1850s and 1860s. They supplied capital for railroad construction and for domestic and foreign state loans. While considerable French accumulation was absorbed in self-financing of entrepreneurial expansion, foreign investment remained a possibility whenever the domestic economy could not readily employ more capital. The expansionist undertakings of Napoleon III's government and a modest deceleration in the domestic economy in the 1860s gradually nudged French investors toward foreign investment. Whereas foreign investment produced about 6 million francs of repatriated income in 1848, by the early 1870s foreign bondholders received an annual income of about 640 million francs.[3]

Nineteenth-century commercial data requires careful interpretation because indirect trade, smuggling, bribery of customs officials, and imprecise bookkeeping affected the figures. While all trading partners may have shared imprecise record keeping, other factors probably differed. Cultural values probably affected the propensity to smuggle or bribe or to prosecute smuggling or bribery, and the state of a nation's merchant marine influenced its indirect trade. The figures for French trade with Central America are misleading because they do not take into account the indirect trade through Belize, Greytown, the Bay Islands, the Hansa cities, or London.

Statistical data on French inhabitants and firms in Central America from 1848 to 1871 reflected the French role in colonization and commerce (Tables 1 and 5). Early in this period, Panama and Costa Rica hosted the largest numbers of French residents, probably due to Gabriel Lafond's colonization project. The French firms on the isthmus were most likely commercial establishments.[4] No statistical data on French investment in Central America in the mid-nineteenth century was located.

France retained a major commercial role in the world. In 1860 its exports represented 60 percent of continental Europe's exports, 16.5 percent of the exports of the industrialized countries, and 12.8 percent of the world's exports. The French commercial role declined thereafter. French exports to Central America followed an erratic course in the 1850s and the early 1860s (Tables 2 and 4). In the late 1860s, French exports to the isthmus increased regularly for seven years, then stabilized until a rapid decline began in the mid-1880s. French imports of Central American products achieved a temporary high level in the late 1850s, then rose and fell erratically until the late 1870s. French trade also suffered because merchants tried to dump inferior products into the Central American market. Thus, French minister Julien Tallien de Cabarrus acknowledged that the Guatemalans preferred common Spanish wines and spirits to the inferior French products being offered them. However, specific French industries—iron, cotton, and woolens—produced on a scale and with an efficiency to penetrate foreign markets.[5]

On average in the 1850s and 1860s, France purchased 3 percent of Guatemalan exports and supplied 15 percent of Guatemalan imports. Costa Rica exported 23 percent of its products to France, but purchased only about 6 percent of its imports there. French vessels supplied between 2 and 4 percent of the vessels and 4 or 5 percent of the tonnage in Guatemalan, Salvadoran, Costa Rican, and Nicaraguan trade.[6]

In the period of political turmoil and the early stages of the development of domestic and international communications, the Central American societies continued to trade largely in the products of the Spanish colonial period. In the 1850s and 1860s, the production of cochineal and indigo in other parts of the world and the development of artificial dyes in Germany undermined the Guatemalan and Salvadoran economies. The landowners in both societies found escape routes. They studied Costa Rica's coffee production and initiated coffee planting. And when the U.S. Civil War disrupted the exportation of Southern cotton, both benefited from the boom in world cotton prices. In fact, all of Central America expanded cotton production in the 1860s.[7]

From 1823 to about 1843, the major objectives of isthmian liberals and metropole promoters were the development of products for world trade, the improvement of roads, harbors, and rivers, and the construction of an interoceanic canal to serve world commerce. The continental powers, as Belgian consul Martial Cloquet maintained, all wanted to preserve the opportunity to enter the isthmian economies, and the metropole entrepreneurs competed for developmental projects in the mid-nineteenth century.[8]

The most intense contest involved British and U.S. diplomatic and military maneuvers to dominate transit routes in the period from 1846 to 1850. Agents from both sides tried to secure a position that assured their country of geopolitical domination of the chief transit options. The two governments accepted a compromise in the [John] Clayton-[Henry] Bulwer Treaty of 1850, which denied either nation control of a Central American canal. This agreement allowed other commercial powers to join the guarantees. This compromise did not, however, establish lasting tranquility on the isthmus. Disgruntled Southerners—who found the expansion of slavery hampered by climate and free soil politics—engaged in filibustering in the late 1840s and 1850s in Cuba, Mexico, and Central America in an effort to obtain new plantation land. The León liberal faction, in conflict with the Grenada conservatives, called the most infamous of these filibusterers, William Walker, to Nicaragua in 1854. Walker and his small band of about fifty-five men grew in numbers and soon displaced the Nicaraguan leaders. Walker became president of Nicaragua in 1856. A coalition of Central American armies (with the assistance of the British and French navies and Cornelius Vanderbilt) defeated Walker's force in 1857, but he returned three more times until captured and executed in Honduras in late 1860.

French chargé Charles Alexandre de Challeye reported in mid-1848 that El Salvador, Nicaragua, and Costa Rica had turned to France for protection against a possible British invasion and U.S. expansionist activity. He found a counterpart to imperial competition in Central American domestic politics; the conservatives favored Britain and the liberals inclined toward France. In late 1848 he warned that if France, rooted in the Roman tradition and Catholicism, did not build "a dam" in Middle America against "the Anglo-Saxon race and the Protestant nations," the United States would "extend the stars and stripes over the two Americas." He argued that well-considered plans for opposing U.S. and British penetration would enhance France's prospects in Central America. In mid-1849 the French government responded to Anglo-American diplomatic moves regarding transit routes in part by authorizing unpaid consular agents for each Central American state.[9]

Despite Challeye's analysis of metropole competition, his hasty and ill-considered actions opened doors for the expansion of U.S. and British influence. In 1848 and 1849, he entangled himself in two ill-tempered disputes with the Guatemalan government. After the *Gaceta oficial de Guatemala* reprinted articles from European newspapers expressing sentiments that he considered insulting to the French Republic, he organized a protest meeting of French residents. The meeting demanded that the *Gaceta* publish a response in French with a Spanish translation. When the Guatemalan government denied responsibility for the reprinted articles, Challeye lowered the French flag, demanded his passport, observed that the French Republic would defend its flag and honor, and left for El Salvador. He returned several months later, after the Guatemalan legislature had expressed its best wishes to the French Republic and the government had fired a 21-gun salute to the French flag. A year and a half later, however, a French diplomat again complained bitterly about reprinted articles critical of France.[10] The favorable view of many Guatemalan leaders toward French civilization declined in the late 1840s.

After his return, Challeye entered into another dispute with the Guatemalan government. He issued passports and identification papers to people he considered to be Spanish subjects. He distrusted the Guatemalan government and wished to protect fellow Europeans, even offering asylum in the French legation to some alleged Spaniards. When Guatemalan officials confiscated the passports and identity papers that he had issued to these individuals, he protested vigorously that they were being fined and burdened because they were accepting his protection. In March 1849, Challeye demanded that all funds collected from people whom he claimed were under his protection be turned over to him within twenty-four hours or that his passport be returned to him. The Guatemalan government pointed out that he had protected many who were not Spanish at all but Guatemalans, and that, in any event, he had no right to extend protection to whomever he saw fit. Challeye again departed after declaring that France would defend its flag, agents, and protectees. This rupture was resolved a year later. The French government conceded that many whom Challeye had tried to protect were indeed Guatemalans. After the embarrassment of

Challeye's ill-considered activities, the diplomat Alfred de Valois described the French role in Guatemala as "a scandalous nullity." Unless France adopted a firm policy in Central America, Valois saw little need for representation there.[11]

The issue of granting asylum to Spanish citizens revealed metropole competition for status and prestige. British chargé Frederick Chatfield was jealous that the Spanish had not turned to him for protection. He bragged, according to a Spanish observer, that "if the Spanish had come to me instead of turning to Challeye, they would not have had to suffer." Guatemala had rejected the French decision to grant asylum, the Spaniard claimed, because it was convinced that France had neither the will nor the power to protect Spanish citizens. The clash between a proud Guatemalan government and assertive French officials over matters of form and prestige and the protection of alleged Spanish subjects troubled Franco-Guatemalan relations for most of the 1850s.[12]

Beginning in the 1820s, but increasingly after the mid-nineteenth century, France struggled for hegemony as a dynamic core power seeking to maximize its role in the world economy (or to maximize its limits under the hegemon—Britain in the nineteenth century and the United States in the twentieth century—within the world economy). The transfer of British hegemony to the United States was hinted at already when the British retreated politically in this peripheral area in the 1850 Clayton-Bulwer Treaty, although they retained a transit role vital to world leadership.Various French interest groups expressed concern over the possible impact on French trade of British and U.S. negotiations for privileged access to Central American transit. The Bordeaux Chamber of Commerce, for example, expected the government to intervene in the negotiations. But French diplomats and businessmen in Central America complained that they received little support from their government. In fact, the home bureaucracy and budget limited the role of French diplomats in shaping the isthmian states. Valois found France's role in Central America exasperating because "with our hands in our pockets, we watch the English and the Americans act and maneuver freely." The inaction especially disheartened him because Guatemala constantly signaled for French protection. Rebuilding France's reputation, he said, would require naval vessels, firm demands regarding reclamations, and an agent with authority to act. French power was presented so feebly that Guatemalans retained little respect for France.[13]

Valois recommended using Belgium—closely linked to France—as a surrogate to block British and U.S. ambitions. When Guatemala considered borrowing a million pesos from England, he countered with a consortium including Belgium, England, and France. But Belgian consul Cloquet was not receptive to cooperation with France. He ridiculed the fickle French, who had sent a parade of agents through Central America while the British had needed only one agent in fifteen years. He observed that French affairs in Guatemala had deteriorated to the point that only small businesses remained in French hands. Chargé Dagobert Fourcade, however, satirized the role of the German and Belgian agents in Guatemala, "who occupy themselves drinking their glass of beer and smoking their pipe." French and Belgian agents were not ready for cooperation.[14]

French agents interpreted the conduct of other participants on the isthmus. Despite France's good relations with the United States, Challeye pondered whether "the civilized world would allow with impunity the American Union to establish its colossal empire over half of the globe." He urged France to seize the Guatemalan port of Santo Tomás as a base to counter British incursions on the Miskito Coast and as part of a program to meet the Yankee challenge—the other parts being regular visits of French vessels to Central American ports and encouragement of French immigration. Fourcade thought that Santo Tomás would offer excellent opportunities for French commerce. Prussian special envoy Franz Hugo Hesse, however, also looked covetously on the disorganized settlement at Santo Tomás, which had become a point of contention between the Belgian originators and the settlers, who were largely German Protestants. French officials paid close attention to this contest to manage Santo Tomás because they perceived a special bond with Belgium and frequently opposed Prussian objectives.[15]

In 1854 the Belgian minister in France, Baron de Behr, opened talks with Guatemalan minister Andrés Santa Cruz regarding colonization of Santo Tomás. The Belgian government wanted to revive the old colonization company, but Foreign Minister Pedro Aycinena of Guatemala was adamant that Guatemala would not revive the onerous contracts or company of the 1830s and 1840s. He complained that previous schemes were often converted into "stock market action without profit for the countries which offered the colonization places." The U.S. government tried to enter the talks about Santo Tomás, but Santa Cruz advised that "the energy with which the Yankees tried to invade us from all sides, makes it necessary to defend ourselves with all means." He expressed the hope that Guatemala would work with Europe to hinder U.S. ambition. Even when the negotiations died, he continued to labor privately to attract colonists, but not from the United States.[16]

After the two Anglo-Saxon states negotiated the Clayton-Bulwer pact, naval captain Cosnier urged the French government to consider some appropriate action to protect important French interests in Central America. In 1850 the U.S. government inquired whether France would join it and Britain in treaties with Nicaragua and New Granada guaranteeing transit routes. If France had reservations about negotiating with these small states, the U.S. government proposed a bilateral treaty to guarantee the transit routes. Cosnier urged French participation because U.S. influence on the west coast of the New World would stagnate after the California gold rush. France should profit from this U.S. loss of status. Meanwhile, he lamented, France's reputation had declined so markedly that many isthmian inhabitants could not even name the French resident diplomat.[17]

During the 1850s, French officials supported the visions of promoter Gabriel Lafond du Lurcy for colonization and transit rights in the Dulce Gulf area at the border of Costa Rica and Panama, and the schemes of the journalist and speculator Félix Belly for acquiring transit rights in Nicaragua. Both men proclaimed the utility of their projects for France's aspirations in the world. Lafond flattered Napoleon III by appealing to the emperor's writings on the role of Central America in building a way to Asia and advancing world trade. In 1846, Napoleon III, son of Louis Bonaparte and the nephew of Napoleon Bonaparte, published a pamphlet, "Canal of Nicaragua, or, a Project to Connect the Atlantic and Pacific by Means of a Canal," while in prison following a second attempt to overthrow the Orléans monarchy. Later, after his rise to emperor of France, Napoleon III retained a deep interest in an isthmian canal and a revived Caribbean empire. In 1850 the French foreign minister assured Lafond, then serving as Costa Rica's consul-general in France, that he would receive assistance "to the limit of international law" for developing his Dulce Gulf concession, which held great promise for French commerce in Middle America. Costa Rica also encouraged Lafond. When the Crimean War made transfers of French funds, colonists, and materials impossible, Costa Rican president Juan Rafael Mora extended Lafond's concession for three additional years.[18]

Gabriel Lafond had been a ship captain, a world traveler, and the director of the assurance company L'Union des Ports before he arrived in Central America. His first trip went to Chiriquí Lagoon on the Panamanian-Costa Rican border in 1851. For more than a decade, he pursued a project to colonize the Chiriquí isthmus and to construct ports and interoceanic transit at that spot. During the 1850s and 1860s, he served both France and Costa Rica in consular and diplomatic posts and wrote several books and articles in praise of the project and the Chiriquí region. Despite Lafond's best efforts, this colonization and transit project made little headway.[19]

Even with a time extension, Lafond's project moved forward slowly. Early in 1852, Costa Rican diplomat Felipe Molina reported that Lafond and his associates were eager to sell their concession for $250,000. When a buyer did not materialize, Lafond renewed the search for support for his colonization scheme. His project received widespread approval in governmental and entrepreneurial circles. In 1855 the Paris prefect of police failed to persuade the French government to send two hundred families from Paris—mostly unemployed citizens—to Lafond's strategically and commercially valuable site. Senator la Barrière and Admiral Alphonse Pellion proclaimed the commercial value of the local coal deposits; Captain Colombel described the site's capacity to absorb Europe's unfortunate population; and civil engineer J. de Courtines envisioned an excellent railroad route within the concession. Lafond advertised the Dulce Gulf as destined to become the entrepôt for the marketing of French products in "California, Polynesia, Australia, Malaysia, China and India."[20] Despite this support, only enough funds materialized to transport a few hundred French colonists to the Dulce Gulf.

In the first years after Napoleon III came to power, officials studied Central American prospects for French merchants, shipping firms, and transit developers. Despite the hopes and schemes of many, statistical evidence shows a weakened trade relationship between the two regions. French ships participated modestly in Central America's trade. The naval commander on the west coast of South America hoped that the economic opportunities at the major Central American harbors—Puntarenas, Realejo, Acajutla, Istapa, Amapala—would attract French shippers. French firms still "enjoyed a good reputation and conducted a commerce of some value" in Nicaragua, Guatemala, and El Salvador. Commonly, French officials advocated Panama and Fonseca Bay as key points in revitalizing French commerce on the isthmus.[21]

Astute leaders in a periphery society could use the national resources—labor, land, and location—to bargain for improved conditions for themselves. The Costa Rican government confronted difficulties in getting its coffee crop to Europe, so it offered to reduce tariffs on French wines and paper carried around Cape Horn in order to attract more French ships. In return it also expected to receive tariff concessions for its coffee and natural products. In the mid-1850s the French purchased about one-fourth of Costa Rican coffee exports. The French commerce minister saw some benefit in the Costa Rican offer for French navigation and in the importation of easily marketable products, but he feared that other nations would request similar advantages. Although Costa Rica was a trading partner of only secondary importance, the French minister underscored its location near transit routes. Costa Rican diplomat Victor Herrán emphasized Costa Rica's potential as a conduit for French trade with the west coast of America, with Oceania, and with Asia.[22] French officials did not respond to the offer of reduced tariffs at this time.

The French government struggled to secure economic advantages for French businessmen in Central America without alienating the region's small states. El Salvador was already a significant market for French commerce, and Costa Rica and Nicaragua were becoming better markets. A French naval officer thought that "wise policies would guide [Central America's] preference for France into material advantages for our commerce and industry," and he claimed that France had captured the sympathy of the isthmian population. Improved commercial relations fostered tariff talks. During tariff discussions in 1857 and 1858, Guatemalan officials argued that they needed tariff policies that better aided Guatemala's development and preserved more of its national wealth. They charged that the French duty on cochineal meant that France benefited from Guatemalan production. French agents proposed to reduce cochineal duties in return for lower tariffs on French liqueurs and on French textiles so that they might better compete with British and Belgian textiles.[23]

Metropole powers commonly used honorary, cultural, and political awards to gain special privileges. A war of honors raged in 1852 and 1853, possibly to acquire influence in the aftermath of the Clayton-Bulwer pact. In 1852, Hesse urged the Prussian government to award medals to key Central American officials who could adopt policies favorable to Prussian interests. Charles Mévil, a Frenchman serving as Nicaragua's consul general in France, sought to negate the Prussian initiative by proposing French honors for Nicaraguan minister José de Marcoleta, Nicaraguan president Francisco Castellón, and several other Nicaraguan officials who had served French interests.[24] The metropole and peripheral states recognized a tie between social status and the control of land, labor, and political authority.

Napoleon III encouraged the idea of a shared Latin culture—language, religion, classical knowledge, and things rooted in the Roman past—to strengthen the appeal of France at the expense of the British and the North Americans. Some Frenchmen dissented, arguing that French commercial ties with the United States were too important and those with Central America too minor to risk alienating the United States. Others responded that alternatives to U.S. wheat and cotton were readily available in Russia, Egypt, South Asia, or South America. Latin Americans who accepted the idea of a fundamental cultural conflict between the Latin and Anglo-American races presumed that they had to look to France for aid.[25]

The Nicaraguan government, lacking the force to resist any determined metropole power, encouraged suspicion among the metropoles. In 1852, Nicaraguan officials believed that both England and the United States threatened their national sovereignty. The Nicaraguan president inquired whether France was disposed to protect Nicaragua if it solicited aid. French chargé Léonce Angrand offered to forward an official request. Simultaneously, the Nicaraguan agent in Paris sought assurance of Napoleon III's support in the face of the persistent British claim to the Mosquito coast.[26]

In 1855 the Nicaraguan government decided that U.S. expansionism had again become such an imminent danger that it had to turn to the French and other European governments for protection. The French consuls interpreted various isthmian events as disguised plans for U.S. control of the interoceanic transit routes. Even before William Walker's filibustering invasion in 1854, they suspected U.S. ties to "liberal" factions that destabilized local governments. The seriousness of U.S. interest in Central America became evident in early 1855 when U.S. diplomats publicly spoke of their fears of European intervention in New World affairs. French agent Alexandre Mellinet interpreted the warnings as an effort to lure the Central American states under U.S. influence. Nicaragua's consul general in Paris solicited assistance because the success of the U.S. filibusterers William Walker, Henry L. Kinney, and Joseph W. Fabens would be fatal for European commerce.[27]

The Nicaraguan government offered France an advantageous commercial treaty if it would guarantee Nicaraguan territorial integrity, either alone or in concert with Britain. Moreover, the Nicaraguans agreed to consider French capital for a canal because U.S. entrepreneurs had falsely indicated that they would construct one immediately. Nicaragua would grant favorable transit concessions, Félix Belly insisted, if Europe could ensure its independence. The Nicaraguan government sought assurances from Europe, but to cover all possibilities, it negotiated to make the country a sort of U.S. protectorate. If the Nicaraguan officials could not obtain commitments from European nations, they would have to come to terms with the U.S. government.[28]

Félix Belly played a significant role in Nicaraguan canal politics in the late 1850s. His determination probably resulted from his personal struggle for achievement. He had lost his father when he was three and matured as much through experience as through formal education. In the mid-1830s, while in his early twenties, he entered journalism. He edited several journals in the 1840s and 1850s, and his work attracted the attention of some powerful figures, including Napoleon III. In 1855 he was awarded the only political decoration the French government granted that year, but he began to have doubts about Napoleon III's rule. He knew of the emperor's interest in the isthmus, and that the Suez project had drawn the attention of world commerce, so Belly studied about Central America and persuaded a few bankers and investors and the French government to support his efforts to obtain a canal concession in Nicaragua. For several years, the idea of a Nicaraguan canal commanded most of Belly's attention and energy.[29]

If French interests obtained a canal concession, activity near the canal route needed reevaluation. The French minister of foreign affairs was intrigued to learn that a French citizen, Augustin Myionet, had obtained a concession from Nicaragua to build a hospice and colony near the transit route. The minister sought the advice of the minister of the navy because Myionet could not undertake his project—which would be in opposition to the Clayton-Bulwer pact—without French protection. The minister of the navy was cautious about placing French colonists in Nicaragua because he saw no threat to French influence from the

Clayton-Bulwer pact, which was expressly open to the adherence of France. Furthermore, the French government would receive no compensation for its expenditures on Myionet's private project. He acknowledged that previously the government had aided similar proposals, such as Lafond's project, but in those the government would eventually become the proprietor of the colony. The naval minister worried that such colonies frequently created onerous complications.[30]

Some Europeans believed that the U.S. government used the Crimean War to divert attention from its expansion into Middle America. Belly charged that the U.S. government intentionally exaggerated the allegations of British recruiting on U.S. soil for the Crimean War and of British misconduct under the Clayton-Bulwer pact. It was hypocritical of the U.S. government to complain of alleged British recruitment on U.S. soil as a violation of U.S. neutrality, he observed, while its own citizens were selling arms to Russia and while it was allowing men, materials, and funds to be raised for filibustering in Central America and the Caribbean. In his view, U.S. society distorted values and ideals during the campaign to absorb much of Latin America.[31]

During the Crimean War, the French were prepared to increase their cooperation with the British government against U.S. expansionism. Knowing this, Costa Rica's chargé requested that France join British naval forces in protecting San Juan del Norte from U.S. filibusterers. He also appealed to the emperor to guarantee Costa Rican nationality and that the French influence would remain in his country. The French government considered the Walker invasion to be a threat to French commerce. In 1856, fearing that Walker's "navy" might attack the coffee ships, Britain and France cooperated in sending vessels to Puntarenas when the coffee was leaving Costa Rica.[32]

Facing the continuing threat of U.S. filibusterers, Costa Rica sought some formal guarantee of support from Europe. Since the isthmian population "hates and fears" the North Americans, a French naval officer claimed that British or French protection would be welcome. In Europe, Adolphe Marie, a longtime resident of Costa Rica and professor of French at the University of Costa Rica, emphasized the dangers to European commerce from U.S. domination of the transit routes. In 1856 the diplomats Juan de Francisco in London and José de Marcoleta in Paris proposed that the British, French, Spanish, and U.S. governments jointly guarantee the independence of Central American states. However, the U.S. government offered to share the guarantee of the transit area, which did not require that the Central American states remain sovereign and independent, with all European states. This gesture undermined the desperate Central American appeals for a patron among the major European powers. The British politely notified the French of their decision not to participate. And the other European powers, while acknowledging the threat that Walker posed to their interests, were not convinced that the U.S. government represented a similar danger.[33]

The Guatemalan government also looked to Europe for protection in the belief that Walker's military success threatened Central American independence and represented an attempt to destroy European influence in the region. Foreign Minister Pedro de Aycinena, a conservative protector of Catholicism and Hispanic culture, asked what steps the British, French, and Spanish governments would take to prevent the Central American states from losing their nationality to the United States. Aycinena, unwilling to rely upon the European diplomats in Guatemala, authorized his agents in Europe to negotiate a convention with France, Britain, and Spain, in which those powers would agree to act justly and generously toward Guatemalan independence and liberty. He presumed that balance-of-power considerations would stimulate French interests because the U.S. government was seeking to dominate both Nicaragua and Panama. He thought that the isthmian societies would be better off in French hands.[34]

In mid-1856, French Foreign Ministry official Adolphe Deshorties expected the U.S. government to use the leverage it had acquired from filibustering to push Britain and the other European powers out of the way. He believed that the European powers could stymie U.S. expansion if they cooperated. One area of potential cooperation was transit. In 1857, Belly, who was alleged to be an agent of either the French government or the large investment firm Crédit Mobilier, argued that French (and European) commercial expansion and security goals required an isthmian canal. He contended that U.S. entrepreneurs had abandoned the project because they were satisfied with the Panama Railroad and that the existence of the railroad at Panama, and the plans for one at Tehuantepec, supported his claim that canals were not feasible at those sites. Finally, if the U.S. government proved ill willed and its citizens again resorted to filibustering, Belly warned that Europe would have to defend Nicaragua and the world canal.[35]

The prospect of great wealth inherent in a canal created tension among the Central American states and thus complicated their relations with the great powers. Only a last-minute agreement at Rivas had kept Nicaragua and Costa Rica from going to war because both states had granted concessions for transit on the San Juan route. Napoleon III's government wished to prevent any such conflict. To undermine U.S. private and governmental proposals aimed at securing dominance of isthmian transit, Napoleon III encouraged Central American alliances under European protection. And he used covert agents to pursue ostensibly private transit concessions. When their competing concessions had threatened to get in the way, Belly persuaded the Nicaraguan and Costa Rican governments to sign the Rivas agreement, which guaranteed Nicaraguan sovereignty over the canal route, while insuring Costa Rican participation in the transit. He sought British and French support for the Rivas Convention and for a concession for a canal along the San Juan River route. The convention and the concession safeguarded world interests during the period when Walker and the U.S. government endangered stability and interoceanic transit on the isthmus.[36] Most isthmian leaders wanted a share of the largesse from a canal. The key concern for many Frenchmen was to obtain assurances of access to any isthmian transit.

Napoleon III's government considered U.S. expansionism the major challenge to the revival of a French empire based upon linking the French colonies and enterprises in the Atlantic and Pacific basins. France needed to divide the Anglo-Saxons. Its dilemma was in having to choose between its traditional enemy, Great Britain, and the rising U.S. nation. In the New World, U.S. expansion clearly posed the largest problem. A French Foreign Ministry study found that the British were bearing the primary burden of defending European interests against U.S. influence. It suggested that "France, with latent interests susceptible to development, was only free to associate itself in that battle to the measure convenient to its moral interest."[37] Not surprisingly, Napoleon III's government drifted toward more cordial relations with Britain and more antagonistic relations with the United States in Central America.

In Belly's operations in Nicaragua and Costa Rica, the U.S. government sensed French opposition to its policy. Belly conspicuously questioned U.S. interests and created the impression that he was a French agent. His scheming convinced the discontented Nicaraguan government to scuttle the unratified U.S.-

Nicaraguan pact of 1857 because it could deal with the French who would make fewer demands. His canal agreement with President Tomás Martínez, however, was rejected because Washington threatened to "immediately and vigorously demand the payment of the indemnities due to its citizens for all the damages which they have suffered in Nicaragua as a consequence of the civil wars and of the filibuster invasion." The French Foreign Ministry found the obstacles to Belly's Nicaraguan canal project to be serious but surmountable.[38]

Foreign Minister Alexander Florian Walewski assured the U.S. government that France had no official relationship with Belly. But Secretary of State Lewis Cass complained that U.S. steamers were being seized and agreements annulled due to Belly's malign influence. Belly's interests in transit did not concern the United States, Cass maintained, as long as they did not interfere with vested U.S. interests. His ominous remark that previous actions "strongly inclined" the United States to suspect that justice would be obtainable only "by the employment of force" was meant for the French and Nicaraguan governments.[39]

The use of force was, however, one significant factor disturbing the isthmus. The presidents of Costa Rica and Nicaragua, Mora and Martínez, jointly appealed to Napoleon III to put an end to the massacres and vandalism of filibusterers "protected by the United States." They tempted the French government with a canal concession, but France wished to avoid confronting U.S. ambition alone. In late 1858, Costa Rican officials proposed cooperating with Britain and France to limit U.S. power in Central America. The French government sounded out the British government regarding cooperation with Costa Rica. A French diplomat in London advised reaching an agreement with Britain before responding to the Mora-Martínez appeal for protection. The British, however, proposed waiting to see if the U.S. Senate actually approved the 1857 U.S.-Nicaraguan pact. As a precaution and as preparation, a French special agent visited the isthmus to remove hindrances to a Franco-Nicaraguan understanding.[40]

The renewal of Walker's filibustering brought the Costa Rican, British, and French governments into cooperation again. The French consul in Central America repeatedly asked Gueydon to intervene against a second Walker invasion. Without specific instructions, however, Gueydon hesitated because the U.S. government appeared to be protecting Walker. Costa Rican consul-general Gabriel Lafond wanted a French vessel assigned to the

Pacific coast to prevent "brigandage" and other outrages by Walker's navy. In October 1858 the British government notified the French government that it would welcome cooperation against Walker's second incursion. The British cabinet authorized royal naval units to defend the coasts from filibusterers if either the Costa Rican or Nicaraguan government formally requested assistance. The French government decided to cooperate. The French chargé in Central America, René-Louis-Marie-Adolphe de Botmilian, reported that in response to the joint British-French naval cooperation, "the [Central American] fears of Walker have naturally disappeared."[41]

In 1859, Walker reentered Central America for the third time. The French naval commander was again ordered to cooperate with the British and to respond to written requests for protection from a Central American government. Since France maintained no consular agents on the west coast of Central America, its naval officers had to turn to British agents for information. These officers used this situation to appeal for a stronger French presence on the isthmus. They argued that the Belly enterprise and other French interests required consuls on the west coast because the British, who were so dependent upon Southern cotton, might not always resist U.S. policy in Central America. In 1861, French officials argued that a successful scientific expedition to the isthmus would promote French commerce, civilization, and influence at the expense of the United States.[42]

The French government wished to place protection of the isthmus under a broader European guarantee. In early 1860, Nicaragua and France negotiated a guarantee for Nicaragua. Before final approval of the pact, France solicited similar guarantees from Austria, Prussia, Russia, Spain, Holland, and Denmark. Their responses were disappointing. Austria agreed to take the matter under consideration; Prussia rejected such a treaty at that time. No country indicated enthusiasm for it.[43] Without European partners, France left the treaty unperfected.

Botmilian was pessimistic about the possibility of developing strong French interests in Central America because local tariffs hindered the importation of wines and other French products. The French commerce minister advocated negotiations with Guatemala and Honduras to rectify the problem of commercial exchange. The Guatemalan government, he observed, "had finally begun to understand how important it was for Central America to strengthen its ties with Europe, if it did not want to see itself exposed again to invasion from filibusterers from the United States." Aycinena really wanted a guarantee of the territorial integrity of Central America based upon its importance as a link between the two oceans. A guarantee might not produce closer political or commercial ties, however. The weaknesses of the Central American societies in the face of U.S. expansion inhibited close links with France.[44]

The Panama transit attracted French strategic concern when several popular disturbances got out of hand in the late 1850s. A riot in Panama in April 1856, commonly called the Watermelon Riot, was directed chiefly against U.S. citizens and particularly passengers on the railroad. New Granada feared that the U.S. response might endanger its sovereignty, so it proposed a joint U.S.-French guarantee of the railroad. Commander Coupvent-Desbois of the French navy did not encourage that course, having concluded that the United States would absorb Panama regardless of European opposition. He had noticed, for example, that French agents had reasonable influence in Panama except when competing with U.S. agents. Later, French officials protested the landing of U.S. forces during an uprising in Panama because they "feared that once settled in the city this force would never reembark." A French naval commander claimed that the Panamanians wanted independence under French or British protection.[45] New Granadan officials probably expected French support because various French entrepreneurs and engineers had speculated in isthmian transit.

French entrepreneurs on the isthmus were engaged in agricultural export production, mining activity, and silk and real estate businesses. French planters helped lead the way when El Salvador copied Costa Rica's success with coffee. And in 1858 the large investment firm Crédit Mobilier operated several of the best and oldest silver mines of El Salvador. In 1860 the firm's superintendent of mines in El Salvador and Honduras inquired whether the Panama Railroad Steamship Company would reduce its rates if he expanded mining operations to produce 1,500 to 1,800 tons of silver ore concentrate for shipment per year. Captain John M. Dow of the Pacific Mail Steamship Company favored this offer, but the company's decision is unclear. In late 1861 the French Foreign Ministry supported an agreement with the Guatemalan government to allow Maison Arles-Dufour to open a "silk-culture" business in Guatemala. French diplomat F. L. Hardy aided Arles-Dufour, but warned of the high risk even with government support. In another instance, the navy aided a private speculator who wanted to deal in land on the Miskito Coast. In fact, French officials facilitated a variety of business ventures.[46]

French enterprises faced more than the activity of the newcomer, the United States, or of the established British. French officials also feared the detrimental impact on French commerce of the German merchant community on the isthmus. By the early 1860s German merchants in Panama offered stiff competition for French importers, and in 1861 the French naval commander reported that the normally large role of French commerce in Costa Rica had become insignificant when compared to British and German activity.[47] In the 1860s, German trade on the isthmus became more active while French commerce deteriorated.

French policies to encourage trade and industry, along with the Anglo-French Commercial Treaty of 1860, fostered business concentration and increased production. French import trade with Central America expanded noticeably from 1855 until 1859, but it returned to pre-1850 levels when the Lafond and Belly colonization projects faded in the early 1860s (see Tables 2 and 3). The Central American states imported European goods —especially from Britain, France, and Germany—because those countries purchased Central American staple crops. The French foreign minister expected statistics "to enlighten our commerce to the new relationships which it could secure in foreign countries."[48]

The ventures of Lafond, Belly, and Archduke Maximilian in Mexico were related to Napoleon III's plan to emphasize a shared "Latin" heritage while building Franco-Latin American ties to hinder U.S. expansion. French geopolitical interests in interoceanic transit and in a broad policy to halt Anglo-Saxon penetration of the Central American-Caribbean region were also at stake in the question of whether to reinforce the French naval squadron in the Antilles and near Mexico. Although Napoleon III's intervention in Mexico was intended to block U.S. expansion, U.S. policy statements revealed that Yankee expansionism was not being held back even by the Civil War. As a countermeasure, Napoleon III's government contacted the Guatemalan government about reorganizing the faltering old Belgian Santo Tomás Company with French capital and colonists. A Franco-Belgian company could make the excellent harbor of Santo Tomás a powerful military point in the Caribbean. A French writer praised Napoleon III's vision of the maximum advantage for French interests on the isthmus and in Asia. The French government encouraged the use of economic and military resources, colonization, and cultural tools to achieve its objectives.[49]

In the 1860s, Central American officials and French promoters and entrepreneurs proposed colonization projects that involved strategic sites and the production of agricultural export crops. The Salvadoran minister failed to secure official French involvement in a scheme to colonize some fertile and healthful land near strategic Fonseca Bay. Neither a projected colony near Santa Tecla, El Salvador, nor Belgian businessman Edward Pougin's project to send six thousand emigrants per year to a site in Costa Rica attracted sufficient support for implementation. In 1866, Captain Imbert appealed in vain for Napoleon III's support of a colonization project near a proposed canal route in Nicaragua. Many of the Central American elite welcomed foreign colonization providing that the location and activity of the colonists suited their own plans for development.[50]

Intrusive metropole projects to dominate a Latin American society usually disturbed all isthmian political factions. The Central American societies, with the exception of Guatemala, were generally not sympathetic to Napoleon III's support for Archduke Maximilian's assumption of the throne in Mexico; the isthmian liberals were opposed, and many conservatives were neutral. Although the Guatemalan government offered modest support for Napoleon III's venture, most Guatemalan liberals and some conservatives organized opposition. *La Revista*—published in New York City, subsidized by the Guatemalan government, and secretly edited by Guatemala's minister in the United States—reported favorably on French activity in Mexico. The Guatemalan government nurtured friendly relations with the Franco-Austrian interventionists because it expected their victory to bring security to its northern border. Since Guatemala continued to claim sovereignty over Chiapas and Soconusco—border areas occupied by Mexican forces in the 1820s—it saw a sign of goodwill in Maximilian's decree announcing that Mexico's southern border would be settled by treaty once the domestic situation became stable. Not all French officials interpreted Central American reaction to Mexico as favorable for French interests. The diplomat Charles de Saulce de Freycinet claimed that the Mexican expedition made France replace the United States as the chief interventionist state.[51]

French officials were often brutally frank when they reported isthmian reaction to Napoleon III's Mexican venture. The chargé reported that Costa Rica, El Salvador, and Nicaragua were passionately opposed to monarchy and feared the loss of national independence to a prince operating under foreign direction. French minister Cabarrus maintained that the Central American population refused to acknowledge any advantages in annexation to Mexico.[52]

After the French military seized Mexico City, it was rumored that agents of Maximilian and Napoleon III were engaged in confidential negotiations with the Guatemalan government. Apprehensive of a new foreign intervention, the Nicaraguan, Salvadoran, and Honduran governments proposed reestablishing a Central American union. Costa Rica hesitated to join, but it was apparently supportive. Salvadoran president Gerardo Barrios, who had resided for a considerable time in France, directed the opposition to the French. Guatemala, however, opposed any union in which Barrios might play an important role. French residents welcomed Guatemala's victory over Barrios in 1863 because the Salvadoran had openly sought a union to oppose French policy. However, even from his exile in the United States, Barrios urged Central American union as a means of defending the region against monarchical objectives.

The British government believed that a union movement could succeed if France, Spain, and Britain were to support it. But France rejected any effort to pressure Guatemala into participating in a Central American union. The French, and probably the Spanish, envisioned halting Anglo-Saxon expansion in the region. Napoleon III's government appealed to shared Latin culture rather than to political union to preserve its influence in Central American societies.[53] The British, however, probably viewed the union movement as a means to frustrate Napoleon III's imperial scheme.

In late 1863 respect for France suddenly surged in Central America. The French image brightened after the success of French forces in Mexico and the emergence of a friendly government in El Salvador. One threat to French influence was the possible return to power of the deposed Salvadoran president Barrios. In mid-1864, Cabarrus reported that all the states except Costa Rica had adopted conservative principles, so that French influence remained preponderant.[54]

Napoleon III's government, to prevent Anglo-Saxon power from spreading south of the Rio Grande, considered various schemes for building interoceanic transit on the isthmus. One involved the formation of a Franco-British firm, the Compagnie

Internationale pour l'Exécution du Canal Maritime de Nicaragua, with the Comte de France (the Count of France, a close relative of Napoleon III) on its board of directors and Gabriel Lafond as its publicist. Lafond listed an impressive group of French and British politicians, businessmen, and naval personnel as "collaborators." The company wanted a French war vessel to visit San Juan del Norte to lend prestige to the project and to bring the Légion d'honneur for President Martínez and decorations for seven other Nicaraguans. Napoleon III's cabinet balked at this request. The government had often used medals to reward those who helped it achieve its diplomatic objectives, but it feared that the French medals would lose their value if they were distributed to support a profit-oriented business. And sending a war vessel could provoke a new U.S. invasion since the company's project would appear to be under French protection.[55]

In the mid-1860s the Frenchman Gustave de Belot, director of the Salvadoran Mint, predicted that U.S. expansionism "could no longer menace [Central America] after the success of the Mexican expedition." He advocated a large French migration to Central America to extract the maximum profit from French influence. He also welcomed the opportunities for French entrepreneurs in the Honduran Interoceanic Railroad project. The railroad intended to exit in Fonseca Bay, which lay alongside one of the major "routes of world commerce" and commanded the Pacific. A French steamer line linked to the Honduran Railroad would allow French products to enter the isthmus directly. Belot considered the Panamanian route a fantasy and the Nicaraguan route unpromising because of U.S. interference. French activity would be especially welcome, Belot said, because all Latin Americans were conscious of their Latin heritage and considered the French character more pleasing than the Anglo-Saxon. He noted, "Whoever opens a new market for his country is a pacific conqueror," linking Central America to French commerce.[56] Belot expected the Honduran Railroad to serve the strategic and commercial interests of France in Central America and the Pacific.

French officials differed on the impact that U.S. control of transit would have upon French commercial interests. In late 1867 the French (and European) role in Panama was clarified in an unfavorable way when North American interests obtained a ninety-nine-year lease on the railroad. French consul in Panama A. Zeltner labored to preserve fair participation for Europe in the transit and in trade with China and Japan. Still, he feared that France would be eternally subordinate to U.S. influence after that country had acquired sole control of the interoceanic communications. In 1869, however, Cabarrus judged that a railroad project that U.S. promoters had negotiated with Costa Rica held great potential as well for European trade with the west coast of America and the Pacific.[57]

In the 1860s, Belot publicized the variety of commercial and investment opportunities that Central America offered to French entrepreneurs and financiers. The commercial section of the French Foreign Ministry insisted that Central America offered good potential for French banking, commerce, and capital. The commander of the French naval division in the Pacific claimed that the steady development of agriculture and commerce in Central America had brought with it to the region a sense of well-being and a rising demand for French luxury goods. Another official reported that French manufacturers could find suitable markets in Middle America if they informed themselves adequately about local tastes. The Costa Rican merchants, he said, impatiently awaited the opening of a French steamer line around Cape Horn to the Pacific, which would offer more reasonable freight rates than the Panamanian alternative. Around 1870, French trade and shipping interests in the Panama area were expected to develop as a consequence of two new shipping lines—the Compagnie Générale Transatlantique and the German Roland line from Bremen to Colón. Yet despite the Compagnie Transatlantique's service, two French firms closed their doors, and the number of French residents diminished.[58]

By the mid-1860s the French navy had such extensive commitments in Mexico, the Mediterranean, the Pacific, and off the coast of Africa that its vessels had ceased visiting Central America. In 1868, when a Prussian vessel was expected on the west coast, the French naval division in the Pacific sent a vessel to Central America to show the flag. The naval commanders operating in Central American waters were admonished not to mix in local politics, but they could take political refugees on board as an act of humanitarianism. In early 1870 the French naval ministry ordered vessels to visit Central America as frequently as possible. Nevertheless, the Pacific division still found it difficult to send a vessel to Central America.[59] Whereas the French government considered the option of greater naval presence, it most commonly resorted to encouragement of technological, cultural, commercial, emigration, or financial activity to mark France's participation on the isthmus.

In summary, in the 1840s and 1850s, French leaders seriously considered a wide variety of steps to secure military, economic, and diplomatic parity with other metropole powers in Middle America. In the early 1850s, French officials were divided over whether the United States or Great Britain constituted the major threat to France's future on the isthmus. Various Central American governments appealed for protection against U.S. expansionism. Although the British were their traditional antagonists, most Frenchmen were convinced by the Walker filibustering expeditions and Anglo-French cooperation during and after the Crimean War that U.S. society was their chief enemy on the isthmus.

Napoleon III's scheme to revive French power and prestige on a world scale encompassed the acquisition of naval support points to protect French commerce and investment. He hoped to rebuild a formal empire to sustain French economic expansion and to recapture glory for the nation (and for his government). He considered the Middle American-Caribbean area the proper place to halt U.S. expansion southward, and his government encouraged the colonization and transit proposals of Belly and Lafond in the 1850s. Many French officials wanted to convert the old Belgian settlement at Santo Tomás in Guatemala into a major naval station, but the failure of France's Mexican venture mooted the question of a joint Franco-Belgian operation there. Napoleon III's new empire planned to expand market areas, security, and investment opportunities and to initiate convenient transit between France's Atlantic and Pacific colonies. The 1860 Franco-British tariff agreement boosted the French economy, which benefited until the costs of the Franco-Mexican venture and the impact of freer trade helped bring it down. After the mid-1860s, Central American affairs faded into the background for most Frenchmen. French financial and security concerns were redirected toward Central Europe as Prussia unified Germany (excluding Austria) under its leadership. The Franco-Prussian War damaged French merchant activity and accelerated the decline of France's role on the isthmus.

Notes

1. Maurice Agulhon, *1848 ou l'apprentissage de la république, 1848–1852* (Paris, 1973); Alain Plessis, *De la fête impériale au mur des fédérés, 1852–1871* (Paris, 1973); Roger Price, *Revolution and Reaction: 1848 and the Second French Republic* (New York, 1975); J. M. Thompson, *Louis Napoleon and the Second*

Empire (New York, 1955); Jean Lhomme, *La Grande Bourgeoisie au pouvoir (1830–1880)* (Paris, 1960), 234–46; Jean Hartmann, *Die Wirtschaftspolitik Napoleons III.* (Bottrop, Germany, 1938), 88–92; John Lough and Muriel Lough, *An Introduction to Nineteenth Century France* (London, 1978), 124–34; Robert Freeman Smith, "Latin America, the United States and the European Powers, 1830–1930," in Leslie Bethell, ed., *Cambridge History of Latin America* (9 vols.; Cambridge, Eng., 1982–1996), 4: 83–119; Jean Bouvier, "Les Traits majeurs de l'impérialisme français avant 1914," in Jean Bouvier and René Girault, eds., *L'Impérialisme français d'avant 1914: Recueil de textes* (Paris, 1976), 305–33.

2. Agulhon, *L'Apprentissage de la république*, 11–12, 102–3, 213–19; Assalein, *Histoire économique de la France*, 2: 138–41; Plessis, *De la fête impériale au mur des fédérés*, 140–51; Caron, *An Economic History of Modern France*, 8–21, 117–34; Maurice Lévy-Leboyer, *Histoire économique et sociale de la France depuis 1848* (Paris, 1952); Maurice Lévy-Leboyer, "Les Processus d'industrialisation: Le cas de l'Angleterre et de la France," *Revue historique* 239 (1968): 281–98. Lévy-Leboyer computed the annual growth of the working population at a more optimistic 0.9 percent for the period from 1866 to 1896, in "La Croissance économique en France au xixe siècle," *Annales: Economies, sociétés, civilisations* 23 (July–Aug. 1968): 788–807.

3. Caron, *An Economic History of Modern France*, 76–85, 104–15, 138; François Caron, "La Stratégie des investissements en France aux xixe et xxe siècles," *Revue d'histoire économique et sociale* 54 (1976): 64–117; Rondo Cameron, "L'Exportation des capitaux français, 1850–1880," *Revue d'histoire économique et sociale* 33 (1955): 347–53; Marcel Blanchard, "The Railway Policy of the Second Empire," in François Crouzet, W. H. Chaloner, and W. M. Stern, eds., *Essays in European Economic History, 1789–1914* (London, 1969); Roger Magraw, *France, 1815–1914: The Bourgeois Century* (New York, 1986), 160–61.

4. Schoonover and Schoonover, "Statistics for the Understanding of the Foreign Intrusion into Central America from the 1820s to 1930, Part 3," 77–119; Paul J. Scheips, "Gabriel Lafond and Ambrose W. Thompson: Neglected Isthmian Promoters," *Hispanic American Historical Review* 36 (May 1956): 211–28; René-Louis-Marie Adolfe de Botmilian to MAE, Feb. 1, 1861, CCC, Guat., v. 6, AMAE; Thomas Schoonover, "Central American Trade and Navigation: Nineteenth Century Data Sources," *Latin American Research Review* 13 (1978): 157–69. For much of the period under discussion in this book, the agents reporting on French settlers commonly cited only the male residents abroad. Although many single French males migrated to Central America, some sent for families and some established families (in this latter case the wives and children were usually considered French citizens). To estimate the number of French residents in Central America at a particular time, the number of settlers (males) must be multiplied by some factor to account for women and children. Based upon the French governmental records, plus private reports and correspondence and information from non-French sources, I have used multipliers of 1.5 or 2.0 to estimate the number of French citizens. When there were large numbers of younger transient workers—such as during the French canal project in the 1880s—I have used a 1.5 multiplier. Where the evidence suggested that many French males were engaged in plantation ownership

or management, or settled commercial activity, I have used the multiplier of 2.0.

5. Julien Dominique M. Edmond Tallien de Cabarrus to MAE, July 1, 1865, CCC, Guat., v. 7, AMAE; Caron, *An Economic History of Modern France*, 105; Bertrand Nagaro and Marcel Moye, *Le Régime douanier de la France* (Paris, 1931), 47–52; Michael S. Smith, *Tariff Reform in France, 1860–1900: The Politics of Economic Interest* (Ithaca, 1980), 28–34; Louis Wolowski, *La Liberté commerciale et les résultats du traité de commerce de 1860* (Paris, 1869); Marcel Rist, "A French Experiment with Free Trade: The Treaty of 1860," in Rondo Cameron, ed., *Essays in French Economic History* (Homewood, IL, 1970), 286–314; Jürgen Schneider, "Terms of Trade between France and Latin America, 1825–1856: Causes of Increasing Economic Disparities?" in Paul Bairoch and Maurice Lévy-Leboyer, eds., *Disparities in Economic Development since the Industrial Revolution* (New York, 1981), 110–19; Roses-Alvarado, "Les Echanges commerciaux entre la France et l'Amérique Centrale"; Jürgen Blankenburg, "Der französische Kapitalexport und seine Rolle als Instrument der Außenpolitik" (Ph.D. diss., Universität Köln, 1966), 98–99.

6. Schoonover and Schoonover, "Statistics for the Understanding of the Foreign Intrusion into Central America from the 1820s to 1930, Part 3," 77–119.

7. Ralph Lee Woodward, Jr., "Guatemalan Cotton and the American Civil War," *Interamerican Economic Affairs* 18 (1965): 87–94; Pérez Brignoli, *Breve historia de Centro-América*, 90–102.

8. Stanley J. Pincetl, Jr., "France and the Clayton-Bulwer Treaty of 1850," *Annales* [Université Aix-en-Provence] 45 (1968): 167–94; Alfred Assollant, "Walker au Nicaragua," *Revue des deux mondes* 26 (Aug. 15, 1856): 872–93; Auguste Laugel, "Les Communications interocéaniques dans l'amérique centrale," *Revue des deux mondes* 27 (Jan. 15, 1857): 436–65; Edouard Vanéechout, "Les Côtes de l'Amérique centrale et la société hispano-américaine," *Revue des deux mondes* 27 (May 15, 1857): 444–65; Emile Chevalier, "Les Américains du Nord à l'isthme de Panama," *Revue des deux mondes* 27 (June 1, 1857): 865–905; Félix Belly, "La Question de l'isthme américain," *Revue des deux mondes* 30 (July 15, 1860): 328–68, 30 (Aug. 1, 1860): 597–633, and 30 (Aug. 15, 1860): 865–902; Elisée Reclus, "Les Républiques de l'isthme américain," *Revue des deux mondes* 38 (March 15, 1868): 479–98; Martial Cloquet to Alfred de Valois, May 6, 1849, CP 1871, Amér. cent., v. 8, AMAE; Paul Lévy, "Amérique centrale de Panama à Managua," *Societé de géographie, Bulletin* 18 (1869): 177–91; Cyril Allen, "Félix Belly: Nicaraguan Canal Promoter," *Hispanic American Historical Review* 37 (Feb. 1957): 46–59; Cyril Allen, *France in Central America: Félix Belly and the Nicaraguan Canal* (New York, 1966); Kühn, "Napoleon III. und der Nicaraguakanal."

9. Charles Alexandre de Challeye to MAE, June 15, 22, July 1, 1848, CP 1871, Amér. cent., v. 7, AMAE; Challeye to MAE, Nov. 18, 1848, Valois to MAE, Feb. 10, Apr. 21, 1849, CP 1871, Amér. cent., v. 8, AMAE; Challeye to MAE, Feb. 20, 1849, MAE to Dagobert Fourcade, May 30, 1849, CCC, Guat., v. 3, AMAE; Comité national du centenaire de 1848, *Documents diplomatiques du gouvernement provisoire et de la commission du pouvoir exécutif* (Paris, 1954), 2: 925–27, 1022–28.

10. Challeye to MAE, June 22, July 1, 1848, CP 1871, Amér. cent., v. 7, AMAE; Challeye to MRE, June 14, 20, Sept. 15, 1848, MRE to Consul-General, June 19, 1848, MRE to MRE(FR), June 20, 1848, Valois to MRE, Aug. 14, 17, 1849, B99-5-6, 4314/93219, Legación y consulado general de Francia, 1846–1851, AGCA.

11. Challeye to MRE, Dec. 19, 1848, March 8, 10, 13, 1849, MRE to Challeye, March 9, 1849, other correspondence, and Franco-Guatemalan agreement, Jan. 24, 1850, B99-5-6, 4314/93219, Legación y consulado general de Francia, 1846–1851, AGCA; Valois to MAE, Feb. 10, Apr. 21, 1849, CP 1871, Amér. cent., v. 8, AMAE; Juan Antoine y Fayas to MAE, Sept. 6, 1849, H2519, Archivo del Ministerio de Asuntos Exteriores, Madrid (hereafter cited as AMAE).

12. Unsigned Spanish document, Oct. 8, 1852, CP 1871, Amér. cent., v. 11, AMAE; M. F. Pavón to MRE, Nov. 11, 1851, Mariano Rodríguez to Prussian, Belgian, and Hansa diplomats, May 9, 1852, MRE to Guat. min. in Fr., Nov. 15, 1853, Angrand to MRE, Dec. 24, 1853, Pedro Aycinena to Angrand, Jan. 24, 1854, and various other correspondence between Angrand and MRE in 1853–1854, B99-5-6/4315/93220, MRE, AGCA; Botmilian to MRE, July 12, 1858, B99-5-6/4316/93221, MRE, AGCA.

13. Vallette to MAE, Jan. 25, 1850, members of Bordeaux Chamber of Commerce to MAE, March 21, 1850, CP 1871, Amér. Cent., v. 9, AMAE; Moges to Min. marine, April 10, June 25, Oct. 24, Dec. 7, 1842, Marine, BB^4 613, AN; Valois to MAE, Feb. 10, Apr. 21, 1849, CP 1871, Amér. cent., v. 8, AMAE; John Laffey, "Municipal Imperialism in Nineteenth Century France," *Historical Reflections* 1 (June 1974): 81–113.

14. Cloquet to Valois, May 6, 1849, CP 1871, Amér. cent., v. 8, AMAE; Fourcade to MAE, Nov. 12, 1849, CP 1871, Amér. cent., v. 9, AMAE.

15. Challeye to MAE, Jan. 7, 1849 (copy in CCC, Guat., v. 3, AMAE), Valois to MAE, Feb. 10, Apr. 21, 1849, CP 1871, Amér. cent., v. 8, AMAE; Fourcade to MAE, Jan. 22, 1850, CCC, Guat., v. 4, AMAE (copy in F^{12} 6543, AN); Frs. Marie Léonce Angrand to MAE, Nov. 26, 1852, CP 1871, Amér. cent., v. 11, AMAE; Angrand to MAE, Feb. 28, 1853, CP 1871, Amér. cent., v. 12, AMAE; Angrand to MAE, Nov. 5, 1853, Jan. 30, Feb. 26, March 1, 1854, MAE to Angrand, Feb. 28, 1854, CP 1871, Amér. cent., v. 13, AMAE.

16. Andrés Santa Cruz to MRE, June 14, Aug. 13, Nov. 13, Dec. 28, 1854, Feb. 14, April 14, May 1, 1855, Pedro de Aycinena to Santa Cruz, Oct. 31 (2 letters, one private), 1854, March 3, 10, 1855, B99-6-5/4476/93432, MRE, AGCA.

17. John Clayton to William C. Rives, Jan. 26, 1850, Record Group 59, Department of State Records, Diplomatic Instructions, France, vol. 15 (microcopy 77/reel 55), National Archives, Washington (hereafter cited as RG 59, DI, France: 15 [M 77/r 55], NA); Cosnier to Fourichon, July 11, 1850, BB4 1596, AAM.

18. Scheips, "Gabriel Lafond and Ambrose W. Thompson," 211–28; Gabriel Lafond du Lurcy to Napoleon, May 9, 1850, MAE to Lafond, May 31, 1850, CP 1871, Amér. cent., v. 9, AMAE; Edward W. Richards, "Louis Napoleon and Central America," *Journal of Modern History* 34:2 (June 1962): 178–84; Gabriel Lafond, *Nouvelle route pour la Californie* (Paris, 1850); Gabriel Lafond, *Notice sur le Golfo Dulce dans l'état de Costa Rica . . . et sur un nouveau passage entre les deux océans* (Paris, 1856); André Broder, "Le

Commerce extérieur," in Fernand Braudel and Ernest Labrousse, eds., *Histoire économique et sociale de la France* (4 vols.; Paris, 1970–80), vol. 3, pt. 1, 340–44.

19. Scheips, "Gabriel Lafond and Ambrose W. Thompson," 212; *Appleton's Cyclopaedia of American Biography* (rev. ed.; 6 vols.; New York, 1900): 592.

20. Felipe Molina to MRE, March 28, 1852, MRE, caja 24, legación de Costa Rica en E.U., Archivos Nacionales, San José, Costa Rica (hereafter cited as AN, CR); Préfet de police to Min. marine et colonies, Sept. 7, 1855, Lafond to Min. marine, Oct. 24, 1855, Marine BB^8 108, Cabinet du Ministre, AN; Lafond to Napoleon, May 9, 1850, MAE to Lafond, May 31, 1850, CP 1871, Amér. cent., v. 9, AMAE.

21. Schoonover and Schoonover, "Statistics for the Understanding of the Foreign Intrusion into Central America from the 1820s to 1930, Part 3," 77–119; Vallette to MAE, Jan. 25, 1850, members of Bordeaux Chamber of Commerce to MAE, March 21, 1850, CP 1871, Amér. cent., v. 9, AMAE; Fourichon to Min. marine, Aug. 29, 1850, Marine BB^4 663, AN; various correspondence, especially "Instructions pour l'étude commerciale des pays du Sud-Américain et de l'Inde Orientale," and [Edmond Dollfus?], "Note statistique sur divers états de Centre-Amérique (Guatemala, San Salvador, Honduras)," F^{12} 7410, AN; T. de Lapelin to Marie-Joseph Alphonse Odet-Pellion, March 26, 1852, Marine BB^4 1596, AAM; Colin W. Newbury, "Aspects of French Policy in the Pacific, 1853–1906," *Pacific Historical Review* 27 (Feb. 1958): 45–56.

22. Costa Rican min. in France to MAE, Aug. 15, 1849, Victor Herrán to MAE, Jan. 28, Feb. 16, 1852, Commerce, F^{12} 8890, AN; Min. de l'intérieur, de l'agriculture et du commerce to MAE, Nov. 19, 1851, Aug. 9, 1852, Négociations commerciales, Centre-Amérique, v. 2, AMAE; Schoonover and Schoonover, "Statistics for the Understanding of the Foreign Intrusion into Central America from the 1820s to 1930, Part 3," 93, 95, 98–100, 107, 109, 113, 115, 117; Victor Herrán, *Notice sur les cinq états du Centre-Amérique* (Bordeaux, 1853); Marie-Joelle Gillet, "Histoire et caractères généraux de l'économie," in *Un îlot de démocratie en Amérique centrale, le Costa Rica* (Brussels, 1979), 186–99.

23. Lapelin to Admiral, June 20, 1852, BB^4 1596, AAM; Pellion to Min. marine, June 12, 1852, Marine BB^4 702, AN; various correspondence 1857 and 1858, B99-5-6/4316/93221, MRE, AGCA.

24. Franz Hugo Hesse to Otto von Manteuffel and August von der Heydt, July 24, Oct. 30, 1852, 2.4.1., Abt. II, Nr. 5198, Bundesarchiv, Merseburg, Germany (hereafter cited as BAM; formerly Deutsches Zentrales Staatsarchiv, Merseburg, DZM); Charles Mévil to Edward Drouyn de Lhuys, Feb. 6, 1853, CP 1871, Amér. cent., v. 12, AMAE.

25. Tom Kemp, *Economic Forces in French History* (London, 1971), 173–78; Henry Blumenthal, *France and the United States* (Chapel Hill, 1970), 66–67.

26. Angrand to MAE, Sept. 1, 1852, CP 1871, Amér. cent., v. 11, AMAE; Castellón to MAE, Sept. 1, 1852, CP 1871, Amér. cent., v. 12, AMAE.

27. Angrand to MAE, Jan. 30, March 1, June 25, 1854, CP 1871, Amér. cent., v. 13, AMAE; Mévil to Drouyn de Lhuys, Jan. 25, 1855, Alexandre Mellinet to AME, June 1, 1855, CP 1871, Amér. cent., v. 14, AMAE; Félix

Belly, "De l'équilibre du nouveau monde," in Félix Belly, *Percement de l'isthme de Panama par le canal de Nicaragua* (Paris, 1858), 121–57.

28. Angrand to MAE, March 30, 1853, CP 1871, Amér. cent., v. 12, AMAE; Angrand to MAE, March 30, 1854, CP 1871, Amér. cent., v. 13, AMAE; Belly, "De l'équilibre du nouveau monde," 121–57.

29. Allen, *France in Central America*, 2–9.

30. MAE to Min. intérieur and Min. marine, Jan. 28, 1853, Fruto Chamorro, Decree, June 7, 1851, Theodore Ducos to MAE, April 11, 1853, CP 1871, Amér. cent., v. 12, AMAE.

31. Allen, *France in Central America*; Pincetl, "France and the Clayton-Bulwer Treaty of 1850," 167–94.

32. Mévil to Alexandre Florian Joseph Colonna Walewski, May 26, 1855, Négociations commerciales, Centre-Amérique, v. 3, AMAE; Lafond to MAE, Nov. 21, Dec. 7, 1855, Jan. 18, 1856, L. Hammond to MAE, Jan. 22, 1856, MAE to Min. marine, Jan. 30, 1856, Min. marine to MAE, Feb. 2, 1856, Henry R. C. Wellesley, Lord Cowley, to Walewski, March 11, 1856, MAE to Cowley, March 21, 1856, CP 1871, Amér. cent., v. 14, AMAE; A. C. LeQuelles to Legeol, Nov. 14, 1856, LeQuelles to commander in the Pacific, Nov. 14, 1856, BB^4 1597, AAM.

33. A. Enguerrand de Marigny, renseignements, *Alcibiade*, Dec. 1856, Marine BB^4 1023, AN; Lafond to Clarendon, April 14, 1856, Lafond to MRE, April 15, 17, Public Record Office, Foreign Office (hereafter cited as PRO, FO 21/8 [r. 2]); Lafond to Vincent Bénetti, April 23, 1856, Francisco Martín, memorandum, July 31, 1856, José de Marcoleta, memorandum, Sept. 1, 1856, George W. F. Villiers, earl of Clarendon, to Cowley, Sept. 5, 1856, Lafond to MAE, May 21, 1858, Lafond to Cowley, May 18, 1856, "L'Amérique Centrale à propos du traité Clayton-Bulwer—1856," Mémoires et documents, Amér., v. 67, AMAE; Luis Felipe González, *Historia de la influencia extranjera en el desenvolvimiento educacional y científico de Costa Rica* (San José, CR, 1921), 253.

34. Juan de Aycinena to Juan de Francisco Martín, Nov. 30, 1855, April 1, 1856, Mellinet to MAE, Dec. 1, 1855, CP 1871, Amér. cent., v. 14, AMAE; Mellinet to rear-admiral, Jan. 6, 1856, BB^4 1597, AAM; Aycinena to Botmilian, Aug. 30, 1856, CP 1871, Amér. cent., v. 15, AMAE.

35. Adolphe Deshorties, "Envahissements du continent de l'Amérique Espagnole par les Etats-Unis: Dangers résultants par les intérêts politiques et commerciaux des nations industrielles et maritimes de l'Europe," June 30, 1856, Mémoires et documents, Espagne, v. 366, AMAE (copy in CP 1871, Amér. cent., v. 15, AMAE); Belly, *Percement de l'isthme de Panama par le canal de Nicaragua*, 5–78; Allen, "Félix Belly," 46–59; Marigny to Min. marine, Jan. 5, 1857, Marine BB^4 746, AN; Thome de Gamond, "Notes extraite de l'avant-projet pour la construction du canal de Nicaragua," in Thome de Gamond, ed., *Carte d'étude pour le tracé et le profil du canal de Nicaragua* (Paris, 1858), 64–90; Louis Napoléon Bonaparte, "Le Canal de Nicaragua," in Gamond, ed., *Carte d'étude pour le tracé et le profil du canal de Nicaragua*, 36–45; Pío Bolaños Alvarez, "Napoleon III y el diplomático nicaragüense Francisco Castellón," *Revista conservadora de pensamiento centroamericano* 16 (Feb. 1967): 42–45.

36. Hesse to Manteuffel, Oct. 29, 1857, March 17, 1858, 2.4.1., Abt. II, Nr. 5247 (AA III, Rep. 14, Nr. 535), BAM; "Suez und Panama Kanäle,"

Westermanns Jahrbuch der illustrierten deutschen Monatshefte 2 (July 1857): 478–80.

37. Clerg, "Convention du 16 Novembre 1857 entre les États-Unis et le Nicaragua, au sujet des passages interocéaniques," Dec. 20, 1857, Mémoires et documents, Amér., v. 67, AMAE (copy in CP 1871, Amér. cent., v. 16, AMAE).

38. Memoranda, "Nicaragua, février 1859, Sr. Marcoleta . . . (affaire Belly)," Note pour le ministre, Dec. 24, 1859, Mémoires et documents, Amér., v. 67, AMAE; Allen, *France in Central America*, 29–66.

39. Lewis Cass to John Y. Mason, June 9, Nov. 5, 1858, April 12, 1859 (two letters, one private and one confidential), DI, France (M 77/r 55).

40. Juan Mora and Tomás Martínez to French emperor, May 1, 1858, Négociations commerciales, Centre-Amérique, v. 3, AMAE; Aimable Pelissier de Malakoff to Walewski, June 4, July 14, 1858, CP 1871, Amér. cent., v. 16, AMAE; André Lavasseur to MAE, June 15, 1859, Note pour le ministre, Dec. 24, 1859, Mémoires et documents Amér., v. 67, AMAE.

41. Lafond to MAE, Jan. 5, 1858, CP 1871, Amér. cent., v. 16, AMAE; Gueydon to Min. marine, Nov. 27, 1857, May 23, June 25, 1858, Marine BB^4 744, AN; James Howard Harris, earl of Malmesbury, to secretary of the admiralty, Oct. 11, 1858, Edmond Hammond to Marcoleta, Oct. 11, 1858 (confidential), Marcoleta to MAE, Oct. 15, 1858, Malmesbury to Cowley, Oct. 21, 1858, MAE to Malakoff, Oct. 30, 1858, Malmesbury to Marcoleta, Oct. 27, 1858, Botmilian to MAE, Jan. 2, 1859, CP 1871, Amér. cent., v. 17, AMAE; Ed. Pénaud to Min. marine, Jan. 3, 1859, Marine BB^4 1650, AN.

42. Louis-Adolphe Bonard to Min. marine, May 3, 1859, Marine BB^4 746, AN; A. Boyer to admiral, June 7, 1861, Marine BB^4 765, AN.

43. Marcoleta to Edouard A. Thouvenel, Feb. 19, 1860, Léonel de Moustier to Thouvenel, March 3, 1860, Thouvenel to Marcoleta, March 9, 1860, Prussian minister to Thouvenel, May 20, 1860, CP 1871, Amér. cent., v. 18, AMAE.

44. Botmilian to MAE, Nov. 27, 1857, CCC, Guat., v. 4, AMAE; MAE to Min. commerce, Aug. 7, 1857, Min. commerce to MAE, Aug. 17, 1857, Commerce F^{12} 6326, AN; Botmilian to MAE, May 7, 25, Oct. 9, 1859, CCC, Guat., v. 5, AMAE; Botmilian to MAE, May 2, 1859, CP 1871, Amér. cent., v. 17, AMAE; René de Botmilian, "Notice sur les états de l'Amérique centrale," *Bulletin de la Société géographie* 44 (Nov. 1865): 465–85.

45. "Communication du Consul de Panama sur les propositions des Etats-Unis pour la réparation demandée par le Gouvt. de Washington à la suite des violences exercées contre les passagers du chemin de fer, le 15 avril 1857," BB^4 1597, AAM; Gueydon to Min. marine, Nov. 27, 1857, May 23, June 25, 1858, Marine BB^4 744, AN; Coupvent-Desbois, renseignements, *Persévérante*, Feb. 1858, Marine BB^4 1023, AN; d'Aignan to admiral, May 14, 1859, BB^4 1596, AAM; report of the commander of the *Bayonnaise*, 1861, BB^4 1596, AAM; Note sur Panama, Feb. 1861, Mémoires et documents, Amér., v. 68, AMAE; Jean-Baptiste E. de Jurien de la Gravière to Min. marine, March 1861, Marine BB^4 1023, AN; Mack, *Land Divided*, 161–68; Mercedes Chen Daley, "The Watermelon Riot: Cultural Encounters in Panama City, April 15, 1856," *HAHR* 70: 1 (Feb. 1990): 85–108.

46. A. Enguerrand de Marigny, renseignements, *Alcibiade*, Dec. 1856, Marine BB^4 1023, AN; Charles Dorat to John M. Dow, June 3, 1858, box 1, folder 1-2, Dow to David Hoadley, Feb. 10, 1860, box 4, letterbook 1858–

1865, pp. 115–23, John M. Dow papers, Cornell University, Ithaca, NY; MAE to F. L. Hardy, Oct. 28, 1861, Hardy to MAE, Feb. 1, 1862, CCC, Guat., v. 6, AMAE; Auguste Bosse to Min. marine, July 2, 1865, Bosse to Baron Dédélot, Aug. 10, 1865, BB[4] 837, AN.

47. Edouard Carpentier to Thouvenel, Aug. 7, 1861, CCC Pan., v. 2, AMAE; Jurien de la Gravière to Min. marine, March 1861, Marine BB[4] 1023, AN.

48. Dow to E. O. Crosby, May 24, 1861, box 4, letterbook 1858–1865, Dow papers; MAE to Hardy, Dec. 15, 1862, Cabarrus to MAE, July 1, 1865, CCC, Guat., v. 7, AMAE; Louis Wolowski, *La Liberté commerciale et les résultats du Traité de Commerce de 1860* (Paris, 1869); Smith, *Tariff Reform in France*, 28–34; Rost, "The Treaty of 1860."

49. Nuguet de Majoureaux, renseignements, *Constantine*, July 1859, Marine BB[4] 1023, AN; *Informe del Secretario de Relaciones Exteriores . . . 1862* (San José, CR, 1862), 5; Edward Loos to Napoleon III, June 18, 1863, analysis of Loos dispatch, July 1863, Mémoires et documents, Amér., v. 68, AMAE; Paul Roger, *De l'intérêt qu'a la marine française à l'ouverture du l'isthme américain par le canal du Darien* (Paris, 1861); Thomas Schoonover, "Black Colonization in Mexico and Central America during the Civil War: Foreign Relations and Imperialism," *Pacific Historical Review* 49 (November 1980): 607–20; L. Y. Cohen, "Note explicative pour servir à élucider la question relative à l'Ile de St. Martin (Antilles)," Dec. 12, 1862, La Roncière le Noury, GG[2] 42, AN; Gueydon to Min. marine, March 26, 1858, Marine BB[4] 744, AN; Hardy to MAE, May 1, 1862, CCC, Guat., v. 7, AMAE; unsigned report, Feb. 24, 1863, Affaires divers politiques, carton 2, folder, Affaires coloniales Belgique, AMAE; Thomas Schoonover, *Dollars over Dominion: The Triumph of Liberalism in Mexican-United States Relations, 1861–1867* (Baton Rouge, 1978); Guy P. Palmade, *Capitalisme et capitalistes français au xixe siècle* (Paris, 1961), 196–98; Blumenthal, *France and the United States*, 79–91; Marvin R. Zahniser, *Uncertain Friendship: American-French Diplomatic Relations through the Cold War* (New York, 1975), 127–47.

50. Herrán to MAE, Nov. 15, 1860, CP 1871, Amér. cent., v. 18, AMAE; Botmilian to MAE, Jan. 11, 1861, CCC, Guat., v. 6, AMAE; Edward Pougin, *L'Etat de Costa Rica* (Anvers, Belg., 1863); Imbert to Napoleon, June 15, 1866, Imbert to Drouyn de Lhuys, Aug. 2, 1866, MAE to Imbert, Sept. 24, 1866, Mémoires et documents, Amér., v. 68, AMAE; Francisco Alvarado to Cabarrus, Oct. 30, 1869, CP 1871, Amér. cent., v. 22, AMAE.

51. Charles de Saulce de Freycinet to Min. marine, [1867], BB[4] 1596, AAM; Gustave de Belot, *Utilité pour Bordeaux d'un dock de marchandises au Centre-Amérique* (Bordeaux, 1862); Enrique del Cid Fernández, ed., *Epistolario inédito de A. J. de Irisarri, 1857–1868* (Guatemala, 1966), 183–225; Schoonover, *Dollars over Dominion*, 166–67, 183, 191–92.

52. Gustave de Belot to Carrera, Aug. 10, 1863, Cabarrus to MAE, April 20, 28, 1863, B99-5-6, 4316/93221, MRE, AGCA; Hardy to MAE, Aug. 6, Sept. 20, 1862, CP 1871, Amér. cent., v. 18, AMAE; Italo López Vallecillos, *Gerardo Barrios y su tiempo* (2 vols.; San Salvador, 1967); Zeltner to MAE, May 1, 1863, CCC, Pan., v. 3, AMAE; Cabarrus to MAE, Dec. 2, 1864, CP 1871, Amér. cent., v. 20, AMAE; Cabarrus to MAE, July 20, 1865, CP 1871, Amér. cent., v. 21, AMAE.

53. British ambassador, note verbale, Dec. 9, 1862, French chargé in London to Louis Alix de Cadore, Dec. 20, 1862, CP 1871, Amér. cent., v. 18,

AMAE; Note pour le ministre, Dec. 1862, Affaires divers politiques, carton 3, AMAE; MAE to Cabarrus, May 30, 1863, Cabarrus to MAE, July 3, 1863, CP 1871, Amér. cent., v. 19, AMAE; Cabarrus to MAE, June 17, October 31, 1863, CCC, Guat., v. 7, AMAE (Oct. 31 letter also in CP 1871, Amér. cent., v. 20, AMAE); Cabarrus to MAE, Jan. 14, 1865, CP 1871, Amér. cent., v. 21, AMAE.

54. Cabarrus to MAE, Nov. 19, Dec. 7, 1863, March 20, 1864, CP 1871, Amér. cent., v. 20, AMAE; Cabarrus to MAE, May 2, 1864, CCC, Guat., v. 7, AMAE.

55. Gabriel Lafond, *Fragments de voyages autour du monde* (Paris, 1863), esp. 191–96, 205; Edward Loos to Napoleon III, June 18, 1863, analysis of Loos dispatch, July 1863, Nathaniel Niles to Drouyn de Lhuys, July 25, 1866, Mémoires et documents, Amér., v. 68, AMAE; Cabarrus to MAE, June 28, 1863, CCC, Guat., v. 7, AMAE.

56. Gustave de Belot, *La République du Salvador* (Paris, 1865); Gustave de Belot and Charles Lindemann, *Amérique centrale: La République du Honduras et son chemin interocéanique* (Paris, 1867); Stansifer, "E. George Squier and the Honduran Interoceanic Railroad Project."

57. Zeltner to MAE, Dec. 22, 1867 (private), CCC, Pan., v. 4, AMAE; Cabarrus to MAE, Feb. 19, 1869, CCC, Guat., v. 8, AMAE.

58. Belot, *Utilité pour Bordeaux d'un dock . . . au Centre-Amérique*; Jean-Louis Joachim Meurant to Min. commerce, May 10, 1869, Commerce, F^{12} 7053, AN; Freycinet to Min. marine, May 21, July 2, 1868, Marine BB^4 865, AN; Min. marine to Lapelin, July 23, 1870, BB^4 902, AAM; Cabarrus to Lapelin, June 5, 1871, BB^4 942, AAM; Charles Emmanuel Pineton de Chambrun to MAE, March 29, 1870, Mémoires et documents, Amér., v. 69, AMAE; Meurant to Min. commerce, July 12, 1870, Charles Cropp to MAE, Feb. 9, 1871, Commerce, F^{12} 7059, AN; Paul Dominique Chevry-Rameau to MAE, Feb. 15, 1871, CCC, Pan., v. 5, AMAE.

59. Freycinet to Min. marine, May 21, July 2, 1868, Marine BB^4 865, AN; Min. marine to Lapelin, July 23, 1870, BB^4 902, AAM; Cabarrus to Lapelin, June 5, 1871, BB^4 942, AAM.

3

Ferdinand de Lesseps and the Panama Canal, 1871–1889

After the Franco-Prussian war ended Napoleon III's empire, the French government reduced its role in Central America. It faced the economic burden of reparations payments, and it needed to repair its position in Europe. French activity on the isthmus eroded until Ferdinand de Lesseps selected Panama as the site to build a second canal connecting the Atlantic-Mediterranean and the Pacific-Indian oceans. De Lesseps's project revitalized the French presence on the isthmus.

De Lesseps grew up in a family of modest means, but with influential and monied relatives. His father and especially his uncle had prominent diplomatic careers, so de Lesseps served overseas for several decades. He happened to be in Egypt in 1839 when a team of French engineers arrived to survey for a possible Suez canal route. Nothing came of this early work, but de Lesseps was attracted to the project and thirty years later stood in the false position of the "Great Engineer." He was not. De Lesseps had no engineering or technical skills, no financial experience, and only modest administrative ability, but his contacts in Egypt and his determination led him to dedicate fifteen years to seeing the Suez project to completion. His role in the Panama project followed his earlier experience. Again he revealed little technical skill or financial or administrative ability, but he had great determination and connections. His capacity to raise enormous sums reflected his prominence and the fact that French investments were spanning the globe in the late nineteenth century.[1] The two de Lesseps canal projects—Suez and Panama—captured the attention of the whole western world, and, a century later, they remained important routes for world navigation.

Historians have clouded the analysis of French expansion in the late nineteenth and early twentieth centuries in two ways: They have exaggerated the role of colonial expansion, at the expense of informal imperialism, and they have overemphasized the hold of nationalism on French foreign relations. The work of Henri Brunschwig illustrates both tendencies. Brunschwig claimed that French expansion fever came from a strong wave of nationalism after the defeat of 1870–71. This is misleading, at least insofar as it implies a discontinuity with earlier expansionist impulses. In fact, early French concession seekers in Middle America sought economic opportunities, naval stations, or communications concessions, and they commonly appealed to nationalism because they required domestic support. Before 1871, Napoleon III and other leaders had tried to restore national glory, to preserve France's "civilizing missions," and to make French entrepreneurs and financiers wealthy.[2]

Brunschwig, after a cursory look at French colonial accounts, uncritically accepted the rhetoric of politicians, some economists, and others who denied the profitability of expansion. But to imply that thousands of entrepreneurs from a dozen materialistically oriented western societies, whose political economies were rooted in the profit motive, conducted business for over a century yet did not "profit" from their ventures suggests a modern miracle. In fact, there was rapid capital accumulation in the industrializing North Atlantic states (commonly from firms or cartels heavily involved in foreign economic activity—Standard Oil, United Fruit, Crédit Mobilier, Crédit Lyonnais, Schneider, or the Comité des Forges) during this era of supposedly costly and unprofitable overseas expansion. Brunschwig suggested that the western societies labored continuously in these unprofitable areas out of a sense of mission, yet these societies have commonly lacked a sense of mission or humanity toward their own unfortunate citizens. Most fundamentally, he confused what it cost imperial governments to secure opportunities abroad with the ledger balances of businesses that took advantage of these opportunities. Imperial governments never collected sufficient revenues in the colonies to cover the expenses of the armies, navies, judicial systems, administrative agencies, and public works required to create opportunities. The businesses, however, often reaped immense gains. The expenses of opening markets were dispersed throughout a broad population base, so the businesses needed to cover only a tiny share of the government's red ink. Their balance sheets, however, showed profit margins that appear obscene in light of the poverty in the host countries. Moreover, the values that the imperial societies extracted from the land, labor, and distribution offered by the colonial areas greatly exceeded the social costs of the metropole societies.

While the industrializing societies of the late nineteenth and early twentieth centuries highlighted capital expansion for growth, labor remained an important ingredient in the formula for production and accumulation. The growth rate of the French population shriveled in the late nineteenth century. It declined to 0.19 percent annually in the 1866–1886 period before falling to 0.08 percent in the years between 1886 and 1901. Caron described a near-stagnant working population, which grew only 20 percent between 1852 and 1896—from 16,240,000 to 19,470,000.[3] France suffered an economic handicap because its labor force (and population) stagnated.

Stagnation in France's domestic workforce encouraged entrepreneurs to find ways to preserve their own accumulation and well-being by collecting the value produced by foreign labor. Metropole entrepreneurs liked the unorganized, subordinated periphery laborer. They could pay such a worker less than a subsistence wage while the household engaged in nonremunerated (by the metropole company) work to sustain the employed laborer's contribution to international trade, thereby transferring the labor value of others (commonly the spouse and children) to the entrepreneur. The driving force of expansion was core, not peripheral, demand—the search for raw materials to cheapen metropole products (and thus the cost of living), not for markets. Except—and it is a significant exception—the development of the periphery required surplus core products to institute the infrastructural changes inherent in liberalism's "progress." A canal, for example, demanded metropole materials, capital, and technology. As domestic profit-making opportunities shrank, France looked to the low cost land and labor in the periphery, where metropole interests competed actively.[4] French interests wished to participate in the subordination and incorporation of Central American labor into the world economy.

Most students of France's economy acknowledge stagnation in the late nineteenth century. Agricultural production, according to Caron, *declined* at an annual rate of 0.15 percent (a negative growth rate) from the mid-1870s to the mid-1890s, a "slump" that paralleled the course of the whole economy (and much of the world) during the "great world depression" (Hans

Rosenberg). Between 1860 and 1913, the French share of continental European exports also declined dramatically.[5] But even as France's foreign commerce stagnated, its leaders had no intention of accepting an inferior position with regard to the other metropoles. They contemplated alternative strategies that used an enlarged financial role, military missions, and cultural tools to preserve a proper role for France on the isthmus.

French commerce, which had challenged British trade for leadership on the isthmus in the post-independence decades, revived noticeably in the last quarter of the nineteenth century. In the 1870s and 1880s, France purchased between 7 and 11 percent of the exports from Guatemala, Nicaragua, and Costa Rica and sold to these three countries between 11 and 15 percent of their imports. France acquired about 13 percent of Salvadoran exports and sent about 21 percent of Salvadoran imports. France supplied between 1 and 6 percent of the vessels and 1 or 2 percent of the tonnage for Guatemalan, Salvadoran, and Costa Rican ports. French vessels represented 18 percent of the ships and 27 percent of the tonnage in Corinto, and 4 percent of the ships and 2 percent of the tonnage at San Juan del Norte. In 1889, Europe dominated Latin America's billion-dollar trade, and U.S. consul James Hosmer expected the European states to struggle to retain this commercial boon.[6]

Economic stagnation in the metropoles increased competition between metropole states and enterprises to guide the material and ideological reformation of the Middle American societies. After a generation of conservative governments, a liberal resurgence began with the political transformations of Costa Rica and Guatemala in 1870 and 1871. In 1870, General Tomás Guardia began a dozen years of moderate liberal reforms in Costa Rica. In Guatemala, Miguel García Granados and Justo Rufino Barrios led the liberals (coffee planters, professionals, and others) who ousted General Vicente Cerna. Barrios then helped liberal factions in El Salvador and Honduras overturn their conservative governments, which he suspected were aiding the defeated Guatemalan conservatives. By 1876, Barrios wielded influence in three isthmian states. Only Nicaragua resisted liberal reform, largely because liberalism was linked to the destructive filibustering of the 1850s. While Costa Rica was pursuing its moderate liberal course, it remained largely isolated from Central American power struggles.[7]

An expanding world economy required institutions to handle the reordered factors of production. It also required intellectual developments to explain the dislocations of lives and the illogical distribution of accumulation. One European (largely French) philosophical movement—positivism—appeared commonly in the statements and writings of the isthmian reformers of the 1870s. Positivism claimed to be a more realistic version of early nineteenth-century liberalism, which was widely discredited for its ineffective reforms in Guatemala during the 1820s and 1830s and for its ties to filibustering. The positivists on the isthmus subordinated political liberty to the need for material progress. They rejected Marxism and socialism because they saw private development as superior. Development and accumulation were expected to produce economic well-being and educational and cultural progress upon which they would found democratic political reform. Order and real material progress had to precede other forms of progress. Positivism, often combined with Herbert Spencer's social Darwinism, lent itself to elitism and authoritarianism, hence it was acceptable to wealthy, landed military, and lay religious people. Despite some sacrifice of political liberty, positivists and social Darwinists thought free market competition and natural selection would produce material success that would ultimately faciliate social and political progress.[8]

Central American leaders often acted as if adopting ideas or terminology from European thinkers was a sign of progress and development. The Central American liberals eagerly championed material progress. They facilitated private acquisition of land, created a wage-dependent labor force, freed domestic capital by undermining the *cofradías* (religiously inspired socioeconomic brotherhoods) and other church-controlled sources of capital, and encouraged the formation of banks (especially hypothecary or mortgage land banks). The isthmian liberals looked to France (or Europe) for inspiration, and their governments offered inducements to foreign settlers and financial and entrepreneurial interests.[9]

Foreign interests took advantage of new liberal laws and decrees to establish enclaves of production in Central America. Enclaves are regions of development in which foreign authority and custom displace domestic law and custom. In the 1880s three such enclaves existed—bananas in Costa Rica, mining in Honduras, and coffee in Guatemala. The banana and mining enclaves—located in isolated areas near the Caribbean coast where Central American authority had traditionally been weak—were characterized by extensive foreign control of the community. In contrast, the German coffee planters and merchants in Guatemala possessed less effective governance over their community because it was near the older settled areas on the Pacific coast. In addition, there was a fourth enclave, of mixed commercial, agricultural, and mining activity, on Nicaragua's Caribbean coast, which had served since the seventeenth century as an adjunct "colony" to British (and later U.S.) commerce and extractive industries (cattle, hides, hardwoods, minerals, and foodstuffs).[10]

The rise of liberalism and enclave exploitation altered much of isthmian society. Most notably, the Indians, who lived a subsistence lifestyle, lost their communal lands. A new tax structure burdened them with cash tax obligations (rather than in-kind services) that compelled them to abandon subsistence farming and enter the wage-labor system. Thus liberal laws transformed the political economy of Indian societies by converting the Indians into a mobile, seasonal, wage-earning labor force employed in enclave projects.[11] This establishment of a forced wage-labor system and related changes produced considerable social tension.

When the peasant communities resisted the new labor role assigned them, the governments adopted metropole-organized and -trained rural police forces and a professionalized military. These new agencies of authority, with increased loyalty to a government rather than to a local caudillo or cacique, enforced the tax collection (accelerating the trend toward wage labor) and assured the privatization of *ejido*, or communal, land. The armed forces acted less regularly to restrict peasant attempts to occupy unclaimed or unused land. Although peasants who settled on vacant lands became less dependent on wage labor, and hence endangered exploitation in the production units geared to a world cash-crop system, the military drove them from the land only when labor was urgently needed in other locations.[12] Indeed, foreign entrepreneurs profited from a system that allowed laborers to feed themselves when not employed yet made them available when needed. And the system protected the foreigner's image because the domestic compradors enforced the unpopular laws.

French entrepreneurs took advantage of these reforms. In the period from 1871 to 1889, the number of French firms conducting business in Central America increased. The firms were most numerous in Guatemala, Costa Rica, and El Salvador (Table 5). Two persuasive indicators of French participation in the "liberal" transformation of Central American societies were the number of French residents on the isthmus and the figures for French commercial activity with Middle America (Table 1). During the 1870s and 1880s, an increasing number of Frenchmen settled in Costa Rica, Guatemala, Honduras, and Panama. In 1872 the French consulate in Guatemala City listed thirty-nine French males matriculated to avoid Guatemalan military conscription. Increased French activity in Central America was consistent with the need of a stagnating domestic economy to develop foreign interests.[13]

In the 1870s, French importation of Central American products was between 500,000 and 1.5 million francs annually (Table 2). After 1878, French importation rose until it reached over 5 million francs in 1887. French exports to Central America were between 2 and 5 million francs annually between 1870 and 1883, when they dipped to about 1 million francs annually until 1896 (Table 4). This commercial decline may have been related to the 1882 failure of the Banque de l'Union Générale and the subsequent recession in France. In fact, the two highest values for French exports to Central America prior to the post-World War I years occurred in 1872 and 1881.

French businessmen were key participants in the liberal transformation and foreign penetration. The first official estimate of French investment in Central America, for 1896, was 270 million francs (Table 7). There is no reason to believe that this figure differs greatly from investment in the 1880s. The French had invested in the Panama Canal project, the Honduran Railroad, and other ventures long before 1896. By the mid-1880s, French capitalists were the largest foreign investors on the isthmus.

In the early 1870s, Minister Cabarrus complained that French residents were treated poorly whereas U.S. interests were respected because U.S. war vessels patrolled both sides of the isthmus. He recommended more frequent visits from French vessels. The commander of the French Pacific Naval Division insisted that his contingent was too small to send a ship regularly to Central American ports. In response, the government in Paris added a ship to his division and assigned it to Middle American duty. This ship's captain argued that the most interesting countries in Middle America were Honduras, due to the interoceanic railroad project, and El Salvador, which was the richest in resources. The ship conducted navigational soundings, searched for sandbars near isthmian harbors, and reviewed the treatment of Frenchmen in Central America. French vessels even appeared on the Atlantic coast. When rumors persisted of disturbances in Omoa, Honduras, the commander of the Division of the Antilles declared that his vessels were "always prepared to defend the interests of French nationals." After decades of unresponsiveness to requests for a naval presence, the French government decided about 1872 (years before de Lesseps's canal project) to bear the cost of assigning vessels to Central American duty.[14] The loss of Alsace-Lorraine compelled French entrepreneurs to find raw materials and investment opportunities abroad. Central America possessed raw materials, investment opportunities, and transit routes.

On a visit to all of Central America in early 1874, Commander Miet was surprised to discover as much French commerce as he did. He found that although the Germans, Americans, and British were the chief commercial partners in the ports on the Pacific, French merchants had made their mark in some spots. Reinforcing this observation, Commander Aube de Seignlay reported in 1876 that French businessmen had a good reputation all along the coast. He concluded that French trade was valued more in La Unión, El Salvador, than elsewhere in Middle America because French merchant vessels visited this harbor most frequently. He warned, however, of a proposal to double the Salvadoran duties on French spirituous liquors and permit German commerce to profit at the expense of French. In Corinto, Nicaragua, the British were barely ahead of French commercial activity. French commerce held a minor position in Panama, Seignlay noted, because French steamers and sailing vessels no longer visited the isthmian ports. On the whole, Miet doubted that French commerce would achieve equality with that of the United States, Germany, England, or Spain in Middle America. Yet French merchants might still develop an advantageous trade. For its part, the French government signaled its intention to match any concessions its competitors might wring from a Central American government.[15]

French officials, like their U.S. and British counterparts, commonly considered the German entrepreneurs to be the most successful businessmen on the isthmus. The French chargé pronounced German goods inferior to French products, but he assigned the stagnation of French imports to the huge German merchant houses that extended special facilities to their Central American consumers. In the mid-1870s, J. Laferrière stated that "all the Central American republics [were] above all exploited by the Germans and the British." "We French," he said, "do not know how to experience the world (to let go of our native-place), we do not have the entrepreneurial spirit." French imports from Guatemala stagnated while German imports augmented yearly, but matters were even worse than the trade statistics indicated. French consul Gustave Langlade claimed that many of the goods recorded as French were, in fact, German products ordered from French wholesalers. The French consul in San Salvador warned that British, U.S., and German merchants appeared more aware of the local demands and would eventually eliminate French merchants and products unless French businessmen adapted to the situation. Nevertheless, he insisted that French products, if properly presented, would fit the tastes and habits of Central Americans.[16] French merchants and commercial agents were fewer and less successful than French officials desired because the Germans were more accommodating.

Compradors in Central America applied simple commercial devices—such as tariffs—to distribute benefits among the metropoles. Central American customs laws placed *ad valorem* duties (a percentage of the certified value listed on the invoice) on imported products. A French consul urged French businessmen to adopt the policy of their British and North American counterparts who reported the value of their goods at the cheaper prices either at the factory or at the port of embarkation rather than at the higher prices of the port of entry. The resulting lower tariffs would help French products compete with British and North American goods. The commerce minister alerted French businesses of this important suggestion. When a chamber of commerce inquired about return cargoes for French freighters, the consul suggested following the British example of accepting credit paper for sales and then using the paper to purchase local products as return cargo. This would eliminate the French merchant's practice of always demanding cash (in French or British currencies), which greatly hindered trade.[17]

The competition between firms often reflected larger national interests. In the late summer of 1873 the Panama Railroad Company rescheduled its Pacific steamers out of synchronization with the Compagnie Générale Transatlantique steamers on the Atlantic coast. French consul Edouard Carpentier claimed that the U.S. firm had done this "with the objective of eliminating at least one of its numerous competitors" and to create advantages for its own and Pacific Mail Steamship Company steamers rather than to serve local needs. A year later the Compagnie

Transatlantique ceased calling at the isthmus.[18] Such assaults upon transit or shipping were particularly threatening because they affected the distribution of metropole production and the return on investment.

The financial difficulties of the Honduran Interoceanic Railroad in the early 1870s jeopardized a sizable French investment (about 50 million francs). Several important Frenchmen supported the project. In 1872, Alfred Neymarck, a respected economist, asserted that the Honduran Railroad bonds of 1869 were a good placement and well guaranteed and that "the project of yesterday is the magnificent reality of tomorrow." French writer Alexandre Bourgeot was convinced that Honduras had overcome the financial problems that had delayed the railroad. He expected that the railroad would help French industry and commerce to satisfy their "need for expansion." But the Honduran Railroad collapsed during the financial panic of 1873. Commander Seignlay attributed this failure chiefly to the sparse population and the lax interest in trade along Middle America's Atlantic coast.[19]

Interoceanic transit was the key to most metropole involvement on or near the isthmus. In the early 1870s, French officials and promoters remained interested in a transit route, particularly to connect France with its Pacific possessions and to facilitate trade with the west coast of the New World and the Pacific islands. In the mid-1870s, U.S. secretary of state Hamilton Fish tried to control the discussion on the canal route. He declared that only Nicaragua was suitable for a canal. Despite Fish's evaluation, in 1876 a French company was formed to undertake a canal project across the Darien isthmus. French leaders and society were looking to repair deflated nationalism after the defeat of 1870–71 and the loss of Alsace-Lorraine. Admiral Daniel Ammen and former president Ulysses S. Grant of the United States supported Aniceto G. Menocal's contract for a U.S. canal at Nicaragua as a counterweight to the Panama project. Ferdinand de Lesseps and the French International Geographical Society had discounted previous U.S. surveys before they called a conference in Paris to consider an isthmian canal route. The U.S. government refused to turn over some maps or to participate officially in the conference. It wanted information regarding French canal plans, but de Lesseps's supporters were beyond its control. Despite the efforts of Ammen, Grant, Menocal, and others, the de Lesseps group selected Panama.[20]

De Lesseps's canal venture from 1878 to 1889 can be easily misinterpreted. For the French it represented an intensified interest in Central American transit and world trade, an outlet for capital, and a source of national pride as France's best promoter undertook a second "impossible" project to benefit humanity, trade, and the nation. France's political economy encouraged searching abroad for new sources of raw materials. The more the French economy demanded the importation of foreign raw materials, the more politicians, economists, and businessmen stressed the major role that opening cheap, convenient access to the Pacific basin would play. Panama was a way station, not an end, for French expansionists. Certainly the health of the labor force would be a key factor in completing the transit, but the French canal company believed that it had selected a decisive leader and the most appropriate and healthiest location.[21]

The canal quickly became the largest French investment in Latin America. The company floated over a billion francs in bonds between 1879 and 1888, but it did not transfer all that capital to Panama. The project attested to the magnitude of surplus capital in France, to the widespread confidence in de Lesseps, and to the French willingness to accept high risk for the chance to revive national glory and dominate world trade. It stimulated other French ventures in Central America. For example, the wealthy Péreire brothers, Emile and Isaac, were approached about supplying capital for Guatemalan president Justo Rufino Barrios's favorite projects—an Atlantic coast railroad and a bank. The Péreires considered the tempting offer. French diplomat Darby P. de Thiersant rejoiced too soon that a Franco-Guatemalan company would construct the Atlantic railroad and stimulate French commercial and industrial interests in Guatemala because the brothers turned it down. Thiersant assured Barrios that while the French government would not involve itself in organizing capital for the Atlantic railroad, adequate private capital was available in France. In addition, French capitalists considered a hypothecary (mortgage) bank in Costa Rica and several new projects in El Salvador.[22] The canal and related projects offered an outlet for mounting sums of investment capital.

The canal stimulated French shipping interests. In 1881, John M. Dow, a senior captain with the Pacific Mail Steamship Company, discovered that French merchants in the various Central American countries were opposing the renewal of Pacific Mail contracts in the hope that a French steamer service would operate on the Pacific coast. In anticipation of the canal, a French naval officer proposed making a hydrographic survey of the Gulf of Panama so that French shipping firms could take full advantage of the canal. He called for French shipping firms to renounce the Cape Horn route and to expand their contact with the New World.[23]

Not all French interests, however, were content with the decision to invest French funds, lives, and reputations in Panama. A number of Frenchmen favored the Nicaraguan canal route. In 1879, Aristide P. Blanchet failed to secure Nicaraguan approval for his plan to construct a Nicaraguan canal. Thiersant, too, believed that the Nicaraguan route was geographically superior. Louis and George Vergrugghe thought the Nicaraguan route was feasible once engineers had dealt with the shifting sandbar blockage of the San Juan River and Greytown port. They urged Central American unification to create the strength necessary "to resist the future covetousness of the United States" and to allow the superior French technical abilities to undertake the transit project. Early during the construction of the Panama Canal, Blanchet warned publicly that the Panama route would be too costly in financial and human terms. Since the completion of the Panama Canal would offer greater commercial advantages to the United States than to France, French industrialist Auguste Lalance was puzzled about why so much French and so little North American money was invested in the project. He advised France to look elsewhere for great projects to complete.[24]

The Central American governments were deeply disturbed by the worldwide commercial and financial crisis of the 1870s. Still, in the late 1870s, Thiersant judged the performance of the French commercial establishment in Central America, and especially in Guatemala, to be satisfactory. He reported that the French mercantile houses prospered because they extracted a greater profit abroad than in France. He noted the lack of capital in Central America and counseled French merchants to act prudently, and he offered his excellent relations with the five Central American states to help France guide them best along the road to progress and civilization.[25]

Many Frenchmen believed that de Lesseps's project offered commercial bonuses if French interests acted wisely. Carpentier, for example, was convinced that French firms would flourish if they set up affiliates in Middle America to distribute their production. He also urged closer contact with the Spanish language and culture. In mid-1879 the French government circulated his proposal to translate French catalogues into Spanish and to adapt the offerings of the École Supérieure de Commerce to attract young Hispanic businessmen. The captain of the *Hussard* assumed that the interoceanic canal would allow the French to capture an appreciable part of the Pacific and Central American trade, even though no French consular agent or important commercial house operated on the Pacific side of Central America. But the competition for the expected boost in isthmian trade was sharp. In late 1882, Carpentier claimed that the Costa Rican tariff-revision committee was a threat to French interests because it contained agents for German, British, and Danish commerce, but not for French. In 1883 the French government ordered Minister Jacques Philippe Auguste LeBrun to report periodically on commercial developments in Guatemala. He formed a commercial committee to advise him, but it functioned ineffectively until it was dissolved three years later. French trade in Central America benefited from the stimulation of de Lesseps's project,[26] but it needed better preparation and representation to avoid squandering the important commercial opportunities arising from the Panama project.

The construction of the canal proceeded slowly as unforeseen problems arose. At first, de Lesseps blamed local conditions such as political disorder, unfriendly climate, unskilled labor, and diseases for delays. Some of the local instability, French writer Edmond Planchut asserted, arose from external forces such as the xenophobia hidden in the shadow of U.S. filibustering. But decisiveness, money, and confidence in the de Lesseps company would lead to a successful canal project. Captain Parizot of the French navy judged that lack of capital and labor hindered the canal's progress. Naturally, de Lesseps's personal appearance in Panama generated enthusiastic demonstrations favorable to France and bolstered optimism about the canal. LeBrun acknowledged the praise, but he was reprimanded for creating the appearance of official support for de Lesseps. Initially, French officials reported good progress in the project.[27]

Despite widespread support in Latin America for a canal, U.S. public opinion remained unfriendly to the de Lesseps project. The countries on the west coast of the isthmus complained that Yankee ingenuity might block the French, but it could not build a canal at an alternative site. The French naval commander described the "detestable impression produced" in Central and South America when President Rutherford B. Hayes opposed de Lesseps's project from which these areas expected so much benefit. Captain Dow feared that the U.S. government would "give another scream and . . . send a squadron" when it learned that the French government was maintaining war vessels on both sides of the canal route to "protect" French interests.[28]

After the Panama project began, Hayes's administration resurrected interest in Ambrose Thompson's Chiriquí concession, which included a transit route in Panama near the Costa Rican border. The U.S. government actually appropriated $200,000 to acquire a naval station there, but the secretary of the navy refused to contract for the sites because of uncertainty about the validity of the concession. When the U.S. government hesitated, Thompson sought unsuccessfully to sell certain of his concession rights to the French Panama Canal Company.[29]

French officials contended that the de Lesseps project diminished U.S. prospects in Nicaragua because both the toll charges and the time of transit would be markedly lower in Panama. They assumed that the U.S. government prolonged its negotiations with Nicaragua only to undermine the Panama work. Since the U.S.-Nicaraguan treaty of 1884 conceded to the U.S. government extensive military control and other broad powers, French officials feared that the agreement might threaten the neutrality of de Lesseps's canal, and they suspected that the United States wanted similar terms from Colombia. They hoped that the North Americans would not risk capital in an enterprise doomed to failure. As a kind of insurance, it was widely rumored, de Lesseps paid Justo Barrios 10 million francs to oppose the Nicaragua canal. In any case, de Lesseps's agents planned to weaken support for an alternative transit route.[30]

The French navy bolstered French interests. In the late 1870s it resumed regular patrolling in Central America. In 1876, Admiral Perigot noted that the second visit of a war vessel to Central America within a six-month period had produced an "excellent effect" for French influence and calmed the consul general. Pleased with this result, he instructed his subordinates to exercise their command with care. They were not to threaten the use of force without specific orders from him, even if French consular or diplomatic officers ordered them to take forceful action. The French navy tried to avoid provoking U.S. public opinion. In response to concerns about possible conflict between the Monroe Doctrine and a French canal, the French government had repeatedly denied any official relationship with entrepreneurial groups involved in isthmian transit. The admiral in command of the Pacific division wanted the *Hussard* to visit each country and, if it could be done discreetly, to contact de Lesseps. He wanted to avoid even the appearance that the French government officially sustained de Lesseps's project. Even to excite U.S. public opinion might endanger the enterprise's international character.[31]

The French government protected the ancillary French commercial and investment activity without relying on force. The navy could show the flag and lend moral support to diplomats, but it was not to use force without specific orders because the French government remained determined to avoid confrontation with the U.S. government. The admiral commanding on the west coast instructed his subordinates that France "had a great interest in not allowing U.S. influence to dominate in South America, but that the French navy's role was limited to informing the government on this subject." Once de Lesseps's project was underway, French vessels appeared less frequently. This disturbed the French diplomat in Guatemala, who reiterated the connection between political influence and frequent visits of men-of-war.[32] But besides jockeying with the United States in Central America, the French government was engaged in colonial campaigns in Tunisia, Indochina, and Algeria.

The U.S. government was determined to undermine French influence. In 1881, despite its repeated calls for nations to use arbitration, Washington resisted the Costa Rican and Colombian attempt to arbitrate their border dispute because these countries preferred the French president to a U.S. representative as arbitrator. The U.S. government claimed that the U.S.-New Granada Treaty of 1846 conceded it a role in selecting the arbitrator, but the Costa Rican government considered this contention merely an attempt to stop the de Lesseps project.[33] U.S. intransigence blocked a settlement of the border dispute for more than a decade—until after the French canal company was in receivership—before the French president was allowed to arbitrate. Metropoles or semiperiphery states commonly adjusted principles that might offer advantages to competing powers.

Franco-Guatemalan relations in the 1880s reflected the competition of metropole capitalists for concessions and the consequences of nationalism and anti-imperial (or anti-metropole) sentiment in a periphery society. In the early 1880s, French diplomats advised a cautious response to Guatemalan overtures to borrow at the Paris Bourse. When one Guatemalan agent,

Crisanto Medina, traveled to France and England to seek a loan and another agent left for France with the Atlantic coast railroad contracts of the former administrator of the Suez canal, Henri Louis Félix de Cottu, Thiersant warned that Guatemala's financial condition and its inability to settle even minor claims suggested insecurity for French capitalists. In addition, he said, Guatemala's border difficulties with Mexico had resurfaced, and these had "thrown" President Barrios into U.S. hands because he needed support. He cautioned that Cottu's railroad concession was short-term and that, after it expired, Barrios, given his dependence on U.S. assistance against Mexico, would grant a successor concession to U.S. entrepreneurs. Moreover, Barrios had already rejected a Franco-Guatemalan guarantee of the concession.[34]

The increased French activity on the isthmus elevated the tension between French and Guatemalan nationalism. Thiersant's personality and exaggerated nationalism involved him, much as Challeye had been thirty years earlier, in several disputes with the Guatemalan government. In late 1881 legation secretary Raymond Pilet was severely wounded in the streets of Guatemala City. Pilet, who held a law degree, was only twenty-seven and a four-year veteran official when he arrived in Guatemala. He rose to the rank of first-class consul and was awarded the chevalier de la Légion d'honneur before he retired in 1912. Thiersant, convinced that the Guatemalan government was behind the attack, made various demands immediately. He remained obsessively critical and hostile even after Guatemalan authorities captured one assassin and sentenced him to ten years in prison and continued its pursuit of other suspects. Simultaneously, Thiersant claimed that an 1856 agreement prohibited the Guatemalan government from separating the French religious order Hermanas de San Vicente de Paul from a hospice in Guatemala City. When the Guatemalan government informed him that it had already sent all the documents on this case to France, where the French government had accepted its position, Thiersant was embarrassed, and his anger from the Pilet incident was magnified. Guatemalan officials reported his persistent complaints and insulting behavior to its diplomat in France.[35]

Shortly after the assassination attempt, Thiersant heard the U.S. businessman General Carlos Butterfield say that even if Guatemala failed to satisfy French demands arising from the attack upon Pilet, the United States would not tolerate strong action being taken against weak Central American states. When the British minister took exception to this remark, Thiersant reported that Butterfield reddened and mentioned the Monroe Doctrine and the U.S. pledge to protect these states. After this confrontation, U.S. minister Cornelius Logan assured Thiersant that Butterfield had no diplomatic status, but he conceded that Butterfield's support might encourage Barrios to be intransigent. Thiersant concluded that France needed to act strongly to preserve its influence. If it was unwilling to insist upon a satisfactory response, he requested permission to move the legation to Costa Rica, where French interests were also appreciable.[36]

The resolution of the Pilet affair proved unsatisfactory to Guatemala rather than France, however. The Guatemalan public was aroused against the French because the French Foreign Ministry had refused to receive the agent Barrios had sent to present his case and the French cabinet had sent its demands on a frigate. The commander of the Pacific division expected that the presence of his vessel and the comparatively soft terms being offered would persuade Barrios to adopt an agreeable course toward French claims. France did not entrust its case to Thiersant. Rather, it had the Spanish diplomat in Guatemala extract from that state a payment of $2,000, prison sentences for all attackers of Pilet, and a note assuring France of satisfaction.[37]

Meanwhile Thiersant was compounding his problems with the Guatemalan authorities. In June 1882 he protested the seizure of 120 bottles of wine, 7 bottles of cognac, and 1 bottle of liquor that he had imported duty free, yet admitted selling because his family had left. The Guatemalan authorities condemned his action as illegal, but decided not to make an issue of it. Thiersant, however, had no shame. On the day Guatemala paid the $2,000 Pilet claim, he requested permission to import goods from Nicaragua duty free and for his secretary to sell wine duty free. Guatemalan officials considered these requests unacceptably bad precedents.[38]

Several years after the Pilet incident, LeBrun reported that the arrival of the *Dayot* at a Guatemalan harbor and the visit of some French officers and men to the capital had created a good impression and displayed the power and capability of the French government. He thought that this friendly visit removed the shadow cast over Franco-Guatemalan relations by the Pilet affair. The arrival of the cruiser *Fabert* in June 1886 further improved Franco-Guatemalan relations. LeBrun requested occasional visits of war vessels similar to the custom of the British and U.S. navies.[39]

Two crises disturbed Central America in early 1885. One was created by Barrios's call for a Central American union, an appeal that ended with his death during a brief war in April 1885. LeBrun welcomed Barrios's proclamation of union because it would check U.S. schemes to absorb Central America and to build the Nicaragua canal. The other crisis was an anti-American riot in Panama. In response to these incidents, the French government ordered vessels to remain near Colón and Panama unless specific problems demanded their presence elsewhere.[40]

The Panama riot had direct bearing upon French interests. In March 1885 a small incident between Panamanians and U.S. citizens on the isthmus had exploded into a riot that caused considerable losses and endangered the property of the French Universal Interoceanic Canal Company, including the Panama Railroad. French officials charged that the U.S. superintendent of the Panama Railroad had responded inadequately to the danger that the riot posed to the canal company's railroad property, wharves, and storehouses and to the property of other French citizens and firms. U.S. officials had built a file of claims against Colombia that could be used to extract concessions that might ruin the canal company. In addition, the superintendent had called upon the U.S. navy rather than the French navy to guard company property, and the U.S. officials at Panama had made no effort to communicate with the senior French officer during the crisis. The French consul warned that U.S. officials were seeking to remove any foreign influence that might undermine their position on the isthmus. He urged the appointment of a Frenchman of rank and authority on the isthmus because although the canal company was international, the capital invested in it was French. Still, the authority Frenchmen could exercise on the isthmus was limited. While the U.S. government might permit a European power to build a canal, it would not accept European nations as joint guarantors of Panamanian transit.[41]

French officials recognized that once a Panama canal was completed, the military situation on the isthmus and in the Caribbean region would change significantly. To start with, the great-power navies would seek to build strength near the transit route. LeBrun was convinced that naval stations would supply the key to metropole power in the area of the canal, particularly on the Pacific side. In early 1884 a French navy survey decided that all Central American ports were weakly fortified, but that Corinto, Amapala, and La Unión could be fortified easily. In the 1880s the French government learned that three islands in Fonseca Bay, suitable for a base, might be purchased: Puntasacate with an area of 994 hectars, Conchaguita with 632 hectars, and Sacate Grande with 4,129 hectars. The family of French vice-consul Octave Courtade owned the first two, and a Frenchman named Leitzelar and former president Marco A. Soto of Honduras owned the third. The French received two offers. Courtade's father offered to sell one island near La Unión for 40,000 pesos, and Leitzelar asked 20,000 pesos for his one-third share of Sacate Grande. All three islands possessed anchorage and ample roadstead, but the naval ministry decided that it was unwise to acquire land without full sovereignty. And the French government rejected all purchase schemes in Fonseca Bay because the acquisition of any of the islands would generate significant problems with Nicaragua, Honduras, El Salvador, and the United States.[42]

French officials considered options further away from mainland Central America that would offer a way station with strategic value in anticipation of the opening of the isthmian canal. They examined Ecuador's Galápagos Islands, Costa Rica's Cocos Island, and Clipperton Island (France, Mexico, the United States, and Britain all suspected they might have claim to this uninhabited island) as possible naval support points. The captain of the French ship *Decree*, for example, looked at the claims of a Frenchman on Foriana Island in the Galápagos chain. Although anxious to avoid trouble with the United States, French officials believed that they had legitimate grounds to obtain a naval base near the Panama Canal to protect their commerce and to assert an appropriate role in the world.[43]

The French government did not lose interest in the islands lying off the west coast of Latin America, in part because de Lesseps's company was reorganized as the New Panama Canal Company. French officials continually evaluated the strategic value of the Clipperton, Cocos (the island group closest to the western terminal of the Panama Canal), and Galápagos Islands. A rumor that U.S. fishermen had raised the flag on Clipperton Island, listed in *Gothas Almanach* as a French possession, prompted the French naval minister to investigate the island's sovereignty. The French sent "investigating and scientific" teams to the Galápagos Islands, which Captain Germinet considered the only useful naval support point in the Pacific near the canal entrance.[44] But as already noted, French officials remained hesitant to pursue maritime bases near the entrances of the canal, fearing U.S. hostility.

Despite a promising start, French interests did not fare well in Costa Rica in the mid-1880s. The Costa Rican government, which claimed an interest in any Nicaraguan canal, shared Nicaragua's disappointment with de Lesseps's project. Both Costa Rican and Nicaraguan leaders recognized that the French project at Panama essentially ended their hopes of attracting a canal to the San Juan River area, from which both nations had expected to reap vast direct and indirect economic gains. The French consul noted, however, that Costa Rica would assume exceptional commercial and strategic importance regardless of whether the canal was completed at Panama or at Nicaragua.[45]

Nicaraguan diplomat Gustavo Guzmán tried to persuade the French to shift their wealth and technology to his country because it offered the only practicable canal. He predicted that France faced a disaster in Panama because a sea-level canal was financially impossible. He concluded: "France is rich enough to pay, at the cost of billions, for the error of one of its most illustrious children. But it is necessary that it hasten to . . . demand of the Nicaragua enterprise . . . that which the deceiving affair of Panama could never offer: the realization of a grand idea, morally and materially profitable to humanity, and financially advantageous for those who would sustain it." Guzmán expressed regret that people of real merit were caught up in the misfortune of the Panama project.[46]

In late 1887 the French consul in Guatemala, Paul Louis Reynaud, reported that the Central American governments were trying to discourage the de Lesseps project. But he accepted wild rumors uncritically. He believed that some U.S. businessmen were plotting to create panic among the supporters of the Panama canal and then acquire this advanced project at a bargain price; these businessmen expected to make a killing off the sale of the Universal Interoceanic Canal Company stock to the U.S. government. In late 1888 a financial scandal involving de Lesseps and the other high officials of the Panama Canal Company undermined the company's ability to raise the funds needed to continue the project; work slowed to a snail's pace. In early 1889 the project was suspended.[47]

Despite the failure of the canal venture, the French government intended to preserve France's commercial and shipping interests in Middle America. French opportunities for trade in the region required monitoring the powerful position of the German Kosmos line and German merchants in the Pacific harbors of Central America. French commerce made headway against the Germans in several places. Naval officer Descamps believed that the French occupied "a very good position" in Nicaragua, and only French firms operated in Amapala, Honduras, and La Libertad, El Salvador. But the French consul in Costa Rica reported that French trade lagged behind German trade, which had "extended considerably into that region," because the Kosmos line offered regular shipping service. He expressed disappointment that the Compagnie Transatlantique had rejected a stop at Puerto Limón that would have helped French merchandise enter Costa Rica. In general, French officials believed that the German shipping industry was instrumental in undercutting France's share of the Central American market.[48]

LeBrun regretted that French companies were not profiting from the opportunities that German and U.S. companies found in Central America. Reynaud warned that the new German-Guatemalan Commerce Treaty of 1887 could lead to German goods replacing French products. With Germany extending its influence into a country that was just entering a development stage, and where French influence had declined since 1870, he pleaded to keep French interests alive and protected. He considered the promotion of German chargé Werner von Bergen to minister as another step in Germany's campaign to achieve a preponderant position in Central America. To halt this trend, Reynaud wanted the French government to match the Germans and the other major powers by naming a minister. Like many Europeans, he became apprehensive when the U.S. government called for a Pan American Conference to meet in Washington, DC, in early 1889. Furthermore, a projected Pan American customs union threatened all European commercial interests. Reynaud expected the French government to respond effectively to the rising German and U.S. influence.[49]

Between 1871 and 1889, French officials and private citizens, bitter over the defeat of 1871, were uniformly unhappy with the growth, expansion, and success of German enterprises on the isthmus. Napoleon III's vision of blocking Yankee expansion faded, but some of his aspirations for France's future on the isthmus remained. In the 1870s, French interests had captured de Lesseps for a project to build a sea-level canal at Panama. French investment and commerce in Middle America rose dramatically. For over two decades after 1880, French capitalists held the largest share of foreign investment in Middle America.

The 1880s represented a peak in French material involvement in Middle America. The canal project increased the interaction of French and Middle American societies. French commerce with the isthmus increased, the number of French residents on the isthmus rose sharply, and the navy made more frequent visits to isthmian ports. The nation's prestige and reputation blossomed. De Lesseps's project educated the French public about transit, colonization, plantations, and business opportunities in the region. Despite the failure of the canal project, French society continued to exert a major influence in the financial and cultural aspects of Central American society into the early twentieth century. Rising U.S. power in the region, however, often prevented Central American affairs from conforming satisfactorily to French expectations.

Notes

1. André Siegfried, *Suez, Panama et les routes maritimes mondiales* (Paris, 1945), 279–84; David McCullough, *The Path between the Seas: The Creation of the Panama Canal, 1870–1914* (New York, 1977), 45–69; Jean-Marie Mayeur, *Les Débuts de la IIIe République, 1871–1898* (Paris, 1973); Jean-Pierre Azéma and Michel Winock, *La Troisième République* (Paris, 1976); Jacques Desmarest, *La France de 1870* (3 vols.; Paris, 1970–1977); Asselain, *Histoire économique de la France*, 2: 159–60; Max Sorre, *Mexique, Amérique Centrale* (Paris, 1928), 215–22; Paul Bairoch, *Commerce extérieur et développement économique de l'Europe au xixe siècle* (Paris, 1976); Paul Bairoch, *Révolution industrielle et sous-développement* (4th ed.; Paris, 1974); William H. Schneider, "Geographical Reform and Municipal Imperialism in France, 1870–1880," in John M. McKenzie, ed., *Imperialism and the Natural World* (Manchester, 1990), 90–117.

2. Henri Brunschwig, *Mythes et réalités de l'impérialisme colonial français, 1871–1914* (Paris, 1960), 185–88; Henri Brunschwig, *La Colonisation française du pacte colonial à l'union française* (Paris, 1949); Henri Brunschwig, *Vom Kolonialimperialismus zur Kolonialpolitik der Gegenwart* (Wiesbaden, 1957); Gilbert Ziebura, "Interne Faktoren des französischen Hochimperialismus, 1871–1914," in Wolfgang J. Mommsen, ed., *Der moderne Imperialismus* (Stuttgart, 1971), 85–139; Archille Viallate, *L'Impérialisme économique et les relations internationales pendant le dernier demi-siècle (1870–1920)* (Paris, 1923); Jean Bouvier, "Encore sur l'impérialisme: Des rapports entre banque et industrie dans l'expansion française au dehors (1880–1914)," *Revue française d'histoire d'outre-mer* 67 (1980): 217–26; Jean Bouvier and René Girault, eds., *Impérialisme français d'avant 1914: Recueil du textes* (Paris, 1976); Roger Magraw, *France, 1815–1914* (New York, 1986), 234–45; Jean-Baptiste Duroselle, "La Politique extérieure de la IIIe République," in *Centenaire de la troisième République. Actes du colloque de Rennes, 15–17 mai 1975* (Paris, 1975), 130–40; René Rémond, *Le xixe siècle, 1815–1914* (Paris, 1974), 208–48; Guy Martinière, *Les Amériques latines: Une histoire économique* (Grenoble, 1978), 324–35; Jean Weiller, "Echanges et politique commerciale de la France," *Économies et sociétés, cahiers de l'institut de science économique appliquée* 3 (Oct. 1969): 1745–1878; Agnes Murphy, *The Ideology of French*

Imperialism (New York, 1968); Winfried Baumgart, "Das größere Frankreich: Neue Forschungen über den französischen Imperialismus, 1880–1914," *Vierteljahrschrift für Sozial- und Wirtschaftsgeschichte* 61 (1974): 185–98; James J. Cooke, *New French Imperialism, 1880–1910: The Third Republic and Colonial Expansion* (Hamden, CT, 1973); L. Salgó, *Du Rôle des facteurs économiques et politiques de la politique coloniale française dans la période d'après 1871* (Budapest, 1975); Raymond Betts, *The False Dawn: European Imperialism in the Nineteenth Century* (Minneapolis, 1976).

3. Caron, *An Economic History of Modern France*, 8–10, 13–21; Michael S. Smith, "Free Trade Versus Protectionism in the Early Third Republic: Economic Interests, Tariff Policy, and the Making of the Republican Synthesis," *French Historical Studies* 10 (Spring 1977): 293–314; Anthony Rowley, *Evolution économique de la France du milieu du xix*[e] *siècle à 1914* (Paris, 1982); Tom Kemp, "Structural Factors in the Retardation of French Economic Growth," *Kyklos* 15 (1962): 325–52. Lévy-Leboyer disagreed. He computed the annual growth of the working population at 0.9 percent from 1866 to 1896 in "La Décélération de l'économie française dans la seconde moitié du xixe siècle."

4. Wallerstein, *Historical Capitalism*, 32.

5. Caron, *An Economic History of Modern France*, 24–25; Jean Bouvier, François Furet, and Marcel Gillet, *Le Mouvement du profit en France au xix*[e] *siècle* (Paris, 1965), 269–77; Rowley, *Évolution économique de la France*, 369–433; Hans Rosenberg, *Große Depression und Bismarckzeit* (2d ed.; Berlin, 1976).

6. Schoonover and Schoonover, "Statistics for the Understanding of the Foreign Intrusion into Central America from the 1820s to 1930, Part 3," 77–119; James Hosmer to William Wharton, Sept. 9, 1889, Consular Dispatches, Guat.: vol. 7, microcopy 337, reel 7 (hereafter, CD, Guat.: 7 [T 337/r 7], NA).

7. Cardoso, "Central America: The Liberal Era, c. 1870–1930"; Woodward, *Central America*, 120–202; Pérez Brignoli, *Breve historia de Centro-América*, 95–106; Jorge Mario García Laguardia, *La Reforma liberal en Guatemala: Vida política y orden constitucional* (Guatemala, 1972), 37–53; Ernesto Chincilla Aguilar, "El positivismo y la reforma en Guatemala," *Antropología e historia de Guatemala* 12 (June 1960): 35–53; Guillermo Molino Chocano, *Estado liberal y desarrollo capitalista en Honduras* (Tegucigalpa, 1976); Héctor Pérez-Brignoli, "La reforma liberal en Honduras," *Ciencias sociales* 2 (1973): 2–19; Ralph Lee Woodward, Jr., "Pensamiento científico y desarrollo económico en Centroamérica, 1860–1920," *Revista del pensamiento centroamericano*, 172–73 (July–Dec. 1981): 73–86; Ralph Lee Woodward, Jr., "Political Economy in Guatemala," *University of Wichita Bulletin* 37 (Aug. 1962): 3–15; David McCreery, *Development and the State in Reforma Guatemala, 1871–1885*, Monographs in Latin America Series, vol. 10 (Athens, OH, 1983).

8. Woodward, *Central America*, 151–61; García Laguardia, *La reforma liberal en Guatemala*, 171–82; Seldon Liss, *Radical Thought in Central America* (New York, 1991), 16–17, 26–27, 98, 128–30, 161–62; Ralph Lee Woodward, Jr., *Rafael Carrera and the Emergence of the Republic of Guatemala, 1821–1871* (Athens, GA, 1993), 330–37; David Bushnell and Neil Macaulay, *Emergence of Latin America in the Nineteenth Century*, 189–90; Burns, *The Poverty of Progress*, 18–19, 46–49.

9. Woodward, *Central America*, 149–202; MRE to Ramón Palacis, July 15, 1871, Feb. 5, 1872, Feb. 6, 1873, B99-5-6, 4355/93261, Legación y Consulado de la República en Francia e Italia, 1867–1874, AGCA; Julien Dominique M. Edmund Tallien de Cabarrus, March 23, 1874, B99-5-6/4318/93223, MRE, AGCA; William J. Griffith, "Attitudes toward Foreign Colonization: The Evolution of Nineteenth-Century Guatemalan Immigration Policy," in *Applied Enlightenment: Nineteenth Century Liberalism* (New Orleans, 1972), 73–110.

10. LaFeber, *Inevitable Revolutions*, 31–34; Karl Bermann, *Under the Big Stick: Nicaragua and the United States since 1848* (Boston, 1986), 103–50; Alison Acker, *Honduras: The Making of a Banana Republic* (Boston, 1988), 55–62; Jim Handy, *The Gift of the Devil: A History of Guatemala* (Boston, 1984), 57–60; Rafael Menjívar, *Acumulación originaria y desarrollo del capitalismo en El Salvador* (San José, CR, 1980), 27–57; Barbara Potthast, *Die Mosquitoküste im Spannungsfeld britischer und spanischer Politik, 1502–1821* (Cologne, 1988); Craig L. Dozier, *"Nicaragua's Mosquito Shore." The Years of British and American Presence* (University, AL, 1985).

11. David McCreery, "Debt Servitude in Rural Guatemala, 1876–1936," *Hispanic American Historical Review* 63 (1983): 735–59; David McCreery, "Coffee and Class: The Structure of Development in Liberal Guatemala, 1871–1885," *Hispanic American Historical Review* 56 (1976): 438–60; Carol A. Smith, *Labor and International Capital in the Making of a Peripheral Social Formation: Economic Transformations of Guatemala, 1850–1980* (Washington, DC, 1984).

12. Woodward, *Central America*, 149–202; Cardoso and Pérez Brignoli, *Centro América y la economía occidental*, 199–320; Handy, *Gift of the Devil*, 65–73.

13. Cabarrus, July 24, 1872, list, B99-5-6/4318/93223, MRE, AGCA.

14. Cabarrus to MAE, July 9, 1872, CP 1896, Amér. cent., v. 23, AMAE; Jean Baptiste Chevalier to MAE, Aug. 7, 1872, CCC, Pan., v. 5, AMAE; Lapelin to Min. marine, Dec. 2, 1872, and correspondence for June 1871, to Feb. 1872, BB^4 942, AAM; various correspondence for 1871–72, particularly Charles de Surville to Commandant *Kersaint*, Nov. 27, 1872, B. de Boissondy to Surville, Jan. 25, 1873, Surville to Min. marine, Feb. 6, 1873; BB^4 954, AAM.

15. Miet to admiral commanding Pacific Division, March 7, April 5, 1874, renseignements, *Hermitte*, commander Miet, Feb.–March, 1874, Jan.–April, 1874, BB^4 1596, AAM; Admiral Albert E. L. Roussin to Min. marine, May 24, 1874, BB^4 962, AAM; Commander Aube de Seignlay to Admiral de Perigot, June 24, 1876, BB^4 1075, AAM; Jean-Louis Joachim Meurant to Min. commerce, May 11, 1872, Commerce, F^{12} 6543, AN.

16. Correspondence for June 1871, to Feb. 1872, BB^4 942, AAM; Cabarrus to MAE, July 27, 1875, Gustave Langlade to MAE, Oct. 22, 1877, André Corne to Thiersant, Jan. 3, 1881, CCC, Guat., v. 9, AMAE; Joseph Laferrière, *De Paris à Guatemala. Notes de voyages au Centre-Amérique* (Paris, 1877), 53–54; David Landes, "French Entrepreneurship and Industrial Growth in the Nineteenth Century," *Journal of Economic History* 9 (1949): 45–61; E. Malcolm Carroll, *French Public Opinion and Foreign Affairs, 1870–1914* (London, 1965); Zahniser, *Uncertain Friendship*, 164–65; Cooke, *New French Imperialism, 1880–1910*, 9–12.

17. Meurant to Min. commerce, May 15, 1874, Commerce, F[12] 7053, AN; Edouard Carpentier to MAE, Dec. 10, 1877, CCC, San José de CR, v. 1, AMAE; Gustave de Belot to MRE (Guat.), Aug. 22, 1872, B99-23-1/6225, MRE, AGCA.

18. Carpentier to MAE, Aug. 19, 1873, CCC, San José de C.R., v. 1, AMAE; Miet to admiral commanding Pacific Division, Jan. 23, 1874, BB[4] 1596, AAM; Langlade to MAE, Oct. 22, 1877, CCC, Guat., v. 9, AMAE; Paul Louis Reynaud to MAE, Dec. 14, 1887, CCC, Guat., v. 11, Reynaud to MAE, March 8, 1888, March 31, 1889, CP 1896, Amér. cent., v. 29, AMAE.

19. Alfred Neymarck, *Le Honduras. Son chemin de fer. Son avenir industriel et commercial* (Paris, 1872); Alexandre Bourgeot, *Le Honduras: Son passé et son avenir* (Paris, 1878); Seignlay to Perigot, June 24, 1876, BB[4] 1075, AAM; E. George Squier, *Honduras Interoceanic Railway* (New York, 1858).

20. Carpentier to MAE, Sept. 22, 1873, CCC, San José de CR, v. 1, AMAE; Henry Bionne, *Le Percement de l'isthme de Panama* (Paris, [1875]); Faucounces to Perigot, Sept. 22, 1875, BB[4] 1597, AAM; Verchère, "Mission d'études d'un canal interocéanique," May 30, 1876, Verchère to MAE, Oct. 19, 1876, Mémoires et Documents, v. 68, AMAE; Fish to Elihu B. Washburne, Nov. 13, 1876, DI, France: 19 (M 77/r 59), NA; William Evarts to Maxime Outrey, Nov. 4, 1878, Notes to For. Leg., France: (M 99/r 21), NA; Daniel Ammen to J. Pouchet and G. Sautereau, April 30, 1878, Thiersant to William Waddington, April 28, 1879, Mémoires et documents, Amér., v. 69, AMAE; Aristide-P. Blanchet, *La Lumière sur Panama. Analyse et critique du rapport lu par M. Ferdinand de Lesseps* (Paris, 1882); Daniel Ammen, *The American Inter-oceanic Ship Canal Question* (Philadelphia, 1880); Daniel Ammen, *American Isthmian Canal Routes* (Philadelphia, 1889).

21. McCullough, *The Path between the Seas*; Edmond Planchut, "Le Futur Canal interocéanique de l'Amérique centrale," *Revue des deux mondes* 39 (Aug. 1, 1879): 668–97; Jacques-Philippe Auguste LeBrun to MAE, Feb. 10, 1879, CCC, Pan., v. 6, AMAE; Ferdinand de Lesseps, "The Interoceanic Canal," *North American Review* 130 (Jan. 1880): 1–15; Gustave de Molinari, *A Panama. L'Isthme de Panama-la Martinique-Haïti* (Paris, [1887]); Henri Louis Gabriel de Bizemont, *L'Amérique centrale et le canal de Panama* (Paris, 1881); Paul Deschanel, *La Politique française en océanie. Apropos du canal de Panama* (Paris, 1884); Schneider, "Geographical Reform and Municipal Imperialism in France, 1870–1880," 90–117; Yasua Gonjo "Le 'Plan Freycinet' 1878–1882: Un aspect de la grande dépression économique en France," *Revue historique* 248 (July–Sept 1972): 49–86.

22. Thiersant to MAE, Aug. 19, 1880, CP to 1896, Amér. cent., v. 24, Thiersant to MAE, Jan. 14, 1880, CCC, Guat., v. 9, AMAE; Skinner, *France and Panama*, 27–46, 239–48, and Appendix B; Weiller, "Study of French Trade Structure," 808–9, 812; Zahniser, *American-French Diplomatic Relations*, 165–69; Blumenthal, *France and the United States*, 139–41; Newbury, "Aspects of French Policy in the Pacific, 1853–1906," 56; J. Fred Rippy, "French Investments in Latin America" *Interamerican Economic Affairs* 2 (1948): 57–58.

23. Dow to B. Mozley, March 8, 1881, box 4, letterbook 1879–1881, Dow papers; Aurélian Parizot to Min. marine, March 12, 1881, Admiral Brossard de Corbigny to Min. marine, March 28, 1881, BB[4] 1121, AAM.

24. Thiersant to MAE, July 2, 1879, CCC, Guat., v. 9, AMAE; Louis and George Vergrugghe, *Forêts vierges: Voyage dans l'Amérique du sud et l'Amérique centrale* (Paris, 1880); Auguste Lalance, "Les Intérêts respectifs du commerce français et du commerce américain dans le canal de Panama," *L'Economiste français* (July 3, 1886): 10–11; Blanchet, *La Lumière sur Panama*.

25. Thiersant to MAE, June 10, 1879, Foreign merchants to Guat. Min. finance, [1879], Thiersant to MAE, Oct. 27, 1879, CCC, Guat., v. 9, AMAE; Thiersant to MAE, Aug. 19, 1880, CP to 1896, Amér. cent., v. 24, AMAE.

26. Carpentier to MAE, Feb. 10, 1879, CCC, CR, v. 1, AMAE; Carpentier to MAE, Aug. 12, 1879, Commerce, F^{12} 7053, AN; Parizot to Admiral Bergasse de Petit-Thouars, Feb. 22, 1880, Chateauminces to admiral, Jan. 7, 1883, Agenor Fournier to admiral, Feb. 19, 1884, BB^4 1596, AAM; Carpentier to MAE, Sept. 14, 1882, Négociations commerciales, Cent. Amér., v. 3, AMAE; LeBrun to MAE, July 30, 31, 1883, Feb. 23, 1886, Affaires divers commerciales, carton 258, AMAE; MAE to Min. commerce, Sept. 26, 1883, enclosing LeBrun to MAE, July 30, 1883, F^{12} 7419, AN; Michel Chevalier, "Le renouvellement des traités de commerce," *Revue des deux mondes* 46 (June 15, 1876): 721–56.

27. Planchut, "Le Futur Canal interocéanique de l'Amérique centrale," 668–97; Parizot, "Panama Canal Interocéanique. Note sur le percement de l'Isthme de Panama," 1880, BB^4 1597, AAM; LeBrun to MAE, Jan. 5, March 30, 1880, CCC, Pan., v. 6, AMAE.

28. Petit-Thouars to Min. marine, Feb. 17, 1881, BB^4 1121, AAM; Dow to Ran Runnels, March 10, 1881, box 4, letterbook 1879–1881, Dow to William Lane, June 26, 1881, box 4, letterbook 1881–1883, Dow papers.

29. Paul J. Scheips, "Gabriel Lafond and Ambrose W. Thompson: Neglected Isthmian Promoters," *Hispanic American Historical Review* 34 (May 1956): 223–25.

30. Vommayrcey to MAE, March 27, 1883, CCC, Guat., v. 70, AMAE; MAE to LeBrun, July 2, 1884, LeBrun to MAE, May 30, 1885, CP 1896, Guat., v. 26, AMAE; Jules Ferry to Théodore J. D. Roustan, Feb. 2, 1885, Mémoires et documents, Amér., v. 70, AMAE.

31. Perigot to du Seignlay, June 13, 1876, Perigot to Min. marine, June 20, 1876, BB^4 1075, AAM; Petit-Thouars to Min. marine, Dec. 3, 1879, Jan. 22, 1880, Petit-Thouars to commander *Hussard*, Dec. 22, 1879, BB^4 1121, AAM; Capt. Parizot, renseignements *Hussard*, Jan. 1880 (2 reports), BB^4 1397, AAM.

32. Corbigny to commander *Dayot*, June 5, 1881, BB^4 1121, AAM; Corbigny to commander *Limier*, April 3, Nov. 19, 1882, BB^4 1152, AAM; Thiersant to Corbigny, March 11, 1881, LeBrun to admiral, Feb. 8, 1884, BB^4 1597, AAM.

33. Werner von Bergen to Otto von Bismarck, Aug. 22, 1881, Abt. IA, Columbien 2, v. 1, Politisches Archiv des Auswärtigen Amts, Bonn (hereafter cited as PAAA); Thiersant to MAE, Sept. 14, 1881, CP to 1896, Amér. cent., v. 25, AMAE.

34. Thiersant to MAE, Nov. 29, 1881, F^{30} 393^1, folder Guat., Archives du ministère de l'économie et des finances (hereafter cited as AMEF); Thiersant to MAE, Dec. 29, 1881, CCC, Guat., v. 70, AMAE; David J. McCreery, "Developmental Aspects of the Construction of the Guatemalan Northern Railroad: The First Attempts, 1879–1885" (M.A. thesis, Tulane University, 1969).

35. Thiersant to Lorenzo Montúfar, July 6, 20, 1880, enclosing memoranda from Pilet, B99-5-6/4318/93223, MRE, AGCA; note verbale, MRE interview with Thiersant, ca. Jan. 15, 1881, B99-5-6/4319/93224, MRE, AGCA; Fernando Cruz to Crisanto Medina, Nov. 14, 16, 1881, Montúfar to Medina, March 19, 1881, Cruz to Medina, Jan. 28, 1882, B99-6, 4358/93269, Leg. y cons. de Guat. en Francia, 1879–1882, AGCA; Monique de Nomazy to author, Feb. 4, 1991, and attachment on career of Raymond Pilet.

36. MAE to Min. marine, Jan. 6, 1882, Min. marine to MAE, Jan. 12, 1882, Thiersant to MAE, Dec. 14, 1881, Jan. 16, March 18, 1882, CP 1896, Amér. cent., v. 25, AMAE.

37. Corbigny to Min. marine, March 16, 1882, A. Pougin de la Maissonneuve to admiral, March 31, 1882, BB4 1152, AAM; MAE to Min. marine, Jan. 6, 1882, Min. marine to MAE, Jan. 12, 1882, Thiersant to MAE, Dec. 14, 1881, Jan. 16, March 18, 1882, CP 1896, Amér. cent., v. 25, AMAE; F. Cruz to Medina, Feb. 17, April 14, 29, June 28, 1882, B99-5-6, 4355, B99-6, 4358/93269, Leg. y cons. de Guat. en Francia, 1879–1882, AGCA.

38. Cruz to Medina, June 14, July 2, 1882, Antonio Batres to Medina, Aug. 3, 1882, B99-6, 4358/93269, Leg. y cons. de Guat. en Francia, 1879–1882, AGCA.

39. "Los Franceses en Asia," *La República* (Guat.), June 5, 1884, CP 1896, Amér. cent., v. 26, AMAE; LeBrun to MAE, March 2, 1885, CP 1896, Guat., v. 27, AMAE; LeBrun to MAE, June 20, 1886, CCC, Guat., v. 11, AMAE; Admiral to Commander, *Dayot*, Jan. 8, 1885, Descamps to Admiral Frauguet, March 6, 1885, BB4 1184, AAM; corres. March 1886, B99-5-6/4320/93225, MRE, AGCA.

40. Min. marine to Admiral, commanding division of the Pacific, March 29, April, 1885, BB4 1181, AAM; LeBrun to MAE, March 12, 18, 1885, CP 1896, Guat., v. 27, AMAE.

41. Capt. Talisman, *Penaud*, "Note sur les événements dans l'Isthme de Panama en Mars-Avril 1885," Franquet to Min. marine, May 2, 1885, BB4 1184, AAM; Charles Armando to MAE, May 25, 1885, CCC, Pan., v. 6, AMAE; Roustan to MAE, March 8, 1885, "Note pour le ministère," n.p., n.d. [circa 1885], Mémoires et Documents, Amér., v. 70, AMAE.

42. Admiral Leferre to Min. marine, Feb. 20, 1889, BB4 1596, AAM; LeBrun to Guat. MRE, June 20, 1886, CCC, Guat., v. 11, AMAE; LeBrun to MAE, April 13, Aug. 28, 1886, Feb. 25, 1887, MAE to LeBrun, June 16, 1886, April 23, 1887, Min. marine to MAE, April 17, 1887, CP 1896, Amér. cent., v. 28, AMAE. See also Bernard Ernst von Bülow to Militär-Cabinet, Sept. 30 1880, Abt. IA, (Handel) II.D.13, v. 1, PAAA.

43. Correspondence, pages 277ff, BB4 1370, AAM; MAE to Min. marine, 28 Oct. 1886, BB4 1391, AAM; Seignlay to Captain La Guerre, Feb. 17, 1887, BB4 1199, AAM; La Guerre to Min. marine, April 29, May 15, 1887, BB4 1204, AAM.; Admiral Jules Charles Auguste Lefèvre to Min. marine, Feb. 20, 1889, BB4 1229, AAM; Min. marine to MAE, Sept. 30, 1886, BB4 1357, AAM; Captain Pottier, report of *Bouvet*, Dec. 1885, BB4 1398, AAM; Frensberg to Bismarck, April 22, 1884, Preußisches Ministerium des Auswärtigen, Nr. 1002/Haiti, Geheimes Staatsarchiv, Berlin.

44. Captain Fort to Min. marine, Dec. 9, 1897, BB4 1299, AAM; Joré to MAE, July 30, 1898, CCC, San José de CR, v. 2, AMAE; Zembsch to Leo von Caprivi, May 15, 1891, Abt. IA, Galápagos-Inseln, v. 1, PAAA; Captain P. Germinet to Min. marine, March 29, 1900, May 31, 1901, BB4 1331,

AAM; Min. marine to commander of Pacific division, April 25, 1900, BB^4 1326, AAM; Walter LaFeber, *The Panama Canal: The Crisis in Historical Perspective* (rev. ed.; New York, 1989), 3–23; McCullough, *The Path between the Seas*.

45. Carpentier to MAE, Sept. 14, 1882, Négociations commerciales, Cent. Amér., v. 3, AMAE; A. Fraysse to MAE, Feb. 10, 1885, MAE to Fraysse, March 18, 1885, CP 1896, Amér. cent., v. 27, AMAE; Thomas Schoonover, "Speculators and Schemers: John C. Frémont, Otto von Bismarck, and the Costa Rican Railroad," in Schoonover, *The United States in Central America, 1860–1911*, 28–45.

46. Gustavo Guzmán, *Canal de Nicaragua* (Paris, 1887).

47. Reynaud to MAE, Dec. 4, 1887, CCC, Guat., v. 11, AMAE; Reynaud to MAE, Nov. 24, 1888, CP 1896, Amér. cent., v. 29, AMAE; Lefèvre to Min. marine, Feb. 20, 1889, BB^4 1229, AAM; Dow noted repeatedly that the project was completely suspended, letterbook 1888–1892, Dow papers; Skinner, *France and Panama*, 27–46.

48. MAE to LeBrun, Nov. 25, 1885, LeBrun to MAE, Jan. 25, 1886, CCC, Guat. v. 11, AMAE; Descamps to admiral, March 7, 1885, BB^4 1398 (see also BB^4 1596), AAM; MAE to Min. commerce Dautresme, Oct. 21, 1887, Commerce, F^{12} 7053, AN; Reinhart Schmelzkopf, "Die Deutsche Dampfschiffahrtsgesellschaft Kosmos-Eine Großreederei, von der nur die Schornsteinemarke blieb," *Schiffahrt international/Seekiste* (Sept. 1972): 361–63; "100 Jahre Südamerika Westküstendienst," Hapag-Lloyd Presse-Information, Oct. 3, 1972; Alfred Marquart, "Historische Entwicklung der Südamerika-Westküsten-Fahrt (Kosmos-Dienst)," March 31, 1942, typescript in possession of the author.

49. LeBrun to MAE, Oct. 25, 1885, Reynaud to MAE, Dec. 14, 1887, CCC, Guat., v. 11, AMAE; Reynaud to MAE, March 8, 1888, March 31, 1889, CP 1896, Amér. cent., v. 29, AMAE; MAE to Min. commerce, July 7, 1888, Commerce, F^{12} 6543, AN; Allan Mitchell, *The German Influence in France after 1870* (Chapel Hill, 1979), 190–93.

4

The Aftermath of the Universal Interoceanic Canal Company, 1889–1903

The collapse of de Lesseps's canal company bankrupted the major French investment in Middle America. It also disrupted the flow of French technology, entrepreneurs, and capital to the isthmus. The canal venture affected the French image and influence in Middle America long after its collapse. Many Frenchmen continued their economic activity on the isthmus after the bankruptcy, and various groups in France argued that the material and human investment of the nation in the canal gave it special rights on the isthmus. Around the turn of the century, French society pursued influence in new ways. It supplemented its cultural policies (for example, programs to send French teachers and books and to monitor French language instruction, and visits of French artists and cultural figures), the canal project, and its commercial and investment activity with military missions and state loans.[1] After the canal company's collapse, other metropole governments and entrepreneurs reconsidered their own transit projects. U.S. policy struggled to erase any lingering influence of de Lesseps's project or of any other French activity that could be considered a danger to U.S. objectives. However, the world economic crisis from 1873 to 1898 and, in particular, the major downturn from 1893 to 1898 burdened any plan to invest in a canal.

The world economy became intense because there were more competitors and higher growth expectations. A nation's well-being and security were bound to a rising growth rate. In this competitive situation, military power increasingly supplemented technology and organization to secure expansion. Overproduction was a sign of the rapid growth and maturation of industrial states (one needs to remember that production was a function of the use of land, labor, capital, and distribution). New markets were not needed for product sales alone, but to acquire cheaper raw materials or food (or a wider variety of food) to satisfy the expectations of laboring groups and entrepreneurs. Just as a material gap between farmers, laborers, or artisans and the landed, commercial, or entrepreneurial elite grew, so did a gap between the core and periphery states.

Competition sharpened as the metropoles struggled to preserve the growth rate that they considered essential for their security and well-being. Exaggerated extraction of value from the domestic laboring class gave way to heightened expectations of wealth from expansion abroad. But metropole competition to derive greater value from formal or informal empire required both better domestic organization and toleration of the poverty created abroad from exploitation. As an alternative, control of information or biased reports of missionary and civilizing activity could veil the reality of the metropole's impact upon the people in the periphery ("the people without history" in the words of Eric Wolf).

French participation in the world economy became better organized about 1890 with the formation of the Union Coloniale Française. Although it focused upon recreating a colonial empire, its activity generated interest in foreign areas, foreign relations, and world economic ties and in promoting markets. French military missions and arms merchants competed successfully against German missions and arms manufacturers on the isthmus. In fact, as tension between the French and Germans increased in Europe, the Balkans, and North Africa, agents and entrepreneurs from these two countries competed sharply in Central America.[2]

The canal venture and other contemporary economic, financial, and commercial activities formed part of the French political economy's response to its domestic economic difficulties and the world economic crisis of 1873 to 1898. The French population reached a nadir with the miniscule annual growth rate of 0.08 percent in the years from 1886 to 1901. From 1901 to 1911, the annual rate recovered somewhat to 0.2 percent. The mean annual increase in working-age population declined from 125,000 in the early nineteenth century to 48,000 in the 1881 to 1911 period. After the working population had remained stagnant at about sixteen or seventeen million from 1852 until 1892, immigrant labor helped it rise to 19,470,000 in 1896.[3]

The increasing accumulation of French investors, the second largest purchasers of foreign debt in the world, forced the

French to search with greater energy for new foreign opportunities. By the 1890s some French statesmen and businessmen were demanding that the nation's surplus capital and industrial production be used to pursue national economic and financial objectives. A call for economic nationalism (especially in areas of competition with Germany) grew stronger after the first Moroccan crisis of 1906. The sharpening diplomatic crisis in Europe and the Mediterranean underlined the wisdom of avoiding difficulties with the United States on the isthmus. Yet many Frenchmen were unwilling to concede to the United States financial, economic, or cultural dominance on the isthmus even while French officials were rejecting any political or diplomatic confrontation.[4]

French officials and business interests warned of the possible dire consequences for French commerce and political interests if the United States used the Pan American Conference of 1889 to build a special market for U.S. goods behind a New World customs union. They worried because a uniform tariff for the New World was consistent with the Western Hemisphere idea that preserved America for the Americans and held Europe politically and commercially distant. A French journalist warned that Europe needed to study New World politics and to protect its commercial interests in Latin America.[5]

Despite the canal company's bankruptcy, until World War I French financial interests remained intrigued with isthmian opportunities for capital placement. In 1891 the *Honduras Mining Journal* reported that French capital had contributed significantly to the development of Honduras. In 1893 a Frenchman outlined a project to build a railroad through Central America into southern Mexico under European supervision. His project reflected European concern with the Pan American railroad idea, which had strong support in the United States. The French consul in Panama considered the project feasible because it would tap areas that the canal could not serve well. Transferring the capital and technology of the vineyard and wine industry also attracted some Frenchmen.[6] French officials and political leaders, recognizing that France's rapidly growing surplus capital required ever-widening areas in which to look for opportunities for profitable lending, encouraged French capitalists to seek an outlet on the isthmus.

The French investment in Middle America in the late nineteenth century has been misunderstood. By 1896, French capitalists had invested 270 million francs ($54 million) in Central

America (excluding about 80 million francs, or $16 million, of principal and interest in Honduran railroad bonds that had not been serviced since the early 1870s; see Table 6). In comparison, U.S. investment on the isthmus (including Panama) totaled about $12 million (60 million francs). The official summary of French foreign investment in 1902 listed 42 million francs (about $8.4 million) as the total for Central America (excluding Panama), which included 10.45 million in El Salvador, 10 million in Costa Rica, 8.62 million in Guatemala, 6.5 million in Honduras, and 6.15 million in Nicaragua. Thus, in dollar terms, French investors had placed about $70 million on the isthmus before the Panama Canal rights were sold to the United States, and $24 million remained after the sale.

The official figures for 1902 underevaluated French capital participation in two ways. First, the evaluation inappropriately dismissed the bonds of the Honduran Interoceanic Railroad. Admittedly, by 1902 the leaders had little hope of receiving full repayment, but to dismiss the sum was to misunderstand international investment. Some money had reached Honduras, a stretch of railroad, harbor, and river improvements had been built, and tools and materials had been sent to Honduras. People, knowledge, and skills had flowed in both directions. In 1902 a length of the Honduran Interoceanic Railroad was still in operation, and French agents continued to assert the validity of this debt. Moreover, the debt influenced the Paris stock exchange whenever a Middle American, and particularly a Honduran, loan was mentioned. Finally, when a U.S.-Honduran loan was negotiated in 1911, the Honduran Railroad bonds were redeemed, although at a price well below their official value. Thus the economists who dismissed the Honduran loan when calculating French investment arbitrarily underevaluated French investment.

The second reservation regarding evaluation of French investment involves the matter of perspective. The Universal Interoceanic Canal Company was evaluated at about 220 million francs, the price it sold for in 1903. Thus the French investment in Middle America totaled 270 million francs (about 350 million francs if the Honduran Railroad debt is included, or even 1,170 million francs, if one counts the full value of shares issued by de Lesseps's company). The figure of 350 million francs would have placed the Middle American states first among the fifteen Latin American nations holding French investment. Of the fifty-eight political units on the world list in the official French evaluation of investments, the isthmus would have ranked eighth. If calculated as investment per capita in the country receiving French funds, Middle America would have ranked near the top of these political territorial units.[7] From 1880 to 1914, Central America was important in France's international financial relations. After the mid-nineteenth century, France's most impressive link to the world economy was as a lender nation, not a trading partner.

The number of French firms and residents on the isthmus indicated a rising involvement in the isthmian economy (Tables 1 and 5). The data on French residents in Central America shows an enormous growth in their numbers in the 1880s and early 1890s. By 1892 the French population on the isthmus was about 4,000 to 5,000 people. About three-quarters of this total lived in Panama, and Costa Rica had half of the rest. By 1900, however, the French were more dispersed among the Central American societies.[8]

The "slump" in French agricultural production (actually a negative growth rate) ended in the late-1890s, and in the two decades before the First World War, agricultural production rose at an annual rate of 1 percent.[9] The French economy shared in a modest worldwide economic "boom" in the early twentieth century. The boom stimulated the demand for raw materials. About 1890 the French economy imported Central American products at its highest levels in the period from 1850 to 1929—7.5 million francs in 1890, but it exported only about 1 million francs annually (Tables 2 and 4) to the isthmian states. At the turn of the century, data on trade between France and Central American republics are sparse. In the 1890s, Costa Rica sold only 1 percent of its exports to France, and French products made up 9 percent of Costa Rican imports and 13 percent of Guatemalan imports. From 1901 through 1903, French interests purchased 32 percent of El Salvador's exports and supplied 11 percent of its imports.[10]

The Central American political economies suffered major disruptions as they were incorporated more closely into the world economy in the late nineteenth and early twentieth centuries. One seldom mentioned socioeconomic disruption was the devaluation of the domestic silver peso. This devaluation eventually compelled the Central American governments to resort to paper currencies. The silver peso, a unifying measure of value on the isthmus, was replaced by divisive, national paper currencies.[11]

Beginning in the late nineteenth century, France joined the liberal industrial states in transferring technology and business organization to the isthmus. Central America experienced communications and other infrastructure development as well as enclave production, especially along the Atlantic coast and in the capitals. Foreign capitalists eagerly sought projects involving railroads, electric power systems, street lighting, sewage systems, streetcar lines, telephones, and water systems. French entrepreneurs played only a modest role in the establishment of Central American enclaves; they operated a banana company, several shipping lines, and some coffee plantation and export firms. The French, like other metropoles, used technology, especially military technology, as an extension of their industrial order, not as a means to transfer the industrial revolution to Central America.[12]

German shipping and investment capital competed aggressively with French enterprises on the isthmus. In 1890, Reynaud warned that large German investments threatened to dominate Guatemala and spread German influence throughout Central America. He complained that Guatemala was inundated with German-made imitations of the products of other nations, including France, and that a German firm was entering Salvadoran coffee production and trade, an area previously dominated by French coffee merchants. Inadequate French maritime services provided German commercial interests with windfall opportunities. The French vice-consul in San José, Costa Rica, complained that because the Compagnie Transatlantique did not stop at Puerto Limón, French products could not compete with German goods, which entered on a direct steamer line. If French entrepreneurs did not compete, he assumed that French influence would be driven from Middle America.[13] His lament was valid for entrepreneurial activity, but ignored French successes in military missions, cultural activity, and portfolio investment.

French minister Casimir Paul Challet observed that German entrepreneurs in Central America had pursued a different course from their French counterparts. The Germans built prosperous enterprises that in turn purchased German products. For example, the German entrepreneurs had used their political, cultural, and economic influence to obtain Guatemala's military supply contracts, to create credit enterprises, and to establish trading houses that used two German shipping firms to exchange coffee and sugar for German manufacturers. Challet hoped that French capitalists would compete in Guatemala because that government seemed well disposed toward them. He regretted that Frenchmen, who needed the aid of their government, were often told by that government that they had assumed the risk and must resolve their problems as best they could. In Guatemalan economic affairs, Challet judged that U.S., German, Belgian, and Spanish interests were doing well, while French businessmen were scarcely represented. And numerous hard-working colonists also strengthened German influence in and extracted benefits from rich Costa Rica. Challet urged greater support for French economic expansion into Central America.[14]

In 1892 the French government cited the low value of Franco-Guatemalan trade to dampen negotiations for concessions aimed at increasing commerce. Foreign Minister Ramón Salazar of Guatemala was unimpressed because the proposed Franco-Guatemalan commercial agreement offered little to encourage the small, indirect commercial exchange. Guatemalan coffee was exchanged for French goods mostly in German or English ports. Reynaud argued that Franco-Guatemalan trade would increase only when better commercial conditions and a direct trade route were established.[15]

A few Frenchmen, attracted to the isthmus because of the canal company, were drawn to other large projects. Several French investment groups bid to build the major railroads of Guatemala. In the early 1880s the syndicate headed by Henri Cottu bid unsuccessfully to purchase the Guatemalan Central Railroad. Cottu was not through. In 1889 he represented one of two French syndicates competing for a concession, valued at $21,300,000 in gold or 106,560,000 francs, to build Guatemala's Atlantic coast railroad and to float a loan. The other French investors, represented by the French engineer H. de Salma, signed a contract, but the U.S.-owned Guatemalan Central Railroad persuaded the Guatemalan legislature to reject it. However, the Guatemalans gave the railroad concession to the Cottu syndicate, not to the U.S. railroaders. Reynaud claimed that his friendship with influential Guatemalans had prepared the terrain for Cottu. The Cottu railroad project promised to carve out a sphere for French influence where German and U.S. traders and investors had previouly dominated. Reynaud foresaw French commerce and industry benefiting from the construction work and related activity.[16]

The U.S. minister, Lansing Mizner, was displeased that French interests had acquired the Atlantic railroad concession. He acknowledged, however, that the railroad would have great value for U.S. enterprises, even though a French loan would displace U.S. interests from an area—Guatemalan railroads—that they had dominated since the early 1870s. U.S. consul James Hosmer remarked: "It is certain that Germany, England, and France are striving in every way to obtain commercial favor with these [Central American] Republics, and the French are making the most out of the matter of the [railroad] 'loan.' " The French were favored because the revived church party was intensely anti-American and sympathetic to European powers. However, the Cottu syndicate withdrew from the railroad contract when it could not raise sufficient capital. The Guatemalan government probably regretted the 34,000 pesos it had spent to celebrate the signing of the contract, particularly after Cottu filed a suit claiming Guatemalan actions had prejudiced his railroad and loan concessions. Cottu agreed to drop his suit against Guatemala if it would concede him its rights and claims against the International Bank of London. Guatemalan diplomat Fernando Cruz endorsed this course because then Guatemala would be free to contract for a loan or railroad concession elsewhere in Europe.[17]

Later, Franco-Guatemalan relations benefited from a series of mutually satisfactory agreements. In the 1890s prominent Frenchmen attempted to preserve a central role for France in the interoceanic transit by appealing to a sense of national duty and honor. Although a group formed in 1876 around Admiral de la Roncière, le Noury and geographers Stanislas C. H. Dupuy de Lôme and E. Levasseur had always considered the Panama project a squandering of de Lesseps's reputation and French investment, it believed that the nation had the duty to complete the project, which would not require large amounts of additional capital and labor. Philippe Bunau-Varilla, who had served as an engineer with the original company, warned that abandoning the canal project would tarnish France's nineteenth-century record just as the loss of India had its eighteenth-century reputation. The project was so far advanced, he contended, that either France or another party could complete the canal successfully. In late 1892 a cholera crisis on the isthmus revealed that the privileges of power had undermined French interests because U.S. and British, but not French, vessels obtained permission to enter and depart Panama's ports. The French consul concluded that French vessels would be denied entrance to the ports for as long as possible to do the maximum damage. He claimed that U.S. interests expected this quarantine policy to give the coup de grâce to the floundering French canal company.[18]

In early 1893, Achille Monchicourt, the liquidator of the Universal Interoceanic Canal Company, sent an agent to negotiate with Colombia. Monchicourt repeatedly requested a brief extension of the concession—about twenty months—to reorganize the company as the New Panama Canal Company and to reinitiate work on the canal. Monchicourt was upset that Colombia was consulting the U.S. government, which, long a determined opponent of the Panama route, was encouraging Colombia's recalcitrance in the liquidation. In his view, only the French government, which spoke for the French savings and lives invested in this undertaking, had the right to be heard regarding the liquidation. French diplomat A. de Routand praised the formation of a New Panama Canal Company as a stimulant for patriotism, prestige, and the revival of France's reputation in Colombia. The completion of the canal would prove French vitality, consolidate its influence throughout Hispano-America, and establish new markets for its products. The French minister in Colombia, however, doubted that the liquidator would succeed against U.S. opposition.[19]

U.S. officials made no secret of their dislike for a foreign canal or their conviction that the U.S. government should dominate interoceanic transit. Secretary of State Thomas F. Bayard suspected that the canal had awoken French desires to influence the Caribbean and Middle American area. While conceding that the liquidation of the Universal Canal Company was a matter between the French and Colombian courts and governments, the State Department found U.S. interests were "of so important a nature" that it needed to be fully informed of all proceedings. Although the U.S. Senate rejected a financial guarantee for the canal, the principal politicians sustained President Hayes's earlier assertion that the canal formed part of the U.S. coastline.[20] The U.S. government commonly perceived French activity in this region as an attempt to obtain special political influence.

Industrial maturity (the age of coal, iron, steel, and steam power) and the age of imperialism were closely connected. The mature industries needed improved distribution, from advertising to steamship lines, to facilitate growth and accumulation. Some leaders viewed culture and social image as a form of advertising and hence a means of softening a market for penetration. Culture was a means of exhibiting status and prestige, but cultural interaction also facilitated the dominant society's influence upon the whole of peripheral society. Thus a nation's "rise to power" was a function of that state's domestic political economy and its culture and of the political economy's capacity to interact with and extract value from the world economy.

French officials sought to avoid confrontations with other metropole political and security objectives, yet to use language and culture as foundation stones to build influence and pursue national goals in foreign areas. In the late nineteenth century, the French government created the Alliance française to disseminate French civilization to the world on a systematic basis. It required its agents in each Central American country to report on the instruction of French. With the best educational system in Central America, Costa Rica also had the best program in French, requiring two years of either French or English in the primary school and two years of French in the six-year secondary school. In the mid-1890s, however, the French-language program deteriorated. French was "smothered" because it was taught at the beginning of the secondary school program and followed by a newly required two years of English. Consul Ritt found that only the Collège des Dames de Sion, where all instructors were French, taught the language effectively. In 1898 he proudly reported that out of the few thousand Costa Rican children who attended secondary school, 694 received instruction in French. To expand France's cultural influence, Consul Emile Joré obtained 400 French grammar books for the Costa Rican lycées. He also sought a competent French educator to serve as director of secondary education for Costa Rica and to head the San José Lycée, the only one authorized to grant diplomas. The Costa Rican elite was impressed with French education.[21]

Ritt surmised that despite the moral sympathy for France in Costa Rica, English had a better hold than French largely due to the commercial preponderance of the British and North Americans. He and other French officials lamented the inadequate support for the Alliance française's program to encourage French in foreign schools.[22] While many French officials expected their cultural policy to facilitate economic penetration, the inability to increase commercial activity undermined the cultural objectives.

French language training was less pervasive in the other isthmian countries. Guatemala had no French schools although secondary schools for boys in Guatemala City (two), Chiquimula, Quetzaltenango, San Marcos, and Antigua and for girls in Guatemala City, Chiquimula, and Quetzaltenango offered French. Four Nicaraguan secondary schools offered French, and so did two Salvadoran schools for girls (both with Frenchwomen as directors) and six for boys. Lacking a report on Honduras, the French Foreign Ministry speculated that French was taught only in Tegucigalpa. The elite in each country except Guatemala was still considered francophile. Thiersant believed that the Central American states recognized that France, another Latin republic, would guide them to progress and civilization.[23]

Irene Peyre founded the Liceo Francés in Guatemala City in 1920. The school remains open in 1999, although it has lost most of its early reputation in education and French language instruction. *Courtesy Ludving Lionel Monroy*

The French government encouraged its citizens in Central America to participate in social, cultural, and humanitarian activity but discouraged involvement in the politics of the host societies. French officials were not always successful. Costa Rica's election in 1894 attracted the participation of numerous foreigners who split along national lines for the two major candidates. The British, Germans, and Spanish residents favored Ricardo Jiménez Oreamuno, and those from the United States, Colombia, and Cuba supported José Joaquín Rodríguez. Some French supported each faction. When war threatened to engulf Nicaragua and Costa Rica in 1898, Joré read French law regarding the loss of citizenship to the leader of some Frenchmen who intended to offer their services to Costa Rica. Joré pointed out that they would have to assume responsibility for any of their actions since Frenchmen also lived in Nicaragua.[24]

French civilization exercised a moral influence in Costa Rica. Under Joré's leadership, the French residents and their supporters built two associations—the French Society for Charity and the French Society of Information—to pursue cultural, humanitarian, and educational objectives. Between 1895 and 1897 the Society of Information gathered 7,000 pesos (= 15,555 francs) in donations. Joré had difficulty getting financial support from France for his associations, but the government finally granted 600 francs for the purchase of books. Since French cultural agencies competed against German influence, he was displeased when the Costa Rican Catholics named another German, Johann Kaspar Storck, rather than a French priest, as successor to German Bishop Bernard August Thiel, who died in 1901. Joré knew that the German priests persuaded some students, who otherwise would have gone to France, to go to Germany. The French foreign minister appreciated Joré's persistent efforts to develop French influence in Costa Rica.[25]

How Franco-Costa Rican cultural cooperation would translate into commercial or financial conduct was not certain until direct communications were established. In 1894 the French foreign minister inquired about negotiating a treaty to facilitate commercial exchange. The Costa Rican minister to France, Manuel María de Peralta, was not very optimistic because reducing the French coffee duty would not be easy, and Costa Rica's chief export product, bananas, was perishable and hence not likely to reach the distant French market even if a direct steamer service existed. French consul Marie Jean Joseph Cravéri recalled that the prior shipping links from Le Havre, Nantes, and Bordeaux to Central American ports had all ceased. Without these direct ties, French products entered Costa Rica through the merchants and vessels of nations that offered lower freight charges (Britain and Germany) or were nearer (United States). There were fine opportunities for French perfumes, wines, and liquors, if merchants could overcome the transit and start-up costs. Cravéri knew that France deserved a better place in the Costa Rican market.[26]

At the turn of the century, French journalist F. Vie compared the successful German commercial colonies in Central America with the French efforts to establish ties between its emigrants and its domestic production. He concluded that France pursued "the illusion of an important colonial duty—a civilizing task which flatters our love of nation, but gives us no other benefit. The Germans on the contrary, without so many distant conquests, methodically increase the spread of their commerce and their nationality."[27] Vie thought that French cultural policy had failed to win commercial benefits or to prepare the field for future gains.

In the late nineteenth century, metropole political economies supplemented the efforts of diplomatic and consular officials to expand commerce with chambers of commerce, fairs, expositions, and traveling salesmen. In 1896 the French government wanted the French residents of El Salvador to form a chamber of commerce. The chamber would be worth the trouble, Challet contended, if a notable increase in trade would follow, yet he doubted that this would occur. A vice-consul in San Salvador would be "a hundred times more useful" to French commerce than a chamber of commerce. The Germans, North Americans, and British did not have trade associations, he remarked, yet all three were successful commercially.[28]

Consul Joré considered the Philadelphia Museum of Commerce and Economics, commonly referred to as the Philadelphia Commercial Museum, a prime example of how U.S. business interests penetrated Latin America. It organized expositions and displays and disseminated information in a wide variety of forms and played an important role in the expansion of U.S. trade in Costa Rica. He encouraged the French Office of Foreign Commerce to undertake similar work. Although growing distrust of the United States tilted Central American sentiment toward French society, Joré believed that French entrepreneurs needed to channel their energy through an organization. Frenchmen and Central Americans shared the desire to stymie U.S. efforts to evict European products from the Latin American market.[29]

The leaders in the periphery borrowed the ideas of fairs and expositions just as they borrowed liberal ideology, positivism, and technology from the metropoles. Central American countries had exhibited at New Orleans in 1883. The Guatemalan government encouraged foreign displays at the Central American exposition in Guatemala in 1897. The agents of the exposition assured the French residents and merchants that a successful display of products such as lingerie, clothes, and furniture, which were eagerly sought in Guatemala, would win France a proper share of a sizable and increasing market.[30] Expositions on the periphery served the needs of the metropole better than they did the needs of the indigenous population.

Despite the caution, French entrepreneurs and President José María Reyna Barrios signed several large contracts related to the Guatemalan Exposition of 1897. In 1894, Guatemalan officials signed contracts worth one million gold francs with the Compagnie Française de Constructions en Acier for materials and another with its affiliate, the Compañía Anónima Nacional de Construcciones de Guatemala, to build a pavilion. The French government demanded 413,000 francs as indemnity to the Compagnie Française de Constructions en Acier for damage caused when the Compañía Anónima Nacional de Construcciones de Guatemala refused to pay for materials delivered. With the support of Reyna Barrios, the police invaded the workplaces of the French company and seized materials. The project failed, and lawsuits and international reclamations followed for over a decade.[31] Despite these problems, Challet rejoiced that Reyna Barrios had granted concessions to several French capitalists.

Although many Frenchmen remained leery of investing in Guatemala, some pursued several railroad projects during the depression of the 1890s. The railroad investment was tied to commercial, financial, or geopolitical opportunities. French capital participated in the Northern Railroad, which promised European products a better route to Guatemalan markets. French commercial interests were attracted to this project because they expected the country supplying the capital to provide the construction materials as well. But then, as Challet noted, Belgian and U.S. funds replaced French capital. Still, Guatemalan minister Muñoz welcomed French capital and engineers as a means to restrict German and North American influence. Guatemalan banks also sought correspondent and agent banking ties in France. Challet continued to hope that nationalism would encourage French commercial institutions to compete against German activity. French businessmen, however, had to be present and making bids for them to offer a more serious image. He could merely support their initiatives. Capital was stagnating at home, he observed, and French capitalists were being offered another opportunity to participate in the Guatemalan Northern Railroad.[32]

Several French cabinet ministers pursued the possibility of attracting bankers to participate in Guatemalan railroad projects. In late 1895 the Guatemalan government wished to float a loan in the French market in order to buy out the U.S. investors and complete the Northern Railroad. French officials in Guatemala welcomed the proposal because it would weaken the competitive position of U.S. capitalists. Challet considered the loan to be politically and economically advantageous and urged French financial establishments such as the Crédit Lyonnais to compete. Two major French credit institutions judged the railroad a worthy investment opportunity, but neither was interested in investing. When the Banque de France recommended against allowing a Guatemalan loan in the Paris financial markets, Challet questioned the information that had led that bank to doubt that Guatemala's financial strength could support a modest loan. If the French did not respond positively, he warned, the Guatemalan government intended to seek German funds. The French government, however, was unable to locate capitalists or broad political support for the venture.[33] Although domestic Guatemalan capital kept the project alive in mid-stage, metropole entrepreneurs and financiers shared in the earlier and final stages of construction and metropole planters, merchants, shippers, and entrepreneurs benefited greatly from its completion.

In 1897, Costa Rican and French officials contemplated closer economic relations if the Costa Rican government would employ a French financial adviser. The French finance minister proposed an experienced adviser who had worked in a similar mission to Guatemala. The Costa Rican government ultimately decided against a financial adviser, but it did explore obtaining a loan from France. The French foreign minister expected advantages for French industry and commerce to follow such a grant of funding. For example, the Costa Rican government preferred a French firm to complete Costa Rica's interoceanic railroad. But the Dayde and Pillet firm, which had shown interest initially, abandoned the project. The foreign minister hoped that other French firms would consider this project, otherwise a North American company would likely participate and thus extend U.S. influence. A French-supported bank or railroad would gain goodwill because the Costa Rican government sought an alternative to the U.S. presence in its political economy.[34]

French officials pursued many paths to encourage French trade and investments in Central America. In the fall of 1898, Costa Rican president Rafael Iglesias Castro traveled to Europe in search of capital for a hypothecary (specializes in real estate mortgages) bank. The French foreign minister persuaded Iglesias that a visit to France might animate financial, industrial, and commercial interests. French bankers, however, showed little interest in the bank. Unwilling to lose the project, the foreign minister conspired to delay Iglesias in France so that the Costa Rican could not search for capital in Italy, Germany, or Spain. By undercutting the participation of other European capitalists, he allowed French investors time to reconsider.[35] While French financial circles were wary of investing in a bank in Costa Rica, a decade later they floated a large Costa Rican state loan, some of which was used to found a bank.

Metropoles competed for banking concessions. The French government discussed two banking projects for Central America. In one, Joré proposed that French capitalists consider opening a hypothecary bank in Costa Rica. French industry and commerce should benefit from such a bank and from the reputation that it would create throughout Central America. Moreover, Joré prophesied that if France did not open such a bank, England, Germany, or the United States would. After the U.S. Senate had approved an international bank with a capital between $5 million and $25 million, he advised that French interests needed their own bank if they did not want to see U.S. banking interests swallowing all of South America. The French cabinet studied his proposal, but the finance minister refused to pressure the Société Générale, which lacked interest in this delicate matter.[36]

The second bank proposal was a grandiose project introduced to the French government in late 1898. Emile Worms, who had contacts with twenty-two South and Central American banks—including some in Guatemala, Honduras, and El Salvador—proposed a bank for international affairs with an effective capital of 200 million francs. Whereas the French foreign minister had endorsed Joré's hypothecary bank, the finance minister was interested in Worms's proposal.[37] Neither project was implemented, so French investors remained without a branch bank even though their investment in Central America remained large in the early twentieth century.

Some French officials urged European cooperation on the isthmus to blunt U.S. interference. The French Foreign Ministry was not enthusiastic when the consul in Guatemala, Eugène Antoine Marcellin Pellet, proposed to undermine a U.S. loan effort with a European syndicate. Since the isthmian countries assumed that the U.S. government would not allow a European military force to collect debts, they would cease repayment to a European syndicate whenever such a course seemed advantageous. The French government recognized that the U.S. government would use force to protect its debt holdings, whereas French or European officials could not realistically consider that alternative.[38] While some French officials continued to conceive of multinational syndicates for isthmian loans, French financiers underwrote the various Central American loans actually authorized for the Paris exchange prior to 1914.

After 1870, French politicians and businessmen often thought in terms of competition with Germany. The French military challenged Germany's leading role in selling military materials in Central America. The French government expected to obtain influence with the isthmian governments by winning contracts for military instructors, equipment, and arms. In 1886 the Guatemalan government arranged for Captain Emile Bruandet of France to serve as instructor of artillery. It repeatedly extended his contract, and in 1890 it asked France to increase the military mission to three infantry and three artillery officers. Minister Reynaud envisioned a vastly improved position for France, if an expanded military mission were to supplement the three advisers in the Guatemalan Finance Ministry and Cottu's railroad project.[39]

Despite the positive trend, several problems arose. Negotiations for the expanded military mission languished, and Cottu's syndicate withdrew from the railroad. Undeterred, the Guatemalan government requested a fourteen-man military mission that the French Foreign Ministry feared might jeopardize its relations with the other isthmian governments. The French government was also concerned that its officers might be activated if Guatemala went to war. Although the contract safeguarded French neutrality, Reynaud advised delaying the mission because maladministration had produced a bad economic situation in Guatemala. Finally, in 1899, Guatemala contracted for Captain Louis Marie Léon Chaigné to serve as military instructor for three years. The small military mission remained for over three decades.[40]

The successful French military mission in Guatemala persuaded other isthmian governments to seek French advisers. Honduras solicited an officer to organize its army. From 1896 to 1901 a French military mission—one captain, one lieutenant, and two noncommissioned officers—served in El Salvador. After 1901 the French shared supplying military services to El Salvador with Chile and Germany. In mid-1899, Nicaragua formally requested a French military mission of six soldiers. French officials assumed that fulfilling the Nicaraguan request would strengthen French prestige in Central America. But a confidential warning (perhaps from Guatemala because President Manuel Estrada Cabrera and Nicaraguan president José Santos Zelaya were bitter enemies) persuaded the French government not to send the mission. When the French withdrew from the contract, German officers ran the Nicaraguan military academy.[41] Each mission boosted French prestige in Central America.

The military missions were expected to nurture economic benefits for the French armaments industry. Costa Rica's population and army were small, so the military powers were less eager to pursue military missions there. However, periodically, Costa Rica acquired arms to maintain its security against Nicaragua and other isthmian armies. In 1890 and 1894, Costa Rican tests proved the French Bange field artillery superior to German Krupp artillery. These tests helped France retain the order, first placed in the 1880s, to furnish field artillery for Costa Rica. Both U.S. arms merchants and Krupp sought expanded sales in Middle America. French officials competed energetically for orders of arms, munitions, saddlery, harnesses, and similar equipment for French firms. The French missions in Guatemala and El Salvador also influenced the acquisition of weapons and military supplies throughout the isthmus.[42]

French officials were interested in the geopolitical competition for naval bases and commercial support points in the vicinity of the terminals of the potential canal and in the development of fledgling navies among the isthmian states. The French navy's annual reports on foreign fleets described a minor naval competition in Central America at the end of the nineteenth century. In 1896 the Costa Rican government considered, then rejected, hiring the French to construct war vessels. At that time, it had the only navy in Central America, one unarmed vessel. The next year, El Salvador acquired a vessel with three guns. By 1900, Costa Rica had four vessels with eight guns, Honduras had two vessels with two guns, Nicaragua had four vessels with six guns, and El Salvador had one vessel with three guns. Only Guatemala resisted the naval competition. The isthmian navies declined after 1900. By 1905, Costa Rica's one ship was in very bad condition, Nicaragua's six vessels were in deteriorated condition, and El Salvador had two vessels without military value. The "naval competition" among the Middle American navies had ended.[43]

The French government weighed the commercial and strategic importance of interoceanic communication in metropole competition. In 1898 a French Foreign Ministry memorandum argued that the New Panama Canal Company offered little chance of completing a canal, but a large possibility of creating problems with the United States. Still, a Nicaragua canal, it conceded, would destroy the last hope of the Panama Canal bondholders for some compensation. It recommended that the New Panama Canal Company sell its interests either to the U.S. government or to a U.S. syndicate so that the French government could avoid future difficulties.[44]

A strike for higher wages by employees of the Panama Railroad refocused the attention of the French government on the difficulties of conducting a multinational enterprise in an area under U.S. influence. Although the New Panama Canal Company owned the Panama Railroad Company, which had an American board of directors, it was unable to control the railroad's U.S. managers, who caused serious injury to the canal company. In 1899 an English-Chilean vessel, anxious to unload despite a strike, offered to pay the difference between the existing wage and that demanded by the striking dockworkers. The superintendent of the Panama Railroad rejected the offer. The French consul condemned the superintendent's decision—which reduced the freight revenues and prejudiced the earnings of a subsidiary of the French canal company—as a "serious war upon French interests on the isthmus to the profit of Americans." In a related situation, a French naval captain disapproved when the U.S.S. *Ranger* was called upon in the contract dispute between the canal company and Colombia. He argued that the large French interests merited that government's intervention into disputes involving the canal.[45]

In mid-1898 the New Panama Canal Company asked the French foreign minister to convey its resolve to complete the canal project to the State Department. The French minister in Washington, Jules Cambon, recognized that the company was concerned because the inferior Nicaragua canal project had mesmerized U.S. politicians and public opinion. He cautioned, however, that "there was no better means to arouse a determined opposition in America than to give the canal question a pronounced foreign twist, such as the French." The French government could do little openly to influence Admiral John G. Walker's Interoceanic Canal Commission, Cambon believed, but it might have some effect behind the scenes; it was conscious of the menace that an alternative canal route posed.[46] The Panama Canal Company recognized that a convincing presentation of its determination to build a canal might facilitate a sale to the United States.

At times French officials felt almost hopeless before U.S. policy. Joré observed that European governments were unwilling to intervene politically to resist U.S. expansion at Europe's expense. He feared that the U.S. victory against Spain in 1898 and the seductive belief that European businesses could acquire wealth where informal U.S. protectorates were in place had lulled European diplomats into inactivity. Even Jules Cambon reconsidered whether his decision not to represent the New Panama Canal Company before the Washington government might not have left a false impression. He intended to correct the impression that France was disinterested in the canal project. While the New Panama Canal Company labored for its life, Joré prepared for the construction of the Nicaraguan canal. Under the pretense of gathering samples of plants, rocks, and other natural items for the Paris Exposition of 1900, he explored sites within Costa Rica, but near the transit, for French colonies. One official hoped that a more visible naval presence in the Caribbean might preserve French interests and prestige.[47]

French agents felt constrained by bureaucratic limitations from giving proper responses to the dynamic U.S. activity. By 1900, Joré was convinced that France would neither resist U.S. influence nor protect French interests in Central America. Thus, French cooperation with the U.S. government would be necessary because the Central American countries were unable to resist U.S. power effectively. Mexico was determined to offer an alternative to Anglo-Saxon influence in Central America, but Joré doubted it would be effective. Because French interests could conceivably benefit from the extension of U.S. political power, and since France and the United States were traditionally friends, Joré reluctantly recommended supporting the U.S. government's policies.[48]

When the final report of the Walker Canal Commission in 1899 recommended a canal at Nicaragua because the New Panama Canal Company had set too high a price, both the French interests and the Colombian government reexamined this matter. Negotiations for the sale of the canal company's concession were complicated because the French, U.S., Colombian, British, German, and Russian governments all wanted to participate, along with agents claiming to speak for Panamanian rebel groups. For example, Dr. Carlos E. Restrepo, an agent for a rebel group, informed Washington that his "government" would not extend the New Panama Canal Company's concession, but it would make the route available to North Americans in return for recognition of belligerency. Since the U.S. government was accustomed to shady characters seeking favors and offering deals, the French diplomats in Washington doubted that Restrepo represented a serious danger to the canal company.[49]

Metropole governments and entrepreneurs often cooperated when the objective was to open an area on the periphery to foreign economic participation or to deny one metropole a privileged position. But metropoles constantly looked for opportunities to achieve a privileged position without undue conflict. In the late 1890s many U.S. officials and businessmen wished to challenge the Clayton-Bulwer pact, which denied any signator the right to fortify transit on the isthmus. The British, however, opposed altering this point, and Cambon wanted all Europe to support Britain's insistence upon a multinational guarantee. The French publicist G. Bailleu argued that U.S. ambitions in the Caribbean-Central American region, evident in the negotiations to revise the Clayton-Bulwer pact, ought to tie the British to continental Europe because access to the canal would define the role of Europe's merchant marine and commerce in the New World. German writer Georg Wegener praised the French canal venture because it involved energy, willingness to sacrifice, and idealism. Paul Dreyfus, writing in *L'Economiste français*, thought that any route built should go across Panama to minimize the loss of the French investors. He welcomed any offer to share Panama with the United States and Great Britain because such a step would minimize French losses by incorporating U.S. and British capital.[50]

Officials and businessmen from both France and Germany were upset when the British surrendered their rights to protect the transit in the [John] Hay-[Julian] Pauncefote agreement of 1901, which came after U.S. officials had made clear their intention to acquire the French canal concession at Panama. Tension developed between French and U.S. objectives in Central America because the isthmus's role in world trade and communications encompassed any core effort to exert the military and economic primacy necessary to secure hegemony. The key was, of course, not the raw materials, trade, or investment options on the isthmus (although they were a bonus), but the trade lines that could be opened to the poorly tapped labor and raw materials of Asia and the Pacific basin.

Colombian officials were disturbed that the New Panama Canal Company negotiated only with the U.S. government for the sale of its rights because competition would maximize Colombia's share of the price of the concession. The Colombian minister in Paris asked the French government to contact Germany and Russia regarding the completion of the canal before it made a decision about an extension of the canal company's concession. In late 1900, when leaders in France, Great Britain, and Germany assumed that the New Panama Canal Company would probably not reach an agreement with the United States, German officials hinted at the possibility of German capital for a joint Panama Canal venture that would "assure the liberty of the seas." Colombia's president, Rafael Uribe, was displeased with the restricted market approach of the French company. He expected the French company to defend its economic stake rather than sell out for a pittance. His agent, however, believed that the canal would be built by the United States or not at all, because England, France, and Germany would not challenge the United States.[51]

In late 1901 it appeared that the German capital market might not support the canal project, but that Russian capital would. French engineer and canal promoter Philippe Bunau-Varilla claimed that the Russian capital market was strong enough to contribute significantly to the project. He was seldom open or honest, however. He campaigned for a sale to the United States when in North America but opposed such a sale while in France. He deceived a naval ministry official into believing that the company was striving to prevent the sale to the United States, when it actually wished to sell to the U.S. government if the terms were acceptable. Most French officials recognized that he played a devious role.[52]

The French consul in Panama noted a watershed in the power situation on the isthmus between the early and late phases of the War of a Thousand Days (October 1899 to late 1902, or between the first Walker Commission's report of 1899 and the second Walker Commission's report of 1902). In the first disturbance, the local officials consulted the U.S., British, and French consuls jointly. In late 1902, however, the Colombian officials consulted only the U.S. consul and admiral. In the post-Spanish-American War years, the U.S. government cast an ever-larger shadow over security for political and economic activity on the isthmus.[53]

In the early twentieth century, several decades of borrowing to finance liberal developmentalist projects combined with the world economic crisis to collapse financial affairs in Central America. Every metropole government shared the concern when the currencies of the isthmian states depreciated markedly. The Central American countries issued paper currencies to allow their domestic economies to function even as the metropole states were draining gold and silver out of those societies to salvage their own economic and social well-being during the depressed periods. In 1902 the metropoles coordinated their reaction when the Guatemalan government collected forced loans, defaulted on bond payments, introduced paper currencies favorable to the domestic economy, and decreed its paper currency legal tender for the payment of public debts. Precious metals were so scarce in the isthmian societies that small quantities could command much land, labor, or other resources. Forcing these economies to pay in precious metals meant transferring greater authority over the local factors of production to foreigners. The French foreign minister expected the legation to prevent French citizens from being compelled to contribute to forced loans. During a debt crisis in Guatemala, a French diplomat called for the cooperation of British, French, German, Belgian, and Italian bondholders. When an agreement seemed near, the British negotiator proposed that the U.S., British, and German governments take official notice of the agreement to assure prompt repayment of Guatemala's bonds. Even though few U.S. citizens held bonds, this action was intended to short-circuit U.S. objections rooted in the Monroe Doctrine. Although the proposal relegated France, Belgium, and Italy to subordinate positions, the U.S. government was unwilling to participate.[54]

In this era of financial crisis and deeply depreciated currencies on the isthmus, metropole powers encountered difficulties in collecting international debts. In 1901 the French government, after a decade of nonpayment of the fees due to it under international postal agreements, laid its claim before the Guatemalan government. The Guatemalan government never denied that it owed France 18,395.34 francs plus interest. It merely neglected to pay. The French applied pressure (while keeping the U.S. government informed so it would not become sympathetic to Guatemala), until Guatemala finally paid in late 1901. The metropoles enforced payments even when the sums seemed small because the principle that governments and enterprises of peripheral areas should meet their obligations was fundamental to the accumulation process of the world economy.[55]

U.S. efforts to use the panamerican movement to link its productive capacity to Latin American markets troubled the Latin states of Europe. A French writer found Spain's call in 1901 for a Hispanic American conference to resurrect the *madre patria*'s historical and cultural roles a proper response to panamericanism, provided that Spain did not undercut the other Latin states—France and Italy. He noted that France exercised a powerful intellectual influence and hoped to expand its commercial and investment roles. French interests wished to halt U.S. penetration of Latin America, but they did not want Spain to undermine their activity in Latin America.[56]

The French government was not prepared to concede ground to other metropole states even in the area of commerce. France had been a premier world trading center, and it had played an important role in Central American trade until late in the nineteenth century. In 1902 the French Senate expected that a Franco-Nicaraguan commercial treaty might improve its deteriorated trade with Nicaragua. The Salvadoran government considered its trade treaty with France a model for negotiations with other European powers. In the early years of the twentieth century, France slowly reduced European and U.S. shares in its commerce as it increased its trade with other parts of the world, including Central America.[57]

Joré measured the comparative success of the U.S. and French programs for developing closer relations with Latin America in terms of the ability of the Buffalo and Paris World's Fairs to attract Latin American nations—in 1901, Buffalo attracted the official participation of sixteen Latin American states and, in 1900, Paris only four. Unofficially, however, all five Central American countries participated in the Paris Exposition. In Paris, Ecuador granted Nicaragua some space, which became a miniature Central American display. Hondurans, Costa Ricans, Guatemalans, and Salvadorans also exhibited in the Nicaraguan area. In addition, two Frenchmen dispensed Guatemalan coffee on Suffren Avenue, and several Salvadorans displayed national products in the Mexican tent.[58] Central America was widely represented at Paris in an unofficial form and in Buffalo officially.

At the beginning of the twentieth century, the French government, entrepreneurs, artisans, import-export firms, and financial establishments remained interested in the development of Middle American economies and cultures. The swelling surplus of capital in France encouraged private citizens and government officials to search for investment opportunities in Central America. French officials sought to develop stronger commercial ties through several processes. First, they sought favorable commercial pacts. Second, they attempted to establish commercial and cultural organizations in Middle America to support trade expansion. Third, they wanted better steamship connections between France and Central America as well as French participation in railroad projects in Guatemala and Costa Rica that were expected to direct these economies toward France (and Europe).

French military missions often pursuaded the Central American governments to purchase French arms and equipment, despite sharp competition from Krupp and other arms sellers. The military mission in El Salvador lasted over twenty years, and the military mission in Guatemala endured forty years. A late 1890s survey of the status of French language instruction in Central America confirmed the hold of French language and civilization upon isthmian societies. But French agents regretfully pointed out that the material assault of U.S. and British money, enterprises, and military power was undermining the Central American elite's tradition of learning French first.

In the 1890s, French investors formed a New Panama Canal Company. The canal project absorbed considerable capital during a period of domestic economic stagnation. A French canal that tied the Atlantic and Pacific half-worlds together and a dynamic steamer service that bound the scattered colonies into a distribution system held out the prospect for rejuvenation of France's geopolitical and economic importance. French officials quietly supported the Panama project and opposed U.S. efforts to develop the Nicaraguan route. In the last decade of the nineteenth century and early years of the twentieth, French influence on the isthmus was linked to the canal, military missions, and cultural institutions.

Notes

1. Wolfgang Klein, "Ein zweitrangiger Imperialismus? Zur Herausbildung des französischen Imperialismus vor 1914," in Fritz Klein, ed., *Neue Studien zum Imperialismus vor 1914* (Berlin, 1980), 165–95; *L'Achèvement du canal de Panama d'après les plans-profils-devis, etc. dressés par la Société internationale d'études* (Paris, 1891); Jean-Marie Mayeur, *La Vie politique sous la Troisième République 1870–1940* (Paris, 1984); Madeleine Rebérioux, *La République radicale? 1898–1914* (Paris, 1975).

2. Christopher Andrew and A. S. Kanya-Forstner, "French Business and the French Colonialists," *Historical Journal* 19:4 (1976): 981–1000; Stuart M. Persell, *The French Colonial Lobby, 1889–1938* (Stanford, 1983), 37–39; François Crouzet, "Recherches sur la production d'armements en France (1815–1913)," *Revue historique* 251 (Jan.–March 1974): 45–84; Christopher M. Andrew and A. S. Kanya-Forstner, "The French 'Colonial Party': Its Composition, Aims and Influence, 1885–1914," *Historical Journal* 14 (1971): 99–128; Paul Lefébure, "A la conquête d'un isthme: Les États-Unis et l'Europe," *Annales des sciences politiques* 16 (Sept. 1901): 600–19; Ernst Daenell, *Das Ringen der Weltmächte um Mittel- und Südamerika* (Berlin, 1919); Eric Wolf, *Europe and the People without History* (Berkeley, CA, 1982).

3. Caron, *An Economic History of Modern France*, 8–21; Rowley, *Évolution économique de la France*, 51–82; Asselain, *Histoire économique de la France*, 1: 152–88; Tihomir Markovitch, "Les Cycles industriels en France," *Le Mouvement social* 63 (April–June 1968): 11–39; Tihomir Markovitch, "L'Industrie française de 1789 à 1964—sources et méthodes," *Cahiers de l'Institut de science économique appliquée*, AF 4, Nr. 163 (July 1965): 1–231. Although Lévy-Leboyer computed the annual growth of the working population more optimistically, he acknowledged a slumping economy in the last third of the nineteenth century, "La Décélération de l'économie française dans la seconde moitié du xixe siècle."

4. Caron, *An Economic History of Modern France*, 78–85; Rowley, *Évolution économique de la France*, 139–84; Raymond Poidevin, "Aspects du nationalisme économique et financier français et allemand au début du xxe siècle," *Mémoires* [Académie National, Metz] 15 (1973): 53–68; René Girault, "Le Milieu bancaire français face aux relations internationales avant 1914," *Relations internationales* 1 (May 1974): 27–37; Emile Becqué, *L'Internationalisation des capitaux. Étude économique, financière et politique* (Montpellier, 1912); Georges Blondel, *La France et le marché du monde* (Paris, 1901); Adeline Daumard, *Les Fortunes françaises au xixe siècle* (Paris, 1973); Tihomir Markovitch, "The Dominant Sectors of French Industry," in Rondo Cameron, ed., *Essays in French Economic History* (Homewood, IL, 1970), 226–44.

5. C. de Varigny, "Un homme d'état américain: James G. Blaine et le congrès des trois amériques," *Revue des deux mondes* 60 (Jan. 15, 1890): 460–62.

6. Reynaud to MAE, Nov. 6, 1891, CCC, Guat., v. 11, AMAE; Coutouly to MAE, May 29, 1893, CCC, Pan., v. 7, AMAE; Cazard to Anguiano, June 6, 1899, B99-5-6/4323/93228, MRE, AGCA; Henry Bourgeois and Manuel Lemus, *Breve noticia sobre Honduras* (Tegucigalpa, 1897).

7. "La Fortune française à l'étranger," *Bulletin de statistique et de législation comparées* 26 (Oct. 1902): 476–77, 483; Rafael-Georges Lévy, "Les Capitaux français à l'étranger," *Revue des deux mondes* 67 (March 15, 1897): 437; Raymond Poidevin, *Les Relations économiques et financières entre la France et l'Allemagne de 1898 à 1914* (Paris, 1969), 36–40; Skinner, *France and Panama*; Richard H. Collin, *Theodore Roosevelt's Caribbean: The Panama Canal, the Monroe Doctrine, and the Latin American Context* (Baton Rouge, 1990), 163–305.

8. Alfred Carpentier to MAE, March 8, 1894, Affaires divers commerciales, carton 258, AMAE. When Guatemala's president ordered the formation of a French chamber of commerce in 1894, the French minister

recorded ninety-eight male names, which suggested about two hundred French residents, lists in Commerce, F[12] 7414, AN.

9. Caron, *An Economic History of Modern France*, 24–25; Rowley, *Évolution économique de la France*, 237–79; Paul Bairoch, "Commerce extérieur et développement économique: Quelques enseignements de l'expérience libre-échangiste de la France au xixe siècle," *Revue économique* 21 (Jan. 1970): 1–33; Eugene Owen Golob, *The Meline Tariff: French Agriculture and Nationalist Economic Policy* (New York, 1944); Daniel Salem, "Sur quelques conséquences du retour de la France au protectionnisme à la fin du xixe siècle," *Revue d'histoire économique et sociale* 45 (1967): 326–80; Wolfgang Göroll, "Die Auseinandersetzung um Freihandel und Protektionismus im Frankreich des 19. Jahrhunderts (1815–1872)" (Ph.D. diss., Universität Erlangen-Nürnberg, 1977).

10. Schoonover and Schoonover, "Statistics for the Understanding of the Foreign Intrusion into Central America," 77–119.

11. Woodward, *Central America*, 149–202; Cardoso and Pérez Brignoli, *Centro América y la economía occidental*, 199–320; Pérez Brignoli, *Breve historia de Centro-América*, 95–106; Daniel R. Headrick, *The Tentacles of Progress: Technology Transfer in the Age of Imperialism, 1850–1940* (New York, 1988), 3–25, 379–84; Raymond Poidevin, "Fabricants d'armes et relations internationales au début du xxe siècle," *Relations internationales* 1 (May 1974): 39–56; François Crouzet, "Recherches sur la production d'armements en France, 1815–1913," in *Conjoncture économique, structures sociales: Hommage à Ernest Labrousse* (Paris, 1974), 287–318.

12. LaFeber, *Inevitable Revolutions*, 31–39; Cardoso, "Central America: The Liberal Era, c. 1870–1930"; Lester Langley, *Struggle for the American Mediterranean: United States-European Rivalry in the Gulf-Caribbean, 1776–1904* (Athens, GA, 1976), 135–93; Achille Viallate, *L'Impérialisme économique et les relations internationales pendant le dernier demi-siècle (1870–1920)* (Paris, 1923).

13. Paul Louis Reynaud to MAE, Jan. 29, 1890, Marie Jean Joseph Craveri to MAE, Nov. 23, 1889, CP 1896, Amér. cent., v. 29, AMAE.

14. Casimir Paul Challet to MAE, June 18, 1895, CCC, Guat., v. 12, AMAE; Francastel to MAE, May 8, 1895, Challet to MAE, May 22, 1895, Joré to MAE, Sept. 29, 1895, CP 1896, Amér. cent., v. 31, AMAE; Challet to MAE, Jan. 3, 1896, F[30] 393[1]: Guat., AMEF; Ignacio Solis, *Sobre el fomento de la inmigración y colonización extranjeras* (Guatemala, 1889); Pierre Guillen, "Opinion publique et politique étrangère en France, 1871–1914: Orientation des études menées en France depuis 1945," in *Opinion publique et politique extérieure* (Rome, 1981), 48–62.

15. Reynaud to MAE, April 12, 1892, CCC, Guat., v. 12, AMAE.

16. "Note," March 15, 1899, and specific items in folder, "Reclamation Bonscayrol contre le gouvernement Guatemaltèque," [Dec., 1899–1902], Georges Thiebaut to MAE, Dec. 20, 1899, various other correspondence in Affaires divers commerciales, cartons 305 and 306, Cent.-Amér., AMAE; various correspondence, Affairs divers commerciales, carton 306[2], Guat. Affaires Buffa, AMAE; Claude-Philibert Darby de Thiersant to MAE, Jan. 14, 1880, CCC, Guat., v. 9, AMAE; Reynaud to MAE, April 24, 1889, Oct. 25, 1892, CP 1896, Guat., Travaux publiques, chemins de fer, navigation, N. S. v. 8, Reynaud to MAE, Oct. 5, 1889, Affaires divers commerciales, carton 543, AMAE (copy in Commerce, F[12] 7054, AN); Reynaud to MAE,

Oct. 8, 1889, CP 1896, Amér. cent., v. 29, AMAE; *El Guatemalteco*, v. 11, Oct. 1, 1889; J. Gaillard to Min. marine, April 3, 1890, BB[4] 1596, Gaillard to Min. marine, March 10, April 1, 1890, BB[4] 1237, Gaillard to Min. marine, March 15, 1890, BB[4] 1255.

17. Hosmer to Wharton, Sept. 9, 1889, Consular Dispatches, Guat.: vol. 7, microcopy 337, reel 7 (hereafter cited as CD, Guat.: 7 [T 337/r 7, NA]; Lansing B. Mizner to James G. Blaine, March 7, 1890, DD, CA: 32 (M 219/r 52), NA; *New York Press*, Jan. 5, 1890, clipping in B99-6-3/4443/93399, MRE, AGCA; Fernando Cruz to Ramón A. Salazar, Jan. 13, April 7, Aug. 24, 1893, B99-6-4/4466/93422, MRE, AGCA; F. Cruz to Salazar, June 25, 1894, and clippings, B. Isaac to Cruz, March 7, 1894, and clippings, B99-6-4/4468/93424, MRE, AGCA; Tom Kemp, *The French Economy, 1913–1939: The History of Decline* (London, 1972), 12–15.

18. Sautereau to Charles L. de Freycinet, Feb. 12, 1891, in *L'Achèvement du canal de Panama d'après les plains-profils-devils, etc. dressés par la société internationale d'études* (Paris, 1891), 2–5 (copy in F[3] 395, Pan., AMEF); Gustave de Coutouly to MAE, Oct. 6, 8, 17, 22, 26, 1892, and pp. 90–300, CCC, Pan., v. 7, AMAE; Maurice Barrès, *Leurs figures* (rprt; Paris, 1967); Philippe Bunau-Varilla, *Panama, the Creation, Destruction, and Resurrection* (London, 1913); Philippe Bunau-Varilla, *Panama: Le trafic. Annexe de l'ouvrage Panama: Le Passé-le présent-l'avenir* (Paris, 1892), esp. p. 54.

19. MAE to Min. finances, Dec. 29, 1892, French min. in Colombia to MAE, June 4, 1894, F[30] 395, AMEF; Achille Monchicourt to MAE, Jan. 21, April 21, 1893, Ed Bruwaert to MAE, Feb. 22, 1893, A. de Routand to MAE, Oct. 16, 1894, Mémoires et documents, Amér., v. 71, AMAE.

20. Thomas F. Bayard to Robert McLane, Dec. 21, 1889, DI, France: 21 (M 77/r 61), NA; John W. Foster to T. Jefferson Coolidge, Dec. 1, 1892, DI, France: 22 (M 77/r 62), NA; "Panama," Aug. 1892, Mémoires et documents, Amér., v. 71, AMAE.

21. Joseph Begueries to MAE, June 26, July 24, 26, 1893, Carpentier to MAE, Jan. 19, 1894, Série C, Administratives, dossier #138, Alliance française, Guat., AMAE; Fonciy to MAE, July 6, 1891, George Ritt to MAE, Nov. 15, 1893, enclosing "Note sur l'instruction publique et l'enseignement du français au Costa Rica," Série C, Administratives, dossier #135, Alliance française, AMAE; Emile Joré to MAE, May 1, July 1, 10, 1898, Affaires divers commerciales, carton 220, Enseignement du français en Amérique latine, folder Cent. Amér., AMAE; Mario Matarrito, "El desarrollo de la educación primaria en Costa Rica: La reforma liberal, 1886–1931," in *Las instituciones costarricenses del siglo xx* (San José, CR, 1986), 151–56; Frédéric Barbier, "Le Commerce international de la librairie française au xixe siècle (1815–1913)," *Revue d'histoire moderne et contemporaine* 28 (Jan.–March 1981): 94–117; Akira Iriye, "Culture and Power: International Relations as Intercultural Relations," *Diplomatic History* 3 (Spring 1979): 115–28; Blumenthal, *France and the United States*, 212, 255; Lafond, *L' Effort français en Amérique Latine*, 67–68.

22. Ritt to MAE, March 3, 1895, CCC, San José de CR, v. 1, AMAE.

23. Thiersant to MAE, Aug. 19, 1880, CP to 1896, Amér. cent., v. 24, AMAE; Begueries to MAE, June 26, July 24, 26, 1893, Carpentier to MAE, Jan. 19, 1894, Série C, Administratives, dossier #138, Alliance française, Guat., AMAE; Ritt to MAE, March 3, 1895, CCC, San José de CR, v. 1, AMAE; Joré to MAE, May 1, July 1, 10, 1898, Affaires divers commerciales,

carton 220, Enseignement du français en Amérique latine, folder Cent. Amér., AMAE.

24. Ritt to MAE, Feb. 12, 1894, CP 1896, Amér. cent., v. 30, AMAE; Joré to MAE, March 6, 13, April 24, 1898, Feb. 14, 1901, CCC, San José de CR, v. 2, AMAE (copy in CP 1918, CR, politique extérieure, N. S. 2, AMAE).

25. Francastel to MAE, May 8, 1895, Joré to MAE, Sept. 29, 1895, CP 1896, Amér. cent., v. 31, AMAE; Joré to MAE, June 30, 1897, MAE to Joré, July, 1897, and other correspondence regarding the Costa Rican associations, Affaires divers commerciales, cartons 305 and 306, Amér. cent., AMAE; Joré to MAE, Jan. 28, 1900, CP 1918, CR, Politique extérieure, N. S. 2, AMAE; Joré to MAE, Oct. 27, 1901, CCC, San José de CR, v. 2, AMAE; Luis Felipe González Flores, *Historia de la influencia extranjera en el desenvolvimiento educacional y científico de Costa Rica* (San José, CR, 1921).

26. Peralta to Ricardo Pacheco, Paris, Dec. 13, 1894, MRE, caja 114, AN, CR; Marie Jean Joseph Cravéri, *La République de Costa Rica. Ses besoins et ses ressources* (Paris, 1895).

27. F. Vie, "Les Colonies commerciales des allemands," *Revue des deux mondes* 68 (Feb. 1, 1899): 696–708.

28. Robert Rydell, *All the World's a Fair* (Chicago, 1980); Min. commerce to MAE, June 25, 1896, MAE to Challet, July 3, 1896, Challet to MAE, Oct. 2, 1896, MAE to Min. commerce, Nov. 17, 1896, Affaires divers commerciales, carton 263, folder San Salv., AMAE; Laffey, "Municipal Imperialism in Nineteenth Century France."

29. Joré to MAE, Oct. 18, 1896, CCC, San José de CR, v. 1, AMAE.

30. J. Tible Machado, *Le Guatemala en 1896. L'exposition Centre-Américaine 1897. Quelques notes* (Bordeaux, 1896).

31. Note verbale, March 30, 1899, B99-6-4/4473/93429, various contracts and correspondence in B99-25-14/6415 to 6417, MRE, AGCA.

32. Challet to MAE, March 18, Aug. 20, Sept. 4, Nov. 12, 1895, Min. commerce to MAE, Oct. 12, Dec. 9, 1895, MAE to Challet, Dec. 28, 1895, Guat., Finances publiques, Emprunts, v. 1 (N. S. 6), AMAE; Challet to MAE, May 22, 1895, CP 1896, Amér. cent., v. 31, AMAE; Challet to MAE, Jan. 3, 1896, F^{30} 393^{1}: Guat., AMEF.

33. Min. commerce to MAE, Oct. 12, Dec. 9, 1895, MAE to Challet, Dec. 28, 1895, Challet to MAE, Jan. 30, 1896, CP 1918, Guat., Finances publiques, Emprunts, v. 1 (N. S. 6), AMAE; MAE to Min. finances, Nov. 22, 1895, Challet to MAE, Jan. 3, 1896, F^{30} 393^{1}: Guat., AMEF; Cruz to Jorge Muñoz, Jan. 14, 1895, B99-6-4/4469/93425, MRE, AGCA.

34. Min. finances to MAE, May 3, 1897, CP 1918, CR, Finances, I, N. S. 3, AMAE; MAE to Min. commerce, June 9, 1897, Commerce, F^{12} 7053, AN; MAE to Min. finances, Sept. 16, 1897, F^{30} 393^{1}: CR, AMEF.

35. MAE to Joré, Oct. 4, 1898, Joré to MAE, Oct. 21, 30, 1898, CCC, San José de CR, v. 2, AMAE; F. Cruz to Muñoz, Dec. 8, 1897, Neuflize to Guat. Cons.-Gen., Nov. 30, 1897, B99-6-4/4471/93427, MRE, AGCA.

36. Joré to MAE, Sept. 7, 1897, June 25, 1898, Min. finances to MAE, Dec. 6, 1897, CP 1918, CR Finances, I, N. S. 3, AMAE; MAE to Min. finances, Nov. 24, 1897, F^{30} 393: CR, AMEF.

37. Emile Worms to MAE, Aug. 17, 1898, Projet de Banque Hypothécaire et commerciale au Costa Rica, [1900], MAE to Min. commerce, Feb. 14, 1898, Commerce, F^{12} 7053, AN.

38. Eugène Antoine Marcellin Pellet to MAE, Nov. 5, 1898, and memoranda to this note, CCC, Guat., v. 13, AMAE.

39. E. Martínez Sobral to Medina, July 18, Sept. 28, 1888, Francisco Anguiano to Medina, Jan. 22, 1891, Emilio de León to Medina, Dec. 22, 1891, B99-6, 4361/93276, Leg. y cons. en Francia, 1887–1892, AGCA; Anguiano to Medina, Nov. 26, 27, 1890, Jan. 22, 1891, B99-6, 4408-13/93364, Leg. y cons. de Guat. en Francia, 1888–1891, AGCA; Reynaud to MAE, Jan. 23, 25, June 3, 1891, CP 1896, Amér. cent., v. 30, AMAE; F. Cruz to Salazar, Jan. 13, April 7, Aug. 24, 1893, B99-6-4/4466/93422, MRE, AGCA; Tom Kemp, *Economic Forces in French History* (London, 1971), 243–47; Poidevin, "Fabricants d'armes et relations internationales au début du xxe siècle," 39–56; Crouzet, "La production d'armements en France."

40. MAE to Guat. chargé, Jan. 19, 1891, Reynaud to MAE, Jan. 23, 25, June 3, 1891, CP 1896, Amér. cent., v. 30, AMAE; Projet de contrat entre Mr. le Ministre de la Guerre de France et Mr. le Ministre Plénipotentiaire de la République de Guatemala à Paris, [1898], Min. guerre to MAE, June 22, 1899, CP 1918, Guat., Défense nationale Armée-Marine, 1, N. S. 3, AMAE; Cruz to Anguiano, Jan. 2, 1900, B99-6-4, 4474/93430, MRE, AGCA; Juan Barrios to Medina, Aug. 29, 1902, B99-2, 4367/93286, Legs. y Cons. en Francia y España, 1900–1902, MRE, AGCA.

41. Min. guerre to MAE, Jan. 17, 1896, CP 1918, San Salv., Politique extérieure, N. S. 2, AMAE; Jean-Jérôme Cazard to MAE, 15 May 1899, Pourtalès-Gorgier to MAE, July 30, 1900, Affaires divers commerciales, cartons 305 and 306, AMAE; Joré to MAE, Oct. 9, Nov. 19, 1899, Jan. 2, March 4, 16, 1900, CCC, San José de CR, v. 2, AMAE; d'Arlot to Stephan Pichon, March 23, April 12, 1908, Min. finances to MAE, Sept. 19, 1908, Francisco de Arce to MAE, Oct. 30, 1908, Min. guerre to MAE, Nov. 10, 1908, CP 1918, Guat., Défense nationale, I, N. S. 3, AMAE; Louis-Jean l'Avril Lévesque to MAE, Feb. 2, 1914, CP 1918, Hond., pol. intérieure, chemins de fer, N. S. 1, AMAE; R. Duval to Min. marine, Feb. 11, 1899, BB^{4} 1319, AAM; Allen Mitchell, *The German Influence in France after 1870* (Chapel Hill, 1979).

42. Craveri to MAE, Feb. 7, 1890, Ritt to MAE, Dec. 9, 1894, CCC, San José de CR, v. 1, AMAE; MAE to French consul, Nov. 30, 1896, and correspondence for late 1896, Affaires divers commerciales, carton 307, Amér., AMAE; correspondence, 1899–1901, Affaires divers commerciales, cartons 305 and 306, Cent. Amér., AMAE; Pourtalès-Gorgier to MAE, Sept. 6, 1900, Louis Chaigné to Min. guerre, Jan. 15, 1901, CP 1918, Guat., Défense nationale, Armée-Marine, I, N. S. 3, AMAE; Poidevin, "Fabricants d'armes et relations internationales."

43. BB^{4} 2452: Listes des flottes étrangères, AAM; various reports, BB^{7} Marines étrangères, 180, AAM.

44. Memo, 1898, CP 1918, Nic., Politique étrangère, N. S. 2, AMAE; Grandprey to Min. guerre, April 1, 1896, F^{30} 393^{2}: Nic., AMEF.

45. S. de Boutaud to MAE, Feb. 1, 16, 1899, CCC, Pan., v. 8, AMAE; Germinet to Min. marine, March 29, 1900, May 31, 1901, BB^{4} 1331, AAM; Skinner, *France and Panama*, 99–126.

46. Conseil de l'administration to MAE, Aug. 29, 1898, including "Notes," A. de Toutand to MAE, Jan. 12, April 30, Dec. 23, 1898, directors, New Panama Canal Company, to MAE, Aug. 29, 1898, Jules Cambon to MAE, June 16, 1899, Joseph Caillaux to MAE, June 29, 1899, CP 1918, Pan.,

Canal Interocéanique, I, N. S. 9, AMAE; Compagnie Nouvelle du Canal de Panama, *Assemblée générale extraordinaire du . . . [year]* (Paris, various years), see esp. 1899 and 1900, copies in 7 AQ 31, AN; Skinner, *France and Panama*, 67–99.

47. Joré to MAE, Oct. 9, 1899, CP 1918, CR, Politique intérieure, N. S. 1, AMAE; Fr. min. to Col. to Germinet, Sept. 14, 1899, BB^4 1597, AAM; Joré to MAE, Nov. 7, 1899, "Mission française au San Carlos et au Río Frío, 1898–1899," CP 1918, Pan., Canal interocéanique, I, N. S. 9, AMAE; J. Cambon to Delcassé, Jan. 28, 1901, F^{30} 394: Pan., AMEF.

48. Challet to MAE, Oct. 8, 1896, CCC, Guat., v. 12, AMAE; MAE to Challet, Sept. 8, 1897, CCC, Guat., v. 73, AMAE; Joré to MAE, March 6, 13, April 24, July 30, 1898, Oct. 9, Nov. 19, 1899, Jan. 2, March 4, 16, 1900, CCC, San José de CR, v. 2, AMAE (copy of some in CP 1918, CR, Politique extérieure, N. S. 2, AMAE); Langley, *Struggle for the American Mediterranean*, 135–93; Jürgen Buchenau, "A Challenge to the 'Big Stick': Mexican Foreign Policy and U.S. Hegemony in Central America, 1882–1930" (Ph.D. diss., University of North Carolina at Chapel Hill, 1993).

49. J. Cambon to MAE, May 4, 1900, CP 1918, Pan., Canal interocéanique, II, N. S. 10, AMAE; "Note sur le canal," May 31, 1901, BB^4 1597, AAM; Boulard-Pouqueville to Delcassé, July 22, 1901, Sept. 13, 1901, F^{30} 394: Pan., AMEF.

50. Edward A. Burke to Policarpo Bonilla, Dec. 10, 1897, Edward A. Burke Papers, Department of Archives and Manuscripts, Louisiana State University; J. Cambon to MAE, Feb. 5, 1900, Paul Cambon to Téophile Delcassé, Dec. 19, 1900, J. Cambon to Delcassé, Jan. 28, 1900, CP 1918, Pan., Canal Interocéanique, II, N. S. 10, AMAE; J. Cambon to Delcassé, Jan. 28, 1901, Delcassé to Caillaux, June 28, 1901, F^{30} 394: Pan., AMEF; G. Bailleu, "L'Europe et le canal interocéanique. Un conflit possible entre les États-Unis et l'Angleterre," *Revue politique et parlementaire* 7 (Jan. 10, 1901): 129–39; Paul Dreyfus, "Le Canal interocéanique entre l'atlantique et le pacifique," *L'Economiste français* (March 4, 1899), in F^{30} 396: Pan., AMEF.

51. Delcassé to Caillaux, July 28, 1899, J. Cambon to Delcassé, Jan. 28, 1901, Boulard-Pouqueville to Delcassé, July 22, 1901, Sept. 13, 1901, F^{30} 394: Pan., AMEF; P. Cambon to Delcassé, Dec. 19, 1900, CP 1918, Pan., Canal Interocéanique, II, N. S. 10, AMAE; MAE to P. Cambon and Emmanuel H. V. de Noailles, April 15, 1901, J. Cambon to Delcassé, May 7, 28, 1901, Boulard-Pouqueville to Delcassé, Nov. 14, 1901, Pierre de Margerie to MAE, Nov. 19, Dec. 3, 18, 1901 (copies of Dec. 3, 18, 1901, in FF^{30} 394, Pan., AMEF), P. Cambon to Delcassé, Nov. 21, 1901, CP 1918, Pan., Canal Interocéanique III, N. S. 11, AMAE; Charles D. Ameringer, "Bunau-Varilla, Russia, and the Panama Canal," *Journal of Inter-American Studies and World Affairs* 12 (July 1970): 328–38; Skinner, *France and Panama*, 219–38.

52. Ameringer, "Bunau-Varilla, Russia, and the Panama Canal"; "Note sur le canal," May 31, 1901, BB^4 1597, AAM; Captain Bernard to Min. marine, July 24, 1901, BB^4 1338, AAM.

53. Deloffre to MAE, May 9, July 30, 1900, Georges Bonhenry to MAE, Nov. 25, 1902, in "Correspondencia de los Consules Franceses Deloffre y Bonhenry," *Lotería* 330–31 (Sept.–Oct. 1983): 157–71; W. T. Stead, *L'Américanization du monde* (Paris, 1902); Thomas Schoonover, "Europe,

the Spanish-American War, and Great Power Activity in the Caribbean and Asia," *SHAFR Newsletter* 28:3 (Sept. 1997): 1–27.

54. Cazard to MAE, May 12, Aug. 28, 1899, MAE to Cazard, July 21, Aug. 25, 1899, CP 1918, Guat., Finances publiques, I, N. S. 6, AMAE; MAE to Boulard-Pouqueville, Dec. 6, 1897, CP 1918, Guat., Politique intérieure I, N. S. 1, AMAE; Edward Monson to Delcassé, March 28, 1901, F^{30} 393^{1}, folder Guat., AMEF; James P. Cooper, memorandum as to the Guatemalan debt negotiations, Nov. 26, 1901, and other correspondence, CP 1918, Guat., Finances-Emprunts, II, N. S. 7, pp. 2–64, AMAE; Donald L. Kemmerer and Bruce R. Dalgaard, "Inflation, Intrigue, and Monetary Reform in Guatemala, 1919–1926," *The Historian* 66 (Nov. 1983): 21–38; Emily and Norman L. Rosenberg, "From Colonialism to Professionalism: The Public-Private Dynamic in United States Foreign Financial Advising, 1898–1929," *Journal of American History* 74:1 (June 1987): 59–82; Elisabeth Glaser-Schmidt, "Amerikanische Währungsreformen in Ostasien und im karibischen Raum, 1900–1918," *Amerikastudien* 33 (1988): 359–75.

55. Min. commerce to MAE, June 7, 1901, MAE to Pourtalès-Gorgier, July 16, 1901, Pourtalès-Gorgier to Delcassé, Sept. [undated], 24, 1901, MAE to F. Cruz, Nov. 4, 1901, CP 1918, Guat., Finances-Emprunts, II, N. S. 7, AMAE; Pourtalès-Gorgier to MRE, Nov. 7, 1900, B99-5-6/4324/93229, MRE, AGCA.

56. Hosmer to Wharton, Sept. 9, 1889, CD, Guat.: 7 (T 337/r 7), NA; Frederick B. Pike, *Hispanismo, 1898–1936: Spanish Conservatives and Liberals and Their Relations and Spanish America* (Notre Dame, IN, 1971); Alcide Ebray, "Une réconciliation. L'Espagne et l'Amérique latine," *Revue des deux mondes* (Nov. 15, 1901): 427–53; Rowley, *Évolution économique de la France*, 402–7; Blumenthal, *France and the United States*, 255–56.

57. Senat, No. 212 (1903), Report on 1902 commercial convention with Nicaragua, F^{12} 8974, AN; Hugo von Radolin to Bernhard von Bülow, Oct. 13, 1902, Abt. IA, San Salv. 1, v. 4, PAAA.

58. Joré to MAE, Sept. 10, 1899, CP 1918, CR, Politique intérieure, N. S. 1, AMAE; Crisanto Medina, *Le Nicaragua en 1900* (Paris, 1900); Folder, Cent. Amér., Affaires divers commerciales, carton 490, Exposition, Paris 1900, AMAE; Cruz to Anguiano, Jan. 26, Feb. 2, March 9, 16, 30, July 6, 1900, Delaunay Belleville to Anguiano, March 22, 1900, Delcassé to Anguiano, March 24, 1900, B99-6-4/4474/93430, MRE, AGCA.

5

Cooperation with the United States, 1903–1914

Most French politicians and businessmen acknowledged U.S. supremacy in Middle America, but at the same time they expected a French commercial revival to vitalize the stagnation in domestic production. Some of France's commercial and imperial goals lay scattered and unfulfilled in Latin America, in the South Pacific, and in Southeast Asia. The failure of de Lesseps's Universal Interoceanic Canal Company and the sale of the successor New Panama Canal Company had burst a bubble. French military missions and financial circles, however, continued to play a major role in Central America. And in the early twentieth century, French leaders wanted to bind France's commercial revitalization to its vision of a civilizing mission. Moreover, they realized that U.S. goodwill might be useful to France in the struggle between it and its Entente allies on the one side and Germany and the Central Powers on the other.[1] In the end, French officials remained divided on the desirability of competing or cooperating with the United States.

Historian Raymond Poidevin has claimed that German and French interests did not compete in Middle America. The Germans sought commercial, industrial, and investment opportunities, he noted, whereas the French invested in government railroad bonds. Poidevin perceived different styles as well. The Germans developed commercial and cultural ties to Middle America (and South America) through numerous colonists who conducted business; France sent few colonists, and those commonly pursued personal, religious, or cultural goals. Colonists facilitated the German commercial success, while the lack of migrants from France made it difficult for the French to hinder the spread of German influence. And the French government did not lend much assistance to the French emigrants who conducted modest business activities. The French chargé in Guatemala conceded the German preeminence in commerce, agricultural exploitation, and ownership of fincas (rural land holdings), yet he nevertheless envisioned various opportunities for Frenchmen.[2]

Poidevin recognized that French governmental and private parties sought wider commercial and financial roles. Metropole businesses and politicians commonly viewed their relationship as competitive, yet they cooperated to obtain common objectives such as access to specific markets for foreign firms and capital. French authorities and businessmen constantly weighed their need to compete against their need to cooperate with others. France (like any core state seeking a hegemonic role) sought access to and a share of the wealth and power from the world system or, if possible, a competitive edge from this region in its quest for preeminence. Since all accumulators competed for limited surplus value, anti-imperialists and compradors in Central America sought a greater share for their own factions. Sometimes they tried to exploit the rivalries among the core states and thereby capture a fair share of Central America's political economy, but they preferred to do so without antagonizing the United States.[3]

French agriculture overcame a stagnant population and labor force to recover its productivity in the two decades before the First World War. The generation-long stagnation of the domestic labor force threatened the nation's productivity and thus to undermine its living standard and its foreign commerce. French businessmen recognized the need either to accept European migrant labor or to exploit overseas labor. From 1901 to 1911, the French population grew at an annual rate of 0.20 percent. In the early twentieth century, when the economy finally overcame the burdens of a population, labor force, and productivity that had remained stagnant, its role in world commerce was greatly reduced. By 1913, France's exports had declined to 12.6 percent of continental Europe's exports (only one-fifth of its share in 1860), 9.3 percent of the exports of industrial countries (70 percent of its share in 1860), and 7.2 percent of the world exports (half of its share in 1860).[4]

The data on French settlers, firms, and trade in Middle America outline, in part, the continuing relationship between the French and the isthmian economies. In the early twentieth century, French firms and entrepreneurs remained well-represented among the foreign participants on the isthmus (Tables 1 and 5). Both nonstatistical observations about French businesses and data on investment and commerce suggest the significant role of French firms in Central America. Between 1903 and 1914, French importation from Central America varied from three to five million francs, while French exports to Central America rose to over one million francs (Tables 2, 3, and 4). Frenchmen often cited their nation's major role in isthmian capital projects, commerce, and culture to justify preserving its share of development.

In the decade before the Great War, France imported from 1 percent to 4 percent of Guatemalan, Honduran, and Costa Rican exports, and French exports made up 5 percent of Guatemalan and Costa Rican imports. The French purchased 21 percent of Salvadoran exports and supplied 7 percent of its imports. Nicaraguan exports to France varied widely, but averaged about 18 percent of Nicaragua's annual exports. On average, Nicaragua received 6 percent of its total importation from France.[5]

Large investments throughout Latin America underscored French interest in New World affairs. Just between 1909 and 1914, French investment in Latin America grew from 1.5 billion to 4.5 billion francs. These figures represented about 10 percent of the total French external investment, including that placed in its colonies. After the sale of the Panama Canal in 1903, France's investment in Middle America fell to about 45 million francs ($9 million) plus over 80 million francs ($16 million) in Honduran Railroad bonds in default (Tables 6 and 7). By 1913, French investment on the isthmus had climbed to about 75 million francs ($15 million, $31 million counting the railroad bonds). Influence followed the capital as the number of French businessmen in Middle America increased (Tables 1 and 5).[6]

Arghiri Emmanuel argues that "unequal exchange" transferred peripheral wealth to core countries. Through price transferring, creative accounting, and control of exchange mechanisms (banks, commodity and currency exchanges, communications, and export-import firms) the profits were organized and manipulated from the core. Core managers determined the policies for bookkeeping and transfers. Management and exchange mechanisms were needed for long-distance trade. Peripheral activity assured that high wages remained in the core, whereas core activity kept low-wage labor in the periphery.[7]

The increased foreign penetration of the isthmus around 1900 hastened the alienation and exploitation of a labor force that had traditionally followed subsistence work rhythms. The liberal order subordinated the native workforce to a wage-labor compensation system to facilitate the exploitation of land and natural resources. Domestic labor leaders (especially those connected with foreign enterprises) struggled to organize unions to strengthen the workers' capacity to bargain with embryo transnational firms for a fair wage, safe workplace, and decent living conditions. An intriguing aspect of the formation of Central American labor movements was their dual anti-bourgeoisie (response to local conditions) and anti-imperialistic (response to the world economy) characteristics, in contrast to early worker organizations in the United States and Europe, which focused upon anti-bourgeoisie activity.[8]

The most dramatic example of foreign manipulation and exploitation of isthmian economic values involved the dual U.S.-French pillaging of the Panamanian isthmus from 1901 to 1903 when the canal concession was sold to the U.S. government. Philippe Bunau-Varilla headed a group seeking to profit from the sale of the New Panama Canal Company. Bunau-Varilla came from a modest background—he was an illegitimate child with middle-class roots. His schooling was about the best France offered. He studied engineering at the École Polytechnique and the École des Ponts et Chaussées. After Bunau-Varilla finished his studies in 1885, de Lesseps's Compagnie Universelle du Canal Interocéanique hired him. His long connection with the project may explain his later determination to extract some wealth from the canal. He and U.S. officials cooperated to encourage revolutionary forces to implement a coup that would gain immense financial benefits for a few speculators who controlled the New Panama Canal Company and enduring political, economic, and security advantages for the United States. After Bunau-Varilla persuaded the revolutionaries to name him as their agent to negotiate with the United States, he bartered away pieces of Panama's sovereignty to assure the profitable sale of the company. In 1903 the French police claimed that a secret dossier existed in the hands of a Professor Izoulet at the Collège de France that revealed the scheme through which builder of the Eiffel tower Alexandre Gustave Eiffel, Letellier, international private banker Gerson von Bleichroeder, and Bunau-Varilla shared a large part of the price of the New Panama Canal Company.[9]

In defense of U.S. conduct during the Panamanian revolt of November 1903, spokesmen for President Theodore Roosevelt's administration charged the French government with threatening U.S. security on the isthmus. Assistant Secretary of State Francis B. Loomis, speaking to the New York Club in December 1903, fantasized that France might have sent troops to Panama if Colombia had expropriated the canal company property. The French, he continued, might have assaulted the Monroe Doctrine, causing a spark that would have ignited a world fire.[10] This defense was illusionary even as a hypothesis. Since the late 1870s the French government had repeatedly demonstrated that it would not intervene on behalf of the canal company.

When the U.S. government purchased the New Panama Canal Company, it created an unexpected opportunity for French shipping interests. The acquisition converted the Panama Railroad from a profit-oriented undertaking to a public service operation. It also terminated the railroad's secret arrangement that conceded to the Pacific Mail Steamship Company reduced charges and favored treatment, and it opened up ship traffic from San Francisco to Panama for competition. The Panama Railroad had consistently adjusted its schedule to the disadvantage of the Compagnie Générale Transatlantique, which ultimately abandoned regular service to the great detriment of French interests. French vice-consul Georges Bonhenry, a career consular official, proposed initiating a regular French postal steamer service to Colón to permit French firms to take advantage of the newly opened arena. The open competition attracted European shipping and lowered the freight rates.[11]

Competition among the metropole states for naval stations on both sides of the Panama Canal assumed urgency after the United States initiated a canal project in 1904. During the period of the French canal companies, various colonial interests had advocated the development of French possessions in the Caribbean and in the Pacific to support trans-Pacific steamship lines. The failure of the New Panama Canal Company had been a rude shock for these parties. They adapted quickly, however, eagerly shifting their expectations to use a U.S. canal to connect the French colonies.[12]

Although the Panama Canal had been the chief French involvement in isthmian affairs between 1878 and 1904, a reviving French domestic economy and the bulging coffers of French investors diversified and expanded the French role in Middle America. Various consular agents promoted commercial and investment ties between France and the isthmus. In 1908 a French consul listed a multipoint program to benefit French relations with Honduras. He suggested establishing a steamship line to carry passengers and cargo between the two countries, participating in a land transportation system and public works to expand France's role in the Honduran market, forming real estate and colonization companies, exploiting mineral, plantation, and manufacturing opportunities, establishing permanent mutual expositions, and, finally, building ship repair facilities in Honduras. These steps, he argued, would augment France's economic and civilizing role in Central America.[13]

The Guatemalan government tried to persuade French businessmen of the stability of its society. In 1907 the government arranged for Agence Havas and other news services to reprint in French papers articles from *El guatemalteco* and *La locomotora* that praised President Manuel Estrada Cabrera and revealed how respected and esteemed he was. The Guatemalan foreign minister was disturbed because he was not receiving the clippings from the French press that he considered necessary to rectify falsehoods and distortions about Guatemala.[14] The touched-up image of Estrada Cabrera was supposed to signal stability and attract French entrepreneurs and investors.

Charles H. Stephan, Guatemala's consul in Paris, encouraged French merchants, investors, and bankers to participate in Guatemala's economy, which was rich in primary materials, particularly forest reserves and agricultural products. He noted that many French products had to enter Guatemala through foreign merchant houses, in part because only nine French firms were involved in Franco-Guatemalan commerce. He estimated the French direct investment in Guatemala at 3.8 million francs: 1.6 million in commerce, 0.9 million in agricultural lands, 0.7 million in real estate, and 0.6 million in banking operations. His evaluation was low, however, because he ignored indirect portfolio participation in non-French firms and Guatemalan state bonds.[15]

A French diplomat believed that Guatemalan railroad construction in the early twentieth century offered multiple new opportunities to French businessmen. Since the inconvenience of the Panama isthmus crossing had hindered previous attempts at achieving a Franco-Guatemalan postal package convention, he expected the railroad terminal at Puerto Barrios on the Caribbean coast to permit a postal treaty and to stimulate direct French exports to Guatemala. In 1908 the Guatemalan government contracted with Minor Cooper Keith, a U.S. railroad contractor and founder of United Fruit, to complete its interoceanic railroad system. When the German and U.S. capital markets could not raise the $5 million needed, Keith looked to Britain and France. The French consul encouraged the sale of bonds by reporting optimistically on Guatemala's economic and political conditions.[16] This issue was not placed in Paris, however, and British and U.S. financiers raised most of the capital Keith needed.

In the early twentieth century the French economy and nationalism reaped benefits from France's military mission in Guatemala. When cavalry captain Louis Chaigné's fourth contract approached its end in 1908, Estrada Cabrera personally requested an extension. The French government cautioned that Chaigné's lengthy stay in Guatemala jeopardized his prospects for promotion. In January 1910, Captain Louis G. J. Salats replaced Chaigné. Before the year was out, however, both Chaigné and Estrada Cabrera requested Chaigné's reappointment, even if it endangered his advancement in the French army. Shortly after Chaigné returned in 1911, he convinced the Guatemalan officials of the superiority of French military equipment. Whereas the Guatemalan government had ordered about one million francs worth of military equipment in the previous ten years, Chaigné persuaded it to replace all of its German artillery with new French cannons thereby breaking the near monopoly of Krupp and other German firms in the sale of military equipment to Guatemala.[17]

In late 1911, Guatemala requested two additional officers. Chaigné viewed this as an opportunity to solidify France's position and to obtain more orders for military equipment. The French War Ministry raised no objection, and in 1913, Chaigné was joined by Captain Gaston Contresty of the artillery and Captain Marcel Escalle of the infantry. The Spanish minister in Central America considered the services of Contresty and Escalle to be "absolutely unnecessary" and a "useless burden for the country." Yet he conceded that the contract that brought the officers to Guatemala "constituted unquestionably an important triumph of French influence."[18]

Chaigné's ability to captivate Estrada Cabrera was widely acknowledged. The Spanish minister believed that Chaigné "enjoys the absolute confidence of the [Guatemalan] chief of state. [Chaigné's] influence was decisive in military questions." Still, an opportunity for Spanish influence rose when Estrada Cabrera decided to utilize Spanish officers, because of their language, as instructors for Guatemala's new military academy. The Spanish diplomat warned, however, that the opportunity could easily

Although frequently called the "Torre Eiffel de Guatemala," the Torre del Reformador was purchased from the Golden State International Exposition in San Francisco in 1933 and reassembled in Guatemala in 1935 for the centennial of the birth of President Justo Rufino Barrios, the leader of the 1870–71 liberal revolution. From *Seis años de gobierno, Presidido por General Jorge Ubico* (Guatemala City: Tipografía Nacional, 1937), 352. *Courtesy Academía de Geografía e Historia de Guatemala*

be reversed once the French officers had learned Spanish well because they were much less expensive. He suspected that Estrada Cabrera wanted European instructors to demonstrate that Guatemala retained vital links to the Old World.[19]

Chaigné's success in Guatemala produced supplementary benefits for the French arms industry with the other isthmian governments. The Honduran military acquired a French officer as adviser in 1911. He and the French consul successfully competed for an order of 30,000 weapons valued at 240,000 francs. In response to the buildup by Honduras, Guatemala requested an additional 100,000 weapons, but it offered less than half the price per weapon that Honduras had paid. To maintain the market and to preserve the appearance of neutrality, the French government insisted that the price had to be the same for Guatemala and Honduras. In 1914, Honduras offered a qualified French junior officer the rank of brigadier general while he organized its army staff, but in the troubled state of European affairs, this possibility was not pursued.[20]

In late 1912 a Krupp agent tried to reacquire Guatemala's artillery order. Although French heavy industry was able to retain Guatemala's order for military equipment, the Krupp challenge confirmed that the situation remained competitive. The success of the French military mission was underlined in 1917 when Guatemala turned to France, not the United States, to modernize its army for a possible call to the European war.[21] The military missions and the arms sales continued to aid France's domestic economy and its influence in Central America.

French investors survived one major misadventure in Central American bonds, the Honduran Railroad bonds of 1869. French bondholders and financiers continually asserted the validity of the bonds after the railroad defaulted in the mid-1870s. In 1903 the Squire investment syndicate—organized in the United States—sought the support of the French government for a loan that would lead to the retirement and partial repayment of the 1869 bonds. Squire was unsuccessful, but in 1909 the French bondholders welcomed from the House of Morgan a loan proposal that would retire the railroad bonds at an acceptable price. The U.S. State Department declared that the Morgan loan proposal would encourage order but that a loan by French banks to Nicaraguan president Zelaya would encourage disorder and injure European creditors. The French minister in Washington interpreted these statements as an indication that the U.S. government intended to supervise the finances of the Central

American countries and to protect U.S., and occasionally European, interests. In his view, the United States would not welcome direct European intervention in Central American financial affairs.[22]

Several French banks pursued investment opportunities in Middle America in the early twentieth century. In mid-1909 the Banque de Neuflize, a private investment bank, sent an agent to Central America to gather information and seek out investment opportunities. He negotiated a loan with Minor Keith that involved shares in the Guatemalan Central Railroad and the Abangaria Gold Mine in Costa Rica as security. He reported extensively on banks, financial houses, large firms, and individual entrepreneurs operating in Central America and arranged for correspondence banks.[23] The bank's agent explored numerous possible investment situations.

The expanding French investment role in Central America worried the U.S. government. For example, France and the United States were the chief competitors for a Costa Rican loan in 1906. The Costa Rican government rejected the good terms offered by the French bankers because it expected to receive better terms from the United States. But Speyer and Company of New York offered onerous terms, which were rejected.[24] The search for a loan continued.

In 1911 the Costa Rican government negotiated with the financial house Behrens in Hamburg and revived contact with Speyer in New York regarding a $7 million loan. It broke off negotiations when Speyer insisted upon a U.S. comptroller for Costa Rican revenues in case of nonpayment of interest. The Costa Ricans turned to the French government, which contacted various financial houses, including a branch of Speyer, about managing the loan in the Paris bond market. But the Costa Rican finance minister, in disagreement with his government, allied with Keith to sabotage a French loan.[25] The loan went forward despite the opposition.

Costa Rican minister to France Manuel Peralta oversaw the arrangements for the loan in France. He worried because Costa Rica had consulted three firms in France—the Littmann firm, Speyer and Company, and Albert Kohn—which were rooted in either Germanic or Anglo-Saxon culture. He suspected that only a French financier could animate public acceptance of the loan. Finally, in December 1911, a Franco-Costa Rican loan for 35 million francs ($7 million) was placed on the Paris market. Peralta was dismayed when the Costa Rican government floated a

£350,000 loan in London simultaneously, because the loans would compete for European funds.[26]

When Nicaragua inquired in mid-1909 about floating a loan for 31.5 million francs ($6.3 million) in Paris, the French foreign minister consulted the U.S. secretary of state, who wanted the French government to make its loan conditional upon Nicaragua arranging its affairs with the United States so that France would not be placed in an adversary role with Washington. France agreed to squeeze Nicaragua. The French consul in Costa Rica warned that the State Department considered President Zelaya "the cause of all the unrest which blocks the material and political progress of Central America" and that any financial collaboration with him would annoy the United States.[27]

The French government, discounting the warning of its consul and misreading the hypocrisy behind U.S. willingness to permit a loan, allowed preparations to go forward. When Nicaragua tried to benefit from the negotiations by announcing the forthcoming loan, the French ambassador to the United States, Jean Jules Jusserand, assured the secretary of state that although a loan had been approved in principle, provided Nicaragua settled with the United States, there was no contract. Later, when the loan was about to be placed on the Paris Stock Exchange, the secretary of state claimed that any money Zelaya might get "would be without doubt spent to purchase munitions to oppress his neighbors." U.S. officials questioned whether the money would be "spent honestly" and expressed fear that the funds would strengthen "Zelaya in his hostility to peace and progress in Central America." The French government, finally realizing that it had to avoid the loan, withdrew permission for it after only a few bonds had been issued. With tension high in Europe, it refused to antagonize the U.S. government over a Central American issue because the French government desired U.S. support in its European problems.[28]

In 1912, with French bankers shunted aside because of U.S. "strategic" interests, and with Zelaya ousted, two U.S. banking firms, Brown Brothers and Seligman, shared the Nicaraguan loan. The projected U.S. loan threatened to injure France in three ways because Brown Brothers had branches in France. First, the U.S. firm might use capital raised in France to the detriment of French interests. Second, France risked sharing the growing unpopularity of the United States in Central America because French capital would support U.S. financial houses. Third, the French government had to prevent the new loan from injuring the few bondholders of the 1909 loan. The U.S. loan did protect the French bondholders.[29]

Although unsuccessful in the Nicaraguan loan, French financial circles sought other Central American loan opportunities. In 1911, French banks evaluated a 50 million franc ($10 million) loan to El Salvador. The bankers consulted the finance and foreign ministries about a syndicate with minority participation by U.S. banks. The finance minister saw advantage in cooperation with U.S. banks only if U.S. investors held some of the bonds. The French banks, however, should not consider the participation of U.S. banks an iron-clad guarantee. The rewards for European bondholders could prove illusory, he cautioned, if the U.S. government considered the loan terms onerous or if it simply did not support the banks participating in the loan. The French foreign minister suspected that certain clauses in the Salvadoran loan contract might produce tension with the United States. There were also expectations of benefit. Since about one-half of the loan was designated for public works, the finance minister hoped that some orders to supply materials for these projects would go to French firms.[30]

The French consul general in New York questioned whether U.S. banks should even be invited to join the Salvadoran loan. In contrast to Honduras, where the United States had a predominant role and excluded foreign creditors, El Salvador had no foreign debt, and the United States exercised no predominant role there. France, he noted, purchased most of El Salvador's coffee. Being the sole source of financial aid should boost France's prestige in a country where its investments had already reached 20 million francs. Finally, many Salvadorans preferred aid from financial institutions without ulterior political motives rather than from U.S. banks that threatened El Salvador's independence.[31]

French financial experts evaluated each loan request after a wide-ranging examination of economic, strategic, and political factors. Not all loan requests met their approval. In 1912, French diplomat Maurice Paléologue recommended reserve toward the special Salvadoran minister who sought a loan in Europe because French holders of Salvadoran railroad bonds had experienced difficulties. He underlined the need for a strong guarantee, but U.S. opposition would surely deny the most effective one, control of the customs. Thus a second Franco-Salvadoran loan was not forthcoming. In 1913, Nicaraguan minister Salvador Castrillo could not obtain a large loan on Wall Street, so the Nicaraguan government planned to seek a $6 million loan in Europe. Jusserand advised great caution because Castrillo was vague about why Nicaragua needed the loan. This loan did not materialize.[32] Although French financiers adjusted their projects to accommodate U.S. security concerns, they never ceased to investigate opportunities.

Chargé Fabre recognized that while the French government maintained its political distance from Central America, French capital searched diligently for opportunities everywhere. He recommended banking as the best area for investing. Thus, in 1905 several French financiers acquired a 20 percent share of the Banco Comercial de Costa Rica, capitalized at 2.4 million francs. French investors also placed small sums of capital in the Nicaraguan canal, electricity, railroads, and other transportation projects, hoping to strengthen French commerce with Central America. Municipal organizations encouraged commercial, communications, and financial policies to expand trade ties abroad. The chambers of commerce of Le Havre, Saint-Nazaire, Nantes, Marseilles, and Bordeaux petitioned to subsidize a regular postal service to Colón. Municipalities wanted to share in the opportunities.[33]

Occasionally, French entrepreneurs also entered agriculture and mining in Middle America. French officials encouraged the development of banana plantations and fruit shipping. Small French banana companies operated in Nicaragua and in the Rio Coclé region of Panama. The French consul asked the Générale Transatlantique to schedule a stop in Panama for a ship with a refrigerated section to transport bananas to France. He hoped that the French would develop a taste for bananas. At times, promoters from the periphery trapped the metropole investors. The French foreign minister warned that an agent for the Guatemala Mining and Development Company, which sought capital in France for a monopoly of Guatemalan mining rights, regularly misrepresented the company's modest financial support. Despite the warning, French investors placed about 500,000 francs in this firm.[34] While French investors exploited the land, labor, and even capital of the periphery, collaborators from isthmian countries could scheme to participate in applying metropole capital to the local land and labor.

French consuls occasionally perceived an opportunity for French firms in the competitive struggles of other metropole enterprises. A major conflict developed in the early 1900s between United Fruit and Atlantic Fruit, which was allied with the

German Hamburg-America line. The struggle was sharpest in the banana area on the border between Panama and Costa Rica. The French consul in Costa Rica speculated that the conflict created an opportunity for Générale Transatlantique to open direct trade because United Fruit might favor a French shipping firm when a German firm aided its competitor.[35]

In the early twentieth century, French officials evaluated the deterioration of France's commercial role on the isthmus in terms of two dynamic isthmian intruders—Germany and the United States. In 1909 the French government received no convincing explanations of why French commerce, especially the sale of wines and alcoholic beverages, in several Central American countries paid tariffs that German, British, and U.S. agents managed to avoid. Jules Jusserand concluded that German programs for penetration of Latin America—particularly military missions and banking—were more advanced than their French counterparts. Since emigration, finance, and commerce had assumed special importance in Europe's relations with Latin America, Jusserand argued that the French needed to learn from the German methods. The foreign minister and Senator A. Gervais found Jusserand's evaluation persuasive. Several French newspapers published articles comparing France with Germany, using an organization and evidence similar to Jusserand's. In 1913 the French minister in Guatemala was instructed to report upon competition with the United States and Germany.[36]

The French struggle for more favorable access to the isthmus encompassed more than investment and commercial elements. In 1906, Fernand-Jean-Baptiste-Marie Bernard, count Montessus de Ballore, published his first book on seismology and firmed up his reputation as one of the world's foremost seismologists. Bernard had begun his studies in El Salvador and carried out the majority of his work in that country. In 1909 a Foreign Ministry report encouraged promoting abroad the same intellectual formation and culture as in France. It recommended diffusion of the French language through the underfunded Alliance française. Chargé Fabre noted the tenacity of French cultural influence in conservative states like El Salvador and Nicaragua. However, other metropoles challenged France in the cultural area. U.S. cultural activity increased steadily, but the German influence was a more serious challenge to the French cultural mission. Panamanians were attracted to French civilization, Fabre contended, but French guidance and material support were inadequate to meet Panama's educational needs. The

French government emphasized that French printed materials and schools should aim to preserve the national identity and culture of inhabitants with French origins.[37]

French commercial relations with Guatemala deteriorated after German business interests became preeminent in the late nineteenth century. French military missions, however, more than held their own against their German counterparts. Nevertheless, the successful French military mission and arms sales did not reverse the commercial decline. Efforts to reverse the decline by negotiating a Franco-Guatemalan trade agreement had failed in 1901. In 1912, however, the Guatemalan government expressed interest in a trade agreement. The French commerce minister contemplated an agreement in which coffee would be exchanged for wine and champagne, French companies would be encouraged to undertake major projects, and French suppliers to municipal and other governmental units would have an advantage. Since France delivered less than 5 percent of Guatemala's imports, there was room for considerable improvement. The French chargé cautioned, however, that the German-Guatemalan commercial treaty prevented Guatemala from granting tariff concessions to France. The writer Alexis Caille reasoned that the fundamental roadblock to enlarged trade was that, because it did not have easy access to the French market, Guatemalan coffee was sold mostly in Germany. Opening French ports to Guatemalan coffee would permit French firms to conduct business on equal terms with German firms. French officials concluded that a treaty was in the best interest of both countries. Whereas French culture and industry had traditionally been appreciated, the officials believed that ways could be found to increase each country's access to the other's market.[38]

In mid-1913 the president of the Association of [French] Manufacturers of Pharmaceutical Products feared that the member firms might get shut out of another Central American market, if French diplomats were not on guard. Costa Rica was effectively closed to French pharmaceutical products in 1912, and El Salvador, France's best customer for pharmaceuticals in Central America, appeared ready to follow. The association president detected a pernicious U.S. influence. A proposed import duty on pharmaceuticals by weight would greatly disadvantage French products, which were often heavy syrups and liquids; U.S. products were commonly light pills. The pharmaceutical association wanted energetic support for *ad valorem* duties.[39]

Europeans unwisely expected North America's "pax americana" in Central America to favor economic development that would benefit the Old World. Central Americans, Fabre observed, recognized that U.S. preeminence produced advantages for Yankee enterprise and little for other countries. For example, in 1912 the State Department maneuvered two North Americans onto the three-member Nicaraguan claims commission. French, German, and British agents immediately complained that this commission was detrimental to their citizens. But the united front dissolved rather than anger the U.S. government. First the Germans rejected a formal protest and withdrew, and then the British retreated. In the end, the French protested alone. The State Department replied disingenuously that French interests were no "less safe" before this body than they would be before a commission consisting entirely of Nicaraguan personnel.[40] Of course, the U.S. government would have considered its own interests "less safe" if the commission had had French representatives, but no North American.

As the Panama Canal approached completion, French officials were reminded of U.S. sensitivity in matters of isthmian canals. When the French financial house Louis Dreyfus and Company negotiated a concession for banks of emission (with the authority to issue currency) and hypothecary in Colombia, U.S. officials objected to locating any European-controlled bank or oil concessions near canal sites. The French government, upon learning of the U.S. position, refused to encourage Dreyfus and Company's or any other French projects near a potential canal route without the agreement of the U.S. government.[41]

The breaching of the isthmus at Panama affected all metropoles. In 1911 the French government pondered the proper technical, material, and mental preparations for the opening of the Panama Canal. It expected French colonies in the Caribbean to flourish because of the increased traffic from new trade and shipping activity. The Chamber of Deputies proposed the integration of France's colonial network to prevent the British from absorbing French international trading routes. It wanted the "metropole" to retain its influence in the Pacific and "to play its historic role in as brilliant a fashion as its rival." The colonies near the main shipping routes through Panama and through Tahiti in the South Pacific needed to offer the multitude of services required for long-distance trade routes: coal, food and other supplies, repair facilities, fresh water, and communications. Jusserand recommended that an interdepartmental committee be set up to study the impact of the canal upon France's role in world commerce.[42]

El Salvador's finance minister, visiting France in the summer of 1912, invited the French government to send a special mission to study his country's economic and financial condition in preparation for the opening of the Panama Canal. The French asked him about the conduct of other metropoles regarding isthmian economic prospects. It learned that U.S. interests labored to take advantage of the opening of the Panama Canal, and that British and German customs officials were already conducting studies similar to the one proposed by El Salvador. French diplomats in Berlin and London underscored the habit of these nations to study Central American trade and shipping regularly.[43]

A cautious commercial policy would not aid French utilization of canal opportunities. In the winter of 1913–14 the French government formed an interministerial committee to aid in maximizing French economic benefit from the canal. The committee examined the means of extending French commerce on the west coast of America, the use of France's land and ocean transport systems in connection with the canal, the orientation of the colonial system so it could extract maximum value from the canal, and various questions related to sanitary measures. It presumed that if it integrated its French Antilles and Pacific possessions wisely, it might increase French trade on the Pacific coast. French shipping firms needed to be more active, yet they hesitated to establish a New World line on the west coast, while the Germans had already initiated several.[44]

French relations with Central America had been unsatisfactory in the early twentieth century because isthmian states tended to allow the United States a growing share of their commerce. At the turn of the century, French investment in Latin America rose dramatically, almost doubling in Central America between the sale of the Panama Canal Company in 1903 and the outbreak of war in 1914. It might have tripled, had U.S. political pressure not undermined loans to Nicaragua in 1909 and to El Salvador in 1912. Much of this French capital was invested in state bonds, and some supported development projects such as railroads, but other investments were inhibited because French officials were uncertain of the attitude the U.S. government would adopt toward foreign debt collection on the isthmus.

Security interests loomed large in both U.S. and French policies. These security interests were part of broader matters of culture, commerce, raw materials, and investment opportunities that were expected to bolster domestic stability and prosperity. The French military mission in Guatemala exercised considerable influence in that country and with its neighbors. Both Honduras and El Salvador negotiated arms and adviser agreements with the French government, in part because of the successful mission in Guatemala. The U.S. canal project stimulated France's government and its commercial, maritime, and colonial interests to evaluate how French possessions in the Caribbean and Pacific might expand their service facilities to meet the anticipated commercial activity. French economic and financial interests expected that a U.S. protectorate over Middle America might offer them more stability for business and loans, more security for foreign residents, and better possibilities for their maritime interests.

Notes

1. Zahniser, *Uncertain Friendship*; Jean-Baptiste Duroselle, *La France et les Etats-Unis: Des origines à nos jours* (Paris, 1976), 53–89; Rebérioux, *La République radicale?*; Roger Magraw, *France, 1815–1914: The Bourgeois Century* (New York, 1986), 255–375; Lester D. Langley, *The United States and the Caribbean in the Twentieth Century* (Athens, GA, 1982); Maurice de Périgny, *Les Cinq Républiques de l'Amérique centrale* (Paris, 1911); Salgó, *Du rôle des facteurs économiques et politiques de la politique coloniale française dans la période d'après 1871*, 5–22; Stanley E. Hilton, "Latin America and Western Europe, 1880–1945: The Political Dimension," in Wolf Grabendorff and Riordan Roett, eds., *Latin America, Western Europe, and the United States* (New York, 1985), 1–39; Andrew and Kanya-Forstner, "French Business and the French Colonialists"; Persell, *The French Colonial Lobby*, 1–6, 37–74.

2. Poidevin, *Les Relations économiques entre la France et l'Allemagne*, 76, 154–56, 241, 333–43; Schoonover, "Metropole Rivalry in Central America"; André M. Jacques d'Arlot de Saint-Saud to Rouvier, Feb. 20, 1906, Commerce, F[12] 7054: Amér. cent., AN.

3. Poidevin, *Les Relations économiques entre la France et l'Allemagne*, 76, 154–56, 241, 333–43; Réné Girault, "Place et rôle des échanges extérieurs," in Fernand Braudel and Ernest Labrousse, eds., *Histoire économique et sociale de la France* (4 vols.; Paris, 1970–80), vol. 4, pt. 1, 229–30; Girault, "Le Milieu bancaire français face aux relations internationales avant 1914"; Blankenburg, "Der französische Kapitalexport," 68–72, 101–5; Lafond, *L'Effort français en Amérique Latine*, 67–71, 97–99; Jean S. Weiller, "Long-run Tendencies in Foreign Trade: With a Statistical Study of French Trade Structure, 1871–1939," *Journal of Economic History* 31 (Dec. 1971): 804–21; Blumenthal, *France and the United States*, 256–57; Jean Malpas, *Les Mouvements internationaux des capitaux* (Paris, 1934); Bouvier, Furet, and Gillet, *Le Mouvement du profit en France au xix*[e] *siècle*, 274–77; Salgó, *Du Rôle*

des facteurs économiques et politiques de la politique coloniale française, 14–20; Kemp, *Economic Forces in French History,* 267–70; Alan S. Milward and S. B. Saul, *The Development of the Economies of Continental Europe,* 1850–1914 (London, 1977), 127–39; Célestin-Pierre Cambiaire, *Le Rôle de la France dans l'expansion des États-Unis* (Paris, 1935), 222–26; Lefébure, "A la conquête d'un isthme: Les États-Unis et l'Europe," 613–14, 618; Wallerstein, *Historical Capitalism,* 62. Often students of French expansion focus upon French colonialism, ignoring informal methods of expanding a political economy. See, for example, Christopher Andrew and A. S. Kanya-Forstner, *France Overseas: The Great War and the Climax of French Imperial Expansion* (London, 1981), 10–17.

4. Caron, *An Economic History of Modern France,* 8–25, 105; Rebérioux, *La République radicale?* 195–208; Rowley, *Évolution économique de la France au milieu du xixe siècle à 1914;* Paul Connac, *La Participation des ouvriers aux résultats de l'entreprise agricole en France* (Paris, 1927).

5. Schoonover and Schoonover, "Statistics for the Understanding of the Foreign Intrusion into Central America," 77–119.

6. Frédéric Mauro, "Les Investissements français en Amérique latine des origines à 1973," *Revue d'histoire économique et sociale* 55 (1977): 234–62; Girault, "Place et rôle des échanges extérieurs," 4: 1: 229–30; unsigned, "Note pour M. le Rapporteur de la Commission de Budget," July 27, 1909, Mémoires et documents, Amér., v. 67, AMAE; MAE to Jean-Jules Jusserand, 17, May 24, June 4, 1909, Jusserand to MAE, May 22, July 1, 1909, Henry White to Stephen Pichon, May 28, 1909, Min. finances to MAE, May 29, 1909, MAE to Min. finances, July 2, 1909, CP 1918, Nic., Finances, Emprunts, N. S. 3, AMAE (copies in F^{30} 393^{1}: folder Nic., AMEF); MAE to Min. finances, May 3, July 2, 17, Aug. 3, 1909, enclosing U.S. min. in CR to Francis Mairs Huntington Wilson, June 19, 1909, Pichon to Min. finances, June 3, 1909, F^{30} 393^{2}: folder Nic., AMEF; R. G. Levy, "Les Capitaux français à l'étranger"; "La Fortune française à l'étranger"; Adeline Daumard, "Les Placements à l'étranger dans les patrimoines des français au xixe siècle (1815–1914)," *Revue d'histoire économique et sociale* 52 (1974): 526–46; Raymond Poidevin, "Weltpolitik allemande et capitaux français (1898–1914)," in Imanuel Geiss and Bernd Jürgen Wendt, eds., *Deutschland in der Weltpolitik des 19. und 20. Jahrhunderts* (Düsseldorf, 1974); Xavier Gorostiaga, *Los banqueros del imperio. El papel de los centros financieros internacionales en los países subdesarrollados* (San José, CR, 1978); Christine Eusebe, "Les Investissements français en Amérique centrale et dans l'aire des Caraïbes" (Mémoire de maîtrise, Université de Paris X [Nanterre], 1972); Lee Ellerich, "France in Latin America," *Current History* 28 (March 1955): 160–67; Jacques Marseille, "L'Investissement français dans l'empire colonial: L'Enquête du gouvernement de Vichy (1943)," *Revue Historique* 252 (July–Dec. 1974): 409–32; Poidevin, *Les Relations économiques entre la France et l'Allemagne,* 76, 154–56, 241, 333–43.

7. Arghiri Emmanuel, *Unequal Exchange* (New York, 1972).

8. Woodward, *Central America;* Cardoso, "Central America: The Liberal Era"; Manuel Roja Bolaños, "El desarrollo del movimiento obrero en Costa Rica; un intento de periodización," in *Desarrollo del movimiento sindical en Costa Rica* (San José, CR, 1981), 13–21; Victor Meza, *Historia del movimiento obrero hondureño* (Tegucigalpa, 1980); Mario Posas, *Luchas del movimiento obrero hondureño* (San José, CR, 1981); Vladimir de la Cruz, *Las*

luchas sociales en Costa Rica, 1870–1930 (San José, CR, 1980); Mario Argueta, *Historia de los sin historia, 1900–1948* (Tegucigalpa, 1992).

9. David McCullough, *The Path between the Seas: The Creation of the Panama Canal, 1870–1914* (New York, 1977), 161–63; Thomas Schoonover, "Morality and Political Purpose in Theodore Roosevelt's Action in Panama in 1903," in Schoonover, *The United States in Central America*, 97–110; LaFeber, *The Panama Canal*, 3–45; Charles Ameringer, "Philippe Bunau-Varilla: New Light on the Panama Canal Treaty," *Hispanic American Historical Review* 46 (Feb. 1966): 28–52; Patricia Pizzurno-Gelos, "Presentación de los documentos de los consules franceses sobre la guerra civil en Panamá," *Lotería* 330–31 (Sept.–Oct. 1983): 146–56; Gustave Anguizola, *Philippe Bunau-Varilla* (Chicago, 1980); Langley, *The United States and the Caribbean in the Twentieth Century*, 3–43; Skinner, *France and Panama*, 219–38; Collin, *Theodore Roosevelt's Caribbean*, 163–305; unsigned memorandum, Dec. 5, 1903, Police générale, F^7 12927: Affaire du Panama, AN; "Le Canal de Panama, la documentation française," *Notes et études documentaires* (March 10, 1950): 1–44.

10. Hermann Speck von Sternburg to Bülow, Dec. 21, 1903, Abt. IA, Pan. 1, v. 4, PAAA; Duroselle, *La France et les Etats-Unis*, 53–89. See also Francis B. Loomis, "The Position of the United States on the American Continent—Some Phases of the Monroe Doctrine," *Annals of the American Academy of Political and Social Sciences* 22 (July 1903): 1–19; Francis B. Loomis, "Attitude of the United States toward Other American Powers," *Annals of the American Academy of Political and Social Sciences* 26 (July 1905): 21–24.

11. Bonhenry to Maurice Rouvier, Aug. 31, 1905, Commerce, F^{12} 7059, AN; Monique de Nomazy to author, Feb. 4, 1991, and attachment on career of Georges Bonhenry.

12. Hautefeuille to Min. marine, Oct. 11, 14, 1904, BB^4 1690, AAM; Hautefeuille to Min. marine, July 12, 1906, BB^4 1701, AAM; A. Goupil, "Note sur le projet de concession de la Baie de Rapa pour l'établissement d'une escale de la navigation transpacifique en vue du percement de l'isthme de Panama," Aug. 17, 1905, BB^4 1597, AAM.

13. Désiré Pector, *Artículos sobre la Mosquitia* (Tegucigalpa, 1908), 99–109.

14. Magraw, *France 1815–1914*, 354–75; René Rémond, *Le xixe siècle, 1815–1914* (Paris, 1974), 208–48; Barrios to Manuel Arroyo, April 30, 1907, Barrios to Enrique Wissbold, July 24, 1907, B99-6, 4409/93365, Legaciones en Francia y España, 1906–1911, AGCA.

15. Charles H. Stephan, *Le Guatemala économique* (Paris, 1907).

16. D'Arlot to Pichon, March 2, 1908, F^{30} 393^1: Guat. folder, AMEF; d'Arlot to Pichon, April 29, 1907, Commerce, F^{12} 8944: Guat., AN.

17. D'Arlot to Pichon, March 23, April 12, 1908, Min. finances to MAE, Sept. 19, 1908, Arce to MAE, Oct. 30, 1908, Min. guerre to MAE, Nov. 10, 1908, and other correspondence, CP 1918, Guat., Défense nationale, I, N. S. 3, AMAE; Augustin Julien Rigoreau to MAE, Aug. 5, 1911, Min. guerre to MAE, Sept. 18, 1911, Min. finances to MAE, Oct. 6, Nov. 24, 1911, Auguste Jean Marie Fabre to MAE, Oct. 8, 1911, Arce to MAE, Oct. 11, 1911, CP 1918, Guat., Défense nationale, II, N. S. 3, AMAE; A. R. Conty to Min. guerre, Nov. 14, 1911, 7N1729, dossier Guat., Archive de l'armée de la terre,

Paris (hereafter cited as AAT); Poidevin, "Fabricants d'armes et relations internationales au début du xxe siècle."

18. Fabre to MAE, Oct. 8, 1911, Arce to MAE, Oct. 11, 1911, CP 1918, Guat., Défense nationale, II, N. S. 3, AMAE; Conty to Min. guerre, Nov. 14, 1911, 7N1729, dossier Guat., AAT; Pablo de Benito to MAE, Feb. 3, 1913, H1609 (Guat.), AMAE, Madrid.

19. Benito to MAE, Feb. 3, 1913, H1609, AMAE, Madrid.

20. Désiré Pector to Jean Cruppi, May 6, 1911, Min. finances to MAE, July 5, 1911, Hond., Pol. intérieure, Armée, N. S. 1, AMAE; L.-M. Alphonse l'Avril to MAE, Feb. 2, 1914, CP 1918, Hond., Pol. intérieure, Chemins de fer, N. S. 1, AMAE.

21. Fabre to MAE, Oct. 15, 1912, José Lardizabal to MAE, Oct. 13, 1917, March 26, 1918, Min. guerre to MAE, Dec. 9, 1917, CP 1918, Guat., Défense nationale, II, N. S. 4, AMAE; Charles Roux to MAE, April 13, 1912, CP 1918, Pan., Canal de Panama VI, N. S. 14, AMAE; various contracts, Nov. 23, 1920, Amér., 1918–40, CA, num. 33, AMAE; Conty to MAE, Nov. 14, 1911, 7N1729, dossier Guat., contracts, 7N3376, Amér. cent., dossier Guat., AAT; François Crouzet, "Recherches sur la production d'armements en France, 1815–1913," in *Conjoncture économique, structures sociales: Hommage à Ernest Labrousse* (Paris, 1974), 313, 315. For a Spanish evaluation of the success of the French military mission in Guatemala, see Benito to MAE, Feb. 3, 1913, H1609, AMAE, Madrid.

22. Tony Chauvin to MAE, July 28, 1909, Pierre Lefèvre-Pontalis to MAE, July 30, 1909, Lefèvre-Pontalis to MAE, Aug. 26, 1909, and other correspondence, CP 1918, Hond., Finances, N. S. 3, AMAE; Chauvin to Morgan, Harjes and Company, July 31, 1909, Chauvin to Min. finances, Aug. 3, 1909, MAE to Min. finances, Sept. 14, 1909, MAE to Min. finances, Sept. 28, 1903, enclosing John Hay to Henry Cabot Lodge, June 10, 1903, F[30] 393[1]: folder Hond., AMEF; Juan E. Paredes, *The Morgan-Honduran Loan, 1908–1911* (New Orleans, 1911); Rosenberg and Rosenberg, "From Colonialism to Professionalism," 59–82; Barbara Stalling, *Banker to the Third World: U.S. Portfolio Investment in Latin America, 1900–1986* (Berkeley, 1987), 58–67.

23. Jacques to patrons [Banque de Neuflize], June 6, July 9, 19, 1909, 44 AQ 19, Banque de Neuflize, folder-Amérique centrale, AN; Jacques to patrons, April 11, 14, 12, 1911, Percy L. Fean, report on Abangarez Gold Fields, Nov. 12, 1909 (updated Feb. 6, 1911), 44 AQ 19, Banque de Neuflize, folder-New York, AN.

24. Joré to Rouvier, Aug. 18, 1905, F[30] 393[1]: CR, AMEF.

25. Jusserand to MAE, April 14, 1911, MAE to Min. finances, May 8, 1911, Fabre to MAE, Dec. 20, 1911, other correspondence, CP 1918, CR, Finances, II, N. S. 4, AMAE.

26. Peralta to Fernández Guardia, March 16, 1910, MRE, caja 197, ANCR; Peralta to Felipe J. Alvarado, Aug. 29, 1911, MRE, l.c. #204, Leg. de CR, 1910–1912, ANCR; Eusebe, "Les Investissements français en Amérique centrale et dans l'aire des Caraïbes," 18ff; Alfredo Figueroa Navarro, "Visión de Panamá durante la época del canal francés," *Lotería* 292 (July 1980): 17–25.

27. MAE to Jusserand, May 17, 24, June 4, 1909, CP 1918, Nic., Finances, Emprunts, N. S. 3, AMAE (copies in F[30] 393[1]: folder Nic., AMEF);

MAE to Min. finances, May 3, July 2, 17, Aug. 3, 1909, enclosing U.S. min. in CR to Huntington Wilson, June 19, 1909, Pichon to Min. finances, June 3, 1909, F^{30} 393^{2}: folder Nic., AMEF; Eusebe, "Les Investissements français en Amérique centrale et dans l'aire des Caraïbes," 18ff.

28. Jusserand to MAE, May 22, July 1, 1909, Henry White to Pichon, May 28, 1909, Min. finances to MAE, May 29, 1909, MAE to Min. finances, July 2, 1909, CP 1918, Nic., Finances, Emprunts, N. S. 3, AMAE (copies in F^{30} 393^{1}: folder Nic., AMEF).

29. Fabre to MAE, Jan. 21, 1912, MAE to ambassador in Wash., April 12, 1912, and other correspondence, CP 1918, Nic., Finances, Emprunts, N. S. 3, AMAE.

30. D'Arlot to Pichon, March 23, April 12, 1908, Min. finances to MAE, Sept. 19, 1908, Arce to MAE, Oct. 30, 1908, Min. guerre to MAE, Nov. 10, 1908, CP 1918, Guat., Défense nationale, I, N. S. 3; Min. finances to MAE, Nov. 13, 1911, MAE to Min. finances, Nov. 23, 1911, F^{30} 393^{2}: folder San Salv., AMEF.

31. Fr. con. gen. to Jusserand, Dec. 14, 1911, CP 1918, San Salv., Finances, N. S. 4, AMAE.

32. Maurice Paléologue to Min. finances, May 11, 1912, F^{30} 393^{2}: folder San Salv., AMEF; Jusserand to Pichon, June 3, 1913, Paléologue to Min. finances, June 2, 1913, F^{30} 393^{2}: folder Nic., AMEF.

33. Fabre to Raymond Poincaré, Aug. 11, 1912, F^{30} 393^{1}: folder CR, AMEF; Eusebe, "Les Investissements français en Amérique centrale et dans l'aire des Caraïbes," 45–48, 57ff; correspondence for March and April, 1914, Commerce, F^{12} 8975, Pan., AN; John F. Laffey, "Municipal Imperialism in France: The Lyon Chamber of Commerce, 1900–1914," *Proceedings of the American Philosophical Society 19* (1975): 2–23.

34. Peralta to Fernández Guardia, March 16, 1910, MRE, caja 197, AN, CR; Henri Barré Ponsignon to MAE, Aug. 10, 1910, CP 1918, Pan., Relations et Conventions commerciales, II, N. S. 8, AMAE; MAE to Min. finances, Feb. 15, 1912, F^{30} 393^{1}: Guat., AMEF; Eusebe, "Les Investissements français en Amérique centrale et dans l'aire des Caraïbes," 57ff; René Girault, "Ein neues Bild des französischen Unternehmers um 1914," in Gilbert Ziebura, ed., *Wirtschaft und Gesellschaft in Frankreich seit 1789* (Cologne, 1975), 202–47.

35. Unsigned, "Note pour M. le Rapporteur de la Commission de Budget," July 27, 1909, Mémoires et documents, Amér., v. 67, AMAE; Subsecretary of Etat des Beaux Arts to MAE, July 6, 1909, Paris, CP 1918, Pan., Travaux publics, N. S. 6, AMAE; Unsigned "Note pour M. le Rapporteur de la Commission de Budget," Aug. 1, 1911, CP 1918, Amér. Latine, Questions générales, N. S. (1908–1914), AMAE; Fabre to MAE, June 2, 1912, CP 1918, Guat., Pol. intérieure II, N. S. 2, AMAE; Ponsignon to MAE, Aug. 1, 1911, CP 1918, Pan., Pol. étrangère II, AMAE.

36. Mamaly to MAE, May 18, July 13, 1912, CP 1918, CR, Travaux publics, affaires économiques et commerciales, N. S. 5, AMAE.

37. "Note sur le commerce, l'industrie et l'agriculture de la Province du Chiriqui," [1910?], CP 1918, Pan., Relations et conventions commerciales, II, N. S. 8, AMAE; Rigoreau to Pichon, Oct. 5, 1910, and other correspondence in CP 1918, San Salv., Affaires commerciales, N. S. 5, AMAE; Jusserand to Pichon, Oct. 26, 1910, MAE to Jusserand, Nov. 17,

1910, A. Gervais, "Le Rôle de la France dans le monde," *Matin*, Dec. 1, 1910, and other newspaper clippings, CP 1918, Amér. latine, Questions générales, N. S. no number, AMAE; MAE to Fr. min. to Cent. Amer., May 21, 1913, CP 1918, Amér. cent., II, N. S. 2, AMAE; Armand Renier, "Fernand-Jean-Baptiste-Marie Bernard comte de Montessus de Ballore," in Montessus de Ballore, *La Géologie sismologique* (Paris: 1924), 453–65.

38. Min. commerce to MAE, Jan. 25, 1912, Fr. chargé to MAE, March 8, 1914, unsigned, "Mémorandum sur l'importance de célébrer une convention commerciale sur les réductions des droites de douane," May 28, 1914, CP 1918, Guat., Négociations et affaires commerciales, N. S. 9, AMAE; François Auguste Arnauné, *Le Commerce extérieur et les tarifs de douane* (Paris, 1911); Charles Augier and Angel Marvaud, *La Politique douanière de la France dans ses rapports avec celle des autres états* (Paris, 1911); Alexis Caille, *Au Pays du printemps éternel. Le Guatemala et son avenir économique* (Paris, 1914).

39. Bertaut-Blancard to MAE, July 30, 1913, Bertaut-Blancard to Min. commerce, Aug. 22, 1913, CP 1918, San Salv., Affaires commerciales, N. S. 5, AMAE.

40. Fabre to MAE, Nov. 3, 17, 1912, CP 1918, Nic., Pol. intérieure, Affaires commerciales, N. S. 1, AMAE; Fabre to MAE, Dec. 29, 1912, MAE to Jusserand, Feb. 25, 1913, Ed. Perelti de la Rocca to Pichon, Aug. 23, 1913, enclosing memorandum of U.S. reply, Aug. 21, 1913, CP 1918, Nic., Pol. étrangère, N. S. 2, AMAE.

41. Min. finances to MAE, Dec. 20, 1913, MAE to Min. finances, Jan. 12, 1914, F^{30} 393^{1} 416: Colombie, AMEF.

42. State of the three ministries, Sept. 18, 1911, "Conséquences du percement de l'isthme de Panama au point de vue des intérêts des colonies, du commerce et de la marine, projet de la marine," [late 1911?], CP 1918, Pan., Canal de Panama, V, N. S. 13, AMAE; Min. colonies to Min. commerce, Jan. 8, 1912, Commerce, F^{12} 7266, Pan., AN; MAE circular, Aug. 29, 1912, CP 1918, Pan., Canal de Panama, VI, N. S. 14, AMAE; Jusserand to MAE, Feb. 24, 1913, Min. commerce to MAE, Oct. 4, 1913, Pan., Canal de Panama, VII, N. S. 15, AMAE; MAE circular to Fr. agents in Europe and Japan, Feb. 17, 1914, Min. marine to MAE, March 18, 1914, Jusserand to MAE, March 31, 1914, "Utilisation du canal de Panama," Feb. 1914, and various other correspondence in this volume, CP 1918, Pan., Canal de Panama, VIII, N. S. 16, AMAE; Henri Simon, "Rapport fait au nom de la commission des affaires extérieures . . ." and annexes, F^{12} 3355, AN; Jusserand to Gaston Doumergne, March 31, 1914, Commerce, F^{12} 8975, Pan., AN; Léon Jacob, "Le Canal de Panama et les colonies françaises," *Questions diplomatiques et coloniales* 33 (Feb. 1912): 193–208.

43. Min. commerce to MAE, Oct. 4, 1913, CP 1918, Pan., Canal de Panama VII, N.S. 15, AMAE; MAE circular, Feb. 17, 1914, "Utilisation du Canal de Panama," Feb. 1914, Min. marine to MAE, March 18, 1914, CP 1918, Pan., Canal de Panama VIII, N.S. 16, AMAE.

44. MAE to ministers in London and Berlin, July 11, 1912, J. Cambon to MAE, July 23, 1912, Aimé de Fleurian to Briand, Aug. 19, 1912, CP 1918, S. Salv., Affaires commerciales, N.S. 5, AMAE; MAE circular, Aug. 29, 1912, CP 1918, Pan., Canal de Panama VI, N.S. 14, AMAE; 2 reports, Oct. 12, 1912, Jusserand to MAE, Feb. 24, 1913, CP 1918, Pan., Canal de Panama

VI, N.S. 15, AMAE; Jusserand to Doumergne, March 31, 1914, Commerce, F^{12} 8975, Pan., AN; "100 Jahre Südamerika-Westküsten-Dienst," Hapag-Lloyd Presse-Information, Oct. 3, 1972, copy in possession of author; U.S. Bureau of Foreign and Domestic Commerce, *Daily Consular and Trade Reports* 16 (Feb. 15, 1913): 818–21.

6

The Great War in Central America, 1914–1920

During and after the Great War, from 1914 to 1920, U.S. expansion pressured not only the Germans but also the British and French in Central America. After war broke out, French officials doubted the wisdom of encouraging trade with Guatemala. German firms had a commanding position in Guatemala and might profit from closer French economic ties to that nation. But ultimately the officials concluded that French merchants could benefit at the expense of German interests throughout Central America. They advocated attracting coffee imports, increasing French exports, encouraging French houses to handle the increased commerce, and acquiring German plantations, shipping lines, and trade firms. They assumed that similar activity in other areas would further weaken German accumulation in the world economy. When the French government finally launched a program to undermine German interests on the isthmus, however, its own deteriorated economic position prevented it from taking advantage of German weakness. In contrast, U.S. agents acquired French and British holdings at bargain prices.[1]

One powerful but often overlooked critique of those nation-states that espoused a liberal marketplace outlook is that their leaders, when confronted with a grave crisis, abandoned the market-oriented economy for a planned economy. They did not use socialist models for these excursions into a centralized planned economy because such models would have restricted private accumulation, required an equitable price-wage mechanism, and directed the use of gain to projects of social utility. Instead, they called upon organized capitalist models that permitted continued privatization of profits, the government-sponsored manipulation of price-wage mechanisms to extract more wealth from the workforce, and the distribution of costs and burdens to the whole society. Even while building the planning agencies, the liberal elite continued to advocate a market economy because the elite needed to justify the personalization of wealth (if wealth is produced by social planning and cooperative effort, no one can claim a grossly larger share of the profits) during the period of planned economic growth. The liberal elite intended to return to a controlled or managed market economy (organized capitalism) at war's end.

During the Great War, French, British, and U.S. businessmen and politicians expected the production, distribution, and financing of wealth to be managed rather than market driven. In the post-World War I years, however, the metropole governments and businesses reinstituted controlled market relations with Central America. Businesses reasserted their authority—shared during the war, but with governments directing survival strategies—over financial and distribution institutions, with government's role reduced. Business and government would guide the trade system so that business could counteract the expected increase in raw material prices.

In part, statistical indicators measure French participation in the isthmian economic order. In 1921 the mission of General Charles Mangin—a hero of French colonial conflicts and World War I—found that there were about 2,000 French citizens dispersed throughout the six countries of Middle America (Table 1). Statistics tracing French trade with Central America are abundant, yet the comparative value of French trade is difficult to measure because the franc (and the isthmian currencies) suffered devaluation both during and after the war. French importation of Central American products rose sharply from 3 million francs in 1914 to 59 million francs in 1920 (Table 3). The French economy absorbed food and raw materials, but it did not export during the war nor in the immediate postwar years. French exports rose slowly, from 1.3 million francs in 1914 to 4.2 million francs in 1919, before shooting up to 10.6 million francs in 1920 (Table 4). French exports commonly represented from 10 to 30 percent of the value of French imports from Central America. Direct purchases of Guatemalan, Honduran, and Costa Rican exports by the French remained about 1 percent during World War I, while France supplied 2 percent of Guatemalan, Honduran, and Costa Rican importation. France purchased 17 percent of Nicaraguan exports and supplied 3 percent of Nicaraguan imports. It remained a strong purchaser of Salvadoran exports at 19 percent of the total, but El Salvador acquired only a modest 4 percent of its imports in France.[2]

French investment in Central America decreased significantly during the war. These holdings, however, responded variously to the devaluation of the franc in the early postwar years. French investment in Nicaragua and El Salvador demonstrates the divergent development. From 1913 to 1919, French capital in Nicaragua declined from 6 million francs to 2.5 million francs, whereas French investment in El Salvador increased from 12 million francs to about 50 million francs (Table 6). Since French entrepreneurs had long invested in Salvadoran coffee plantations and mining operations, the dramatic rise in postwar trade may have reflected, in part, an expansion of investment, a return of capital, and a correction of underestimated investment. Of course, the devalued franc also helped to explain the dramatic rise.

The severe disturbance of the Central American political economies, a by-product of liberal penetration and improved incorporation into the world's cash-crop market order, encouraged the rise of political strongmen to serve as collaborators or compradors. Further economic disruptions marked the years from 1900 to 1921. While the metropole economies expanded their shipping capacity and employed most of their domestic labor force, the Central American populations faced rising unemployment and greatly reduced national revenue and personal income for wage earners. Central American governments relied upon customs revenue, but imports dropped as the great powers redirected their productive capacities to fill the needs of the war economy. Competition was more prevalent among producers of primary products in the periphery than among metropole firms, which utilized capital-intensive high technology. The (Central American) periphery could not even sell products essential to metropole needs (rubber, balsa wood, some minerals, modest quantities of cacao and coffee, and hardwoods) unless another nation assigned transportation and financing.[3] Central American leaders discovered that the social and economic objectives of their societies, and even their need for metropole products or capital, were given a low priority by metropole states during a world crisis. They were allowed only minimal participation in decisions about access to the resources they needed (capital, shipping, or technology) or in the allocation of land, labor, capital, or the means for the distribution of production.

In the autumn of 1914 the French minister in Central America described a publicity contest between the Allied and the Central Powers for the minds of Central Americans. The large, economically strong German element in Guatemala launched a multimedia propaganda campaign to influence public opinion and advance German imperial objectives. Newspapers, speakers, and pamphlets informed Guatemalans that friendship with Germany and neutrality in the war were the wisest options. French agents in Honduras, El Salvador, and Nicaragua reported similar propaganda activity in their jurisdictions. A small group of French, British, and Belgian residents in Guatemala founded a newspaper, *Le National*, to counter the German effort. A French diplomat in Guatemala considered the population sympathetic to the Allied cause despite the German propaganda.[4]

The credibility of France's declaration of war and its appeal for support was undermined when local French enterprises retained German employees. The French minister in Central America found it scandalous that Martell, Hennessy, the Reims Company, and other firms marketed their products through German distributors who boldly advertised their agency for French firms. In another example, an absentee French proprietor in Costa Rica retained a German administrator for his property, who used the French firm to conduct business for other Germans. The minister called upon French firms and entrepreneurs to stop employing German agents and to conduct business in accordance with national war policy.[5]

Substituting French expertise or capital would not be easy because French firms faced established German enterprises. However, the Guatemalans were disturbed about the impact the war might have on their economy because it was so closely tied to Germany. Guatemala allowed its commercial treaty with Germany to expire in 1915. But the French minister failed to see any benefit from a new Franco-Guatemalan commercial treaty unless French industry could find markets in Guatemala. Markets would occur, he assumed, only if French products were granted a special tariff—which seemed unlikely in the face of the German influence. In 1915 the French commerce minister described possibilities for selling French automobiles in Central America, but the war prevented auto shipments. The French minister to Central America believed that German firms had formed the Economic Association for South and Central America because they were apprehensive about their capacity to continue business in the event of a long war. He saw an opportunity for French merchants and industrialists to surpass "the competitor of yesterday and the enemy of today."[6]

French officials wanted to displace German businessmen with French entrepreneurs. Most of the important firms in Guatemala, El Salvador, and Panama were German. The French war minister expected these businesses to encounter difficulty in obtaining goods and credit, thus providing an excellent opportunity for Allied trading firms. But German trade continued under dummy firms. For example, French agents alleged that the Nederlandsche Handel Maatshappy was a disguised German agency and that Holland and the Scandinavian countries were the intermediary destinations for much German trade with Central America.[7]

The Allied countries imposed a blacklist on Central American firms trading with the Central Powers (Germany, Austria, and the Ottoman Empire), but it was less effective than expected. German businessmen simply operated through straw men. Guatemalan president Estrada Cabrera used straw men to maintain his ties with Germans in the coffee and sugar trade, and he allegedly earned fifty cents for each sack of coffee exported. A German-Alsatian resident claimed that he sold his coffee through a Spanish middleman. Some firms with a minority German interest had escaped blacklisting by arranging a sham sale of their German-held shares, but French agents warned that pursuing these firms might injure their Guatemalan and Allied associates. When the Allied countries abandoned the blacklist in May 1919, the Germans resumed unrestricted trading.[8] It appears that, at most, German coffee and merchant interests had been inconvenienced.

Blacklisting involved French opposition to Central Power activity, but the French were caught in the middle when President Woodrow Wilson's administration repeatedly refused to recognize the Costa Rican government after the secretary of war, General Federico Tinoco, and his brother, Joaquín, deposed President Alfredo González Flores in a coup. The Tinocos requested French mediation, and Costa Rican minister Peralta solicited assistance from the U.S. ambassador to France, William Graves Sharp, in altering U.S. policy. Sharp advised the Costa Ricans to persuade France and Britain to exert their influence in Washington. The chief of the political section of the French Foreign Ministry, Pierre de Margerie, sympathized with Costa Rica's position, and he accompanied Peralta on a visit to the British ambassador. Margerie and the British diplomat proposed a joint appeal by their ministers in Washington in favor of extending recognition to Tinoco's government. The appeal, however, was not successful. Although France and Great Britain had followed the U.S. lead in not recognizing Tinoco's government, neither could persuade the U.S. government to change its policy.[9]

U.S. officials charged that several French banks (which they could not identify) were making funds available to Tinoco's government. Unofficially, the U.S. government wanted the French government to block funds for Tinoco's regime. The French foreign minister, wishing "not to indispose the U.S. government in a question which appears to lay on their heart," asked the finance minister to investigate "which French banks might be meant by the State Department complaint, and, if the transfers occur, what measures are possible to make these banks cease their cooperation with the government of General Tinoco?"[10]

The French finance minister uncovered the truth behind the allegations. Wartime financial problems in Central America had brought down the Banco Comercial de Costa Rica while it was still holding $150,000 to pay the interest due French investors on the Franco-Costa Rican loan of 1911. Since the Costa Rican government could not obtain alternative foreign exchange to service its debt, a French firm suggested that Costa Rica export 600,000 sacks of coffee to France to earn enough revenue for that purpose. The finance minister felt obliged to help Costa Rica obtain the funds to pay the French bondholders. Besides, in this transaction no money reached Tinoco.[11]

Many Costa Ricans were dissatisfied with the weak European response when President Wilson punished their nation under Tinoco's rule by denying it trade and finances. Costa Rica's *Nuevo tiempo* claimed that the European powers paid for U.S. entry into the Great War by acquiescing in U.S. domination of the New World.[12] Although the Costa Rican government and some of the public were displeased by European acquiescence in Wilson's nonrecognition policy, they had few options beyond further appeals to France and other European nations for recognition.

The French writer Maurice de Périgny noted that Costa Rica had paid its debts despite the great economic hardship it had suffered during the war. The Costa Rican government had maintained neutrality during most of the war, but its citizens had exhibited sympathy for the Allies. Although Costa Rica had to come to terms with U.S. imperialism, Périgny expected an improved atmosphere for French enterprise into Costa Rica because of its intellectual and moral debt to France. The Costa Rican government needed colonists to develop its agricultural potential and to avoid a dangerous dependency on North Americans. Périgny believed that French emigrants and businessmen had major roles to play in Costa Rica.[13]

The French military recognized the geopolitical value of Central and Latin America. After the U.S. government entered the Great War, a French study of Latin America conceded that "it would probably be inopportune for France to seek to extend its influence" in the area because "the United States considers this region too close to the Panama Canal to permit even its best friends to take a hold there." The French military considered the raw materials near the Panama Canal inaccessible because of their high geopolitical value to the United States. Germany also recognized the geopolitical value of this region to the United States. Prior to the U.S. entry into the war, Bunau-Varilla had alleged German conspiratorial efforts to sabotage the canal. Once the U.S. government did enter, he reconfirmed his allegations.[14]

During World War I, France and the Central American states used symbols and gestures to demonstrate mutual sympathy. Each Central American state declared July 14 (Bastille Day) a national holiday. In a further gesture of support, Costa Rica offered France two brand-new U.S. cannons from its arsenal. In mid-1918, French consul Désiré Pector expressed the hope that French businessmen would take advantage of a strong wave of sympathy to negotiate profitable postwar concessions.[15]

In the fall of 1918 the French government used its system of honor awards as a weapon against the powerful German interests in Guatemala. It granted Estrada Cabrera the Grand Croix de la Légion d'honneur and another official the Croix d'Officier. Estrada Cabrera had assured the French minister Camille Joseph Alexandre Chayet that he would act vigorously to halt German economic activity, but he did not do so despite repeated reminders. Late in the war, Estrada Cabrera appointed A. Matos as chargé to France. A French intelligence source identified Matos as a man with Hungarian citizenship who would spy for the Central Powers in France. Chayet accused Estrada Cabrera, who was more Indian than Spanish, of having little sense of honor; according to Chayet, in repayment for France's most coveted honor, Estrada Cabrera had put a Central Power spy in Paris and had done little to curtail the activities of German coffee barons.[16]

Furthermore, Estrada Cabrera was serving the interests of the utility company Empresa Eléctrica de Guatemala, a subsidiary of the German Siemens firm. His support allowed the German stockholders to profit from that enterprise during the war. He was, according to French sources, in league with a coterie of evil, anti-Allied influences: the Italian Divizia de Monforte, the Swiss agents Benz and Koller, the Austrian Max Vogl, one Schwartz (a German Jew who had become an American citizen), and Schwartz's partner, a man named Rosenthal. Finally, French agents suspected that Monforte, under the alias Max Dorsal, had conducted an anti-French campaign in Central America. Chayet considered Estrada Cabrera an enemy of France.[17]

Leaders of the Guatemalan economy, which had suffered greatly during the war, welcomed the return of European entrepreneurs. The French residents who returned to Guatemala reestablished their businesses, often rehiring their employees from the prewar period. Chayet warned that it would not be easy to persuade the Guatemalan government to act against the returning German entrepreneurs, however. Germans, he said, owned about half the property in Guatemala (a valid estimate in terms of the export economy). If the German market were excluded, Guatemala either would have to find other buyers for its coffee or would face financial ruin. Yet the French government was in no position to purchase a large share of the coffee crop. In fact, German managerial, commercial, and financial resources were so essential to the Guatemalan economy that the prosperity of other metropole interests was linked to German economic activity.[18]

Presumably, U.S. enterprises, which had pushed aside not only Germans but all European competitors during the war, would continue to do so in peacetime. Chayet claimed that French shipping and commercial interests confronted unfair U.S. practices. Before the war, French exports commonly passed through German, British, or U.S. ports to enter Central America. After the war began, the German and British routes were either closed or severely restricted. This left only the route through U.S. ports, but these port authorities favored U.S. goods destined for Latin America. Since U.S. authorities were discouraging Latin Americans from purchasing European goods, Chayet argued that only direct navigation lines that stopped at a port in each isthmian country could save European commerce. Furthermore, he was appalled to learn that U.S. businesses in Central America were using German firms seized during the war to undermine basic French export industries. For example, a U.S. firm used the confiscated Bayer drug firm to market aspirin in

Central America, thus squeezing the French aspirin producers Rhodins and Urodonal out of the market. Chayet suggested that a consortium of French pharmaceutical firms build a large advertising budget and issue a Spanish-language journal to inform the Latin American medical profession about French pharmaceutical products.[19]

French agents found no significant German property holdings in Central America outside of Guatemala. In 1919, French officials estimated German property in Guatemala at over $100 million (867,000,000 marks), in Nicaragua at $2.5 million, and in Panama at $200,000. The French government wanted the Panamanian government to confiscate German property. Panama was willing to do so, but the costs were excessive in relation to the small amount of property.[20] Some German property in Guatemala was seized, but little was confiscated elsewhere.

Rumors abounded that Estrada Cabrera was friendly toward the Germans because he owned property in Frankfurt and Hamburg valued at between $8 million and $20 million. Disgruntled Frenchmen wanted his property seized after the war because he had not fulfilled the promises he had made during the war. In particular, Chayet and U.S. chargé Walter Clarence Thurston were disappointed with Estrada Cabrera's foot-dragging in selling off confiscated German coffee plantations. Chayet assumed that Estrada Cabrera was waiting until he had profited from the 1919 crop. Chayet's proposal to place the proceeds from the sale of the 1918 and 1919 crops in the war debt fund was rejected.[21]

French diplomats complained that British minister Alban Young often supported Estrada Cabrera's policy of sheltering Germans and German businesses. Young also protected Germans who were conducting trade through British Honduras. He vehemently insisted that there was no reason to intern all Germans; after all, many were "Israelites." In addition, he considered confiscation of German property contrary to international law. He defended German firms threatened with the blacklist without irrefutable proof of their guilt. Chayet complained that Young laid full responsibility for the blacklisting of German firms on the French, and that along with Colonel J. P. Armstrong, he encouraged British capitalists to acquire German property. Thus the Germans received a good price for their property, and British interests obtained a stronger position in Guatemala.[22] In this case, British activity aided the Germans and injured the French.

In Chayet's judgment, key North American figures conducted themselves no better than Estrada Cabrera or the British. In

1918, Guatemalan officials seized the German-owned Empresa Eléctrica company and employed an American to administer it. To Chayet's dismay, the American retained some German staff because there were no suitable replacements. Chayet had wanted French interests to be able to bid for the Empresa Eléctrica and to pursue new opportunities on the isthmus.[23]

In France commercial associations and local governments lobbied to have their objectives in the world economy elevated into national policy. Even though the Guatemalan government had supported German businessmen until the last months of the war, the Bordeaux Chamber of Commerce protested that Guatemalan coffee did not enjoy the minimum tariff. It pretended that Guatemala's attitude in the Great War had been francophile in order to argue for a tariff adjustment to permit the exchange of coffee for French wines, liqueurs, and other products. A deputy from Le Havre (another potential coffee port), who was a spokesman for the National Coffee Association, insisted that Estrada Cabrera had turned against Germany after 1914. He wanted to open France's doors to Guatemalan coffee in order to reward Guatemala and divert the market from Germany. Guatemalan officials also encouraged a revival in Franco-Guatemalan trade.[24] The French officials may not have been blind to Guatemalan conduct, but they were more determined to undermine Germany's role on the isthmus.

The desire of French entrepreneurs and political leaders to rebuild commercial links to the isthmus in the postwar era encouraged the French government to mediate between the U.S. and Costa Rican governments. Although the U.S. government remained hostile to Tinoco's regime, the French government included Costa Rica on the list of invitees to the Paris Peace Conference of 1919. President Wilson insisted that the Central American state be stricken from the list. Peralta undertook to persuade the French government, or the delegates attending the Paris Peace Conference, to reverse Wilson's decision. After meeting with many delegates and officials, he concluded: "The allies, and France in particular, owe too much to the United States. They currently are in such an absolute adoration before this idol [Wilson] that France is unable to exercise its rights as host and instead allows this arbitrariness to occur." Several nations promised to support Costa Rica's petition for inclusion, but Peralta knew that "our friends cannot do anything if Mr. Wilson does not relent or if the great powers permit him to have a free hand in Latin America in order to obtain his support in other places."[25]

In February 1919, Peralta complained to the Peace Conference that of the states that had declared war on the Central Powers only Costa Rica was not invited to the conference. Later, he petitioned the conference to demand Costa Rica's inclusion and to issue a formal complaint over Costa Rica's exclusion. He blamed the French delegation for the inadequate response to his proposals. He wrote that "the tiger," Premier Georges Clemenceau, was reserving his energies for defending French interests rather than leading a noble defense of Costa Rican rights. The French Foreign Ministry offered its sympathy, but Peralta reported that "neither France nor Great Britain . . . wish to oppose their main ally. When the United States recognizes us, they will [do so] immediately." He advised the Latin American delegates to check Wilson's megalomania by working for a clause in the peace agreement that would undermine the onerous Monroe Doctrine. Still, he did not expect success for Costa Rica's case unless France or Britain were to assume leadership.[26]

French cultural policies implemented on the isthmus during the Great War persisted after Germany's defeat. Charles Houssaye arrived in Costa Rica in September 1918 to assume control of French propaganda work. He persuaded the local daily, *La información*, to hire the Havas news service (his former employer) in addition to Reuters and the Associated Press. He urged local groups to distribute French books, pamphlets, and films to combat "Teutonic" publicity. Moreover, Chayet distributed French films for propaganda and commercial purposes until the French Office of Foreign Commerce decided to curtail such film distribution. But films were only one cultural bond between the two societies. And in Franco-Guatemalan relations cultural ties were not the vision of just government officials.[27]

Chayet expected stronger representation in postwar Central America to use cultural policy to expand and diversify French influence in El Salvador as well. Since El Salvador lacked foreign schools and was burdened with a poor education system, the French vice-consul inquired about creating French schools in San Salvador. And he suggested that a visiting theater troupe, a library, and films would be appropriate cultural supplements. He proposed a career consul be named because a numerous French colony in El Salvador owned wealth estimated at $10 million. According to Chayet, El Salvador had not joined the Allies during the Great War because of effective German propaganda.[28] He ignored the possibility that Salvadorans had had little interest in the war.

In Guatemala the French military mission remained in good favor throughout the war, and Guatemala turned to France to modernize its army for possible service in Europe. France, despite the war, contracted for two of its officers to serve in Guatemala to preserve French influence at the expense of Germany. However, since Estrada Cabrera used the military for personal purposes, the army continued to suffer from apathy and lack of initiative. Chayet was not impressed with the French military mission, which, to the dissatisfaction of its distinguished officers, accomplished little. For example, the Guatemalan president had granted Captain Contresty's request to purchase an artillery battery on one day and then countermanded the order on the next. Still, in 1920 the two governments agreed to increase the maximum size of the mission to five officers.[29]

The Paris Peace treaties complicated the continued sale of French armaments in Central America because the signator nations agreed not to sell arms to nonsignator states, which included Nicaragua and El Salvador. In July 1920, Nicaraguan chargé Carlos Villanueva wanted to purchase a long list of war materials and munitions. The French government avoided negotiations because it believed Villanueva might represent a rebel faction that suspected French support for the existing government. In August 1920, El Salvador inquired about purchasing 13 artillery batteries, 12,000 rifles, 1,000 carbines, 68 heavy machine guns, 2 airplanes, 9,000,000 rounds of small arms munitions, and 36,000 rounds of artillery ammunition. The French government observed that as a signatory of the St. Germaine Treaty (1919), it could not sell a Central American state military materials. El Salvador claimed that it had adhered to the pact by joining the League of Nations, but the French government pointed out that the St. Germaine Treaty was a separate agreement.[30] Thus the French government sidestepped the requests of both Nicaragua and El Salvador. Although metropoles often manipulated military supplies and services in competitive situations, France, in the immediate postwar years, was in no condition to use military policy to challenge U.S. preeminence in Central America.

Some French businessmen argued that if their government did not take an active role in revitalizing trade in the postwar years, French commercial interests would miss opportunities to penetrate Central American markets and fall even further behind those of the United States. In Panama, merchants organized a permanent "commercial museum" to display French products and build ties between French chambers of commerce and manufacturers and Panamanian customers. French businessmen also sought government support for a mobile trade exposition in Middle America. In 1920 the Guatemalan government wanted to renew trade with France, and the French chargé boasted that if French officials negotiated wisely, France might regain its former trading role and clip the wings of its chief competitor.[31]

Occasionally, French business interests encountered unexpected difficulties in the New World. Over time, French investment and entrepreneurial activity outside of France actually established competition for French commercial firms. The vineyards of French immigrants in Chile, California, and Argentina competed effectively in Central America with French regional wines in the modest to low price ranges. In another example, the consul in Costa Rica reported that some local firms were placing deceptive labels on perfumes to make them appear French. Costa Rica also increased its tax on champagnes and spirits.[32] But perfumes, wines, champagnes, and spirits were prime French export goods that attracted investment projects as well as commercial activity.

In 1919, French officials were dissatisfied with the French role in Costa Rican trade. They wanted a Costa Rican customs policy that would be more favorable to French products. They assumed that suppressing the tariff advantage conceded to Costa Rican coffee would capture the attention of officials and businessmen because coffee generated most of the country's revenues. The French vice-consul hoped that the small French colony in San José would be animated by the Spanish colony to take a larger role in Costa Rican commerce.[33]

Several Frenchmen—Enrique Peyroutet, Emile Bousque, and Ernesto Martin—promoted a colonization project to increase the meager number of Frenchmen living in Costa Rica. In 1919 they advertised in France to attract colonists to the 40,000-hectare La Palma finca. The prospectus outlined plans for the colonists to enter the lumber, cattle, and rice businesses. Most of the two-score colonists attracted to La Palma quickly returned to France or left the settlement. Although the organizers were said to have made huge profits, the former residents and other observers reported much suffering, hardship, and forced labor among the colonists. The French government filed claims against Costa Rica for inadequate supervision of the concession but had no success in court.[34]

For a brief moment in the early postwar years, Honduras appeared on the verge of initiating close ties with France. In mid-1919 the new Honduran minister to France, former president Policarpo Bonilla, proposed an ambitious plan that included sending young Hondurans to attend French military schools, hiring a Frenchman to reorganize the national police force, initiating regular direct ship service, establishing a French branch bank and a Honduran central bank with French capital, and appointing a French technical commission to conduct an economic survey of Honduras. After the French government selected a man to organize the Honduran police, Bonilla departed urgently for Washington. He never returned to France, and no one pursued his proposals.[35] French capitalists had viewed Honduras with suspicion since the default of the Honduran Interoceanic Railroad debt. Bonilla might have overcome the resistance, but his interest was too transitory.

It was easier for the French to restart economic activity in Guatemala (or in Costa Rica or El Salvador), where they had long had extensive business contact, than in Honduras. French interest in banking opportunities on the isthmus revived in the postwar years. When Chayet learned about the formation of the Banque Française d'Exportation, he investigated the banking system of Guatemala. The Banco Colombiano was the only reliable option as a correspondence affiliate. French diplomat Henri Aymé-Martin reported that "among the great powers, France sparkled alone by its absence" in branch banking in Guatemala. He expected that a French bank would facilitate currency exchange and thus invigorate the trade between France and the New World.[36]

In the postwar years, French entrepreneurs reexamined old Central American projects and searched for new areas of investment. In 1920 the Compagnie Foncière et Agricole de l'Amérique Centrale petitioned the French government for permission to issue 500,000 francs in new stock. Paris authorities, without information about this company, queried the chargé in Guatemala. He discovered that the company had been organized in 1912 and was active throughout Central America, but especially in the Nicaraguan departments of Zelaya and Río Grande. Its directors were solid capitalists. The company was linked to the Banana du Río Grande, which claimed a capitalization of 2.5 million francs. In 1916 the Banana du Río Grande's property had been sold to the Nicaragua Fruit and Steamship Company. The Compagnie Foncière had tried to repurchase the property, but the Nicaragua Fruit Company kept improving the land to drive up the price. The chargé recommended against allowing the new stock issue, however, principally because the Compagnie Foncière was too weak financially to reacquire the Banana du Río Grande.[37]

After World War I, the search for a new energy source, petroleum, led most metropoles to Central American sites. Petroleum companies and speculators suspected that there were oil fields in Costa Rica, Honduras, and Guatemala. In late 1919, Minister Peralta recommended Bénard Frères of Paris for petroleum exploration in Costa Rica, in part because the predecessor firm, Bénard et Javislowsky, had successfully managed the Franco-Costa Rican loan of 1911. He hoped this firm would be given every consideration consonant with the best interests of Costa Rica.[38]

The scent of oil on the isthmus reshaped alliances made during the Great War. In 1920 former president Cleto González Víquez of Costa Rica remarked that the foreigners flocking to his country were like "sharks . . . attracted by the smell of petroleum." The Amory Company, an American oil firm in league with British interests, and the Sinclair Oil Company competed for concessions. Good relations might be important. The U.S. government delayed recognition of the government that succeeded Federico Tinoco, but Britain extended recognition quickly. The French consul in San José, Paul Adolphe Serre, presumed that his nation would remain loyal to the U.S. government in the question of recognition and in the struggle for oil concessions, even though the United States had "abandoned" France in Europe (that is, had refused a joint military alliance against Germany). The U.S. government would not exchange support for France on the Rhine for French support in Central America. The United States, outmaneuvered by the British and eager to build support in Costa Rica for its petroleum interests, extended recognition two days after the British. The French were caught off guard by the reversal of the U.S. position; France extended recognition several days later. Despite Serre's speculations, the French government had withheld recognition to obtain leverage for the settlement of outstanding claims against Costa Rica. Serre foresaw difficult times ahead for both British and French oil interests because only the U.S. government, sustained by the Monroe Doctrine and cruisers, ever found justice in the Costa Rican courts. In 1921, when it seemed that the U.S. and British oil concession seekers might join hands in a Honduran scheme, a French diplomat proposed trying to participate in the venture.[39] Although small quantities of oil and gas were located, no find merited commercial development.

World War I had greatly shaken the French political economy at home and abroad. The French economic stake in Central America declined precipitously. European purchases in Central America were disrupted, capital and income were diverted to European consumption, and shipping and cargo space were too scarce to load much coffee, fruit, cotton, or sugar. During the war, the French government had augmented its military mission in Guatemala in an effort to strengthen its influence on the isthmus at the expense of Germany. French officials and residents labored to counter the active propaganda of the pro-German elements, especially in Guatemala. British and French agents cooperated, though some British agents appeared soft on the treatment of German coffee barons, and some French firms had relied upon German merchant and coffee expertise during the war. Historian James Cooke claimed that the French victory over Germany in 1918 spelled the death knell for the new French imperialism because its raison d'être—to help rebuild France so it could defeat Germany—had disappeared.[40]

The French policy of promoting its cultural and civilizing mission paid dividends during the Great War when most Central American societies expressed solidarity with France. Such gestures of sympathy from the populace as well as the elites in Central America were seldom made toward the United States, Germany, or Great Britain. Despite the bad experience of its award of high honors to Estrada Cabrera, after the war the French government granted honors to various Central Americans who had rendered wartime services to France. In addition, the French government sympathized with the Costa Rican government's desire to join the Paris Peace Conference, but it was unwilling to confront President Wilson's unrelenting opposition. French officials limited themselves to offering advice and best wishes to the Costa Ricans.

The post-World War I French economy allowed no speedy rebuilding of its position in Central America. The new element—competition for oil—loomed as potentially unsettling. French agents attempted, with little success, to persuade French businessmen to adopt programs aimed at exploiting the rumored oil resources in Central America. In the immediate postwar years, though the isthmus region was not forgotten, a renewed cultural program would be France's chief activity in the area, since

French economic and security concerns were focused more sharply on Central Europe.

Notes

1. Caron, *An Economic History of Modern France*, 202–48; Alfred Sauvy, *Histoire économique de la France entre les deux guerres* (4 vols.; Paris, 1965–75), 1: 295–313; Duroselle, *La France et les États-Unis. Des origines à nos jours*, 91–129; Philippe Bernard, *La Fin d'un monde, 1914–1929* (Paris, 1975), 40–41, 110–14, 131–32; Asselain, *Histoire économique de la France*, 1: 201–21, 2: 9–18; Christopher Andrew and A. S. Kanya-Forstner, "The French Colonial Party and French Colonial War Aims, 1914–1918," *Historical Journal* 17: 1 (1974): 79–106; Claude Bresson, "L'Image économique de l'Amérique Latine dans *L'économiste français* durant la 1ere Guerre Mondiale, 1914–1918" (Maîtrise, Université de Paris X-Nanterre, 1978); Min. CA to MAE, Nov. 22, 1914, F30 3931: folder Guat., AMEF.; Min. CA to MAE, Feb. 23, Aug. 5, 1915, Min. commerce to MAE, Sept. 7, 1915, MAE to Min. commerce, Oct. 20, 1915, Commerce, F12 8944, AN; Larroque to director, National Office of Foreign Commerce, Oct. 12, 1914, Commerce, F12 7226, AN; Larroque to Théophile Delcassé, Oct. 30, 1914, F30 416: Colombie, AMEF; Min. CA to MAE, March 8, 1914, March 24, 1915, memorandum, May 28, 1914, CP 1918, Guat., Négociations et affaires commerciales, N. S. 9, AMAE; Germanicus, "The Central American Question from a European Point of View," *American Journal of International Law* 8 (1914): 213–23; A. O. Tuaner, "La maîtrise du Pacifique et la diplomatie yankee au dix-neuvième siècle," *Revue d'histoire diplomatique* 30 (1916): 268–301.

2. Schoonover and Schoonover, "Statistics for the Understanding of the Foreign Intrusion into Central America," 77–119.

3. Cardoso, "Central America: The Liberal Era, c. 1870–1930"; Woodward, *Central America*, 177–223; Pérez Brignoli, *Breve historia de Centro-América*, 107–32; Pierre Léon, *Histoire économique et sociale du monde* (6 vols.; Paris, 1977), 5: 470–77; Otto Damblé, "Die Wandlung des französischen Außenhandels in der Nachkriegszeit" (Ph.D. diss., Universität Köln, 1932).

4. Min. CA to Delcassé, Nov. 22, 1914, CP 1918, Guat., Négociations et affaires commerciales, N. S. 9, AMAE (copy also in AMEF, F30 3931: folder Guat., AMEF); Larroque to Delcassé, Oct. 30, 1914, F30 416: Colombie, AMEF.; Min. CA to MAE, Feb. 23, Aug. 5, 1915, MAE to Min. commerce, Oct. 20, 1915, Min. commerce to MAE, Nov. 30, 1915, Commerce, F12 8944, AN; Larroque to director, National Office of Foreign Commerce, Oct. 12, 1914, Commerce, F12 7226, AN; Jean Ganiage, *L'Expansion coloniale et les rivalités internationales* (2 vols.; Paris, 1973); Jean Ganiage, *Les Relations internationales de 1890 à 1914* (Paris, 1972).

5. Min. CA to Briand, Nov. 8, 1915, Commerce, F12 7222—Cent. Amér., Chile et La Paz, AN; Camille Joseph Alexandre Chayet to MAE, Sept. 19, 1918, Amér. 1918–40, CA (Guat.), num. 20, AMAE; Paul Serre to MAE, May 2, 1919, Amér. 1918–40, CA, num. 53, AMAE.

6. Min. CA to MAE, March 24, 1915, CP 1918, Guat., Négociations et affaires commerciales, N. S. 9, AMAE; Larroque to director, National Office of Foreign Commerce, Oct. 12, 1914, Commerce, F12 7226, AN; Min.

CA to Aristide Briand, Nov. 8, 1915, Commerce, F[12] 7222—Cent. Amér., Chile et La Paz, AN.

7. Min. guerre to MAE, June 19, 1916, CP 1918, Guat., Négociations et affaires commerciales, N. S. 9, AMAE; Paul Ernest Joseph Bizel to MAE, July 22, 1915, CP 1918, Pan., Canal de Panama, X, N. S. 18, AMAE; Armando Cohens and Co. to [?], Nov. 13, 1915, F[23] 157, Services extraordinaires des temps de Guerre, 1915–1920, AN; James A. Farrell, "Central and South American Trade as Affected by the European War," *The Annals* 40 (July 1915): 60–68; John Hay Hammond, "Trade Relations with Central and South America as Affected by the War," *The Annals* 40 (July 1915): 69–71; Henri Hauser, *Les Méthodes allemandes d'expansion économique* (Paris, 1916).

8. Chayet to MAE, Sept. 19, 1918, Amér. 1918–40, CA (Guat.), num. 20, AMAE; Serre to MAE, May 2, 1919, Amér. 1918–40, CA, num. 53, AMAE; Chayet to MAE, July 26, 1919, Amér. 1918–40, CA, num. 75, AMAE.

9. Peralta to Carlos Lara, Oct. 10, 1917, MRE, caja 236, leg.-Francia III, AN, CR; N. Gordon Levin, Jr., *Woodrow Wilson and World Politics* (New York, 1968); Suzanne M. O'Connor, "Costa Rica in the World Community of Nations, 1919–1939: A Case Study in Latin American Internationalism" (Ph.D. diss., Loyola University of Chicago, 1976).

10. MAE to Min. Guat., April 24, 1917, P. Cambon to MAE, June 15, 1917, CP 1918, CR, Pol. extérieure, N. S. 2, AMAE; Oct. 17, 1917, and following correspondence, CP 1918, CR, Pol. intérieure, N. S. 1, AMAE; Pierre de Margerie to Min. finances, Oct. 22, 1917, Min. finances to MAE, Oct. 29, 1917, F[30] 1926, CR, AMEF; Federico Tinoco to Lara, Oct. 16, 1918, Record Group 165, Military Intelligence Division, file 10674-2, NA (hereafter cited as RG 165, MID, 10674-2, NA); Lardy to MAE, Jan. 21, 1916, CP 1918, CR, Finances II, N. S. 4, AMAE.

11. Min. finances to MAE, [Jan. 10, 1918], F[30] 1926, CR, AMEF.

12. Henri Eugène Aymé-Martin to Pichon, Oct. 8, 1919, Amér. 1918–40, Dossiers Généraux, num. 59 (CR), AMAE; Charles Ludovic de Francqueville to MAE, Sept. 9, 10, 1918, April 11, 1919; Serre to MAE, Oct. 13, 1919, Amér. 1918–40, CA, num. 64, AMAE.

13. Maurice de Périgny, *La République de Costa Rica: Son avenir économique et le canal de Panama* (Paris, 1918), 226–31.

14. Unsigned, "Notes succinctes sur les ressources présentées par les principaux Etats de l'Amérique du Sud et Centrale," May 1917, 7 N3375, dossier 3, AAT; Philippe Bunau-Varilla, *The Great Adventure of Panama: The German Conspiracies against France and the United States* (New York, 1920).

15. Peralta to Pichon, [July 8, 1918], Francqueville to MAE, July 20, 1918, CR chargé to Pichon, Aug. 10, 1918, "Note pour le Cabinet du Ministre," Jan. 25, 1919, Amér. 1918–40, CA, num. 48, AMAE; Fr. con. gen. to MAE, July 11, 1918, MAE to Min. Guat., July 12, 1918, Min. Guat. to MAE, July 14, 1918, Amér. 1918–40, num. 68 (Nic.), AMAE; Pector to Pichon, July 19, 1918, Amér. 1918–40, CA, num. 1 (générale), AMAE.

16. Chayet to MAE, Jan. 20, Feb. 6, 18, March 4, April 26, 30, 1919, Amér. 1918–40, CA (Guat.), num. 21, AMAE; Chayet to MAE, July 8, 1919, Amér. 1918–40, CA, num. 6, AMAE; MAE, "Note pour la direction des affaires politiques et commerciales," March 18, 1919, lists, March 21, 1919, Amér. 1918–40, CA, num. 10, AMAE.

17. Chayet to MAE, Oct. 27, 1919, Amér. 1918–40, CA, num. 30, AMAE.

18. Chayet to MAE, July 26, 1919, Amér. 1918–40, CA, num. 75, AMAE; Chayet to MAE, Sept. 19, Oct. 1, 1918, Amér. 1918–40, CA (Guat.), num. 21, AMAE.

19. Chayet to MAE, Nov. 29, 1919, Amér. 1918–40, CA, num. 37, AMAE; Min. CA to Pinchon, Sept. 19, 1919, Commerce, F[12] 7222-Cent. Amér., Chile et La Paz, AN.

20. Chayet to MAE, Jan. 21, 1919, Amér. 1918–40, CA, num. 68 (Nic.), AMAE; Ernest Maurice de Simonin to MAE, Jan. 21, 24, Feb. 2, 1919, Amér. 1918–40, CA, num. 96 (Pan.), AMAE.

21. Chayet to MAE, Nov. 30, 1918, CP 1918, Amér. cent., II, N.S. 2, AMAE; Chayet to MAE, Dec. 15, 1919, Amér. 1918–40, CA, num. 29 (Guat.), AMAE.

22. Pichon to Min. Guat., Sept. 7, 1918, Chayet to MAE, Sept. 19, 1918, Amér. 1918–40, CA (Guat.), num. 20, AMAE.

23. Correspondence, Nov. 1918–Jan. 1919, Amér. 1918–40, CA, num. 6, AMAE; Chayet to MAE, Nov. 30, 1918, CP 1918, Amér. cent., II, N.S. 2, AMAE.

24. John Laffey, "Municipal Imperialism: The Lyon Chamber of Commerce, 1914–1925"; Secretary, Bordeaux Chamber of Commerce, to Min. commerce, Dec. 14, 1918, Commerce, F[12] 8944, Guat., AN; George Ancel to MAE, June 26, 1919, Amér. 1918–40, CA, num. 37, AMAE; G. Aguirre to Guillermo Matos Pacheco, May 27, 1919, B99-6/4411/93367, MRE, AGCA.

25. Peralta to Tobías Zúñiga Montúfar, Feb. 6, 1919, MRE, caja 247, leg.-Francia III, AN, CR.

26. Peralta to president and delegates of the Paris Peace Conference, Feb. 24, 1919, Peralta to Zúñiga Montúfar, March 25, 1919, Peralta to Lara, April 11, 1919, MRE, caja 247, leg.-Francia III (1919), AN, CR.

27. Francqueville to MAE, Sept. 23, 1918, Amér. 1918–40, CA, num. 64, AMAE; Min. Directeur de l'office national du commerce extérieur to MAE, Feb. 28, 1920, Amér. 1918–40, CA, num. 1, AMAE; Virgilio Rodríguez Beteta to Rafael Vehils, May 14, 19[17?], "Le Guatemala au point de vue international," n.d., Commerce, F[12] 7949, AN.

28. Chayet to MAE, Nov. 30, 1918, CP 1918, Amér. cent., vol. 2, N. S. 2, AMAE; Chayet to MAE, Feb. 4, 1919, Amér. 1918–40, CA, num. 4, AMAE; Chayet to MAE, Nov. 9, 1919, Amér. 1918–40, CA, num. 75, AMAE.

29. Chayet to MAE, March 31, 1919, Amér. 1918–40, CA (Guat.), num. 21, AMAE; José Lardizabal to MAE, Oct. 13, 1917, March 26, 1918, Min. guerre to MAE, Dec. 9, 1917, CP 1918, Guat., Défense nationale, II, N. S. 4, AMAE; contracts, 7N3376, Amér. cent., dossier Guat., AAT; contract, June 9, 1918, Nov. 23, 1920, and other correspondence, Amér., 1918–40, CA, num. 33, AMAE.

30. Carlos Villanueva to MAE, July 20, 1920, Amér. 1918–40, CA, num. 68, AMAE; MAE to chargé in Guat., Dec. 22, 1920 (secret), Amér. 1918–40, CA, num. 69, AMAE; Pedro Jaime Matheu to MAE, Aug. 17, 25, 1920, MAE to Matheu, Aug. 23, 28, Amér. 1918–40, CA, num. 75, AMAE.

31. Simonin to MAE, Dec. 20, 1918, Amér. 1918–40, CA, num. 94, AMAE; Priquet [?] to Pichon, n.d., April 30, June 16, 1919, Amér. 1918–40, CA, num. 8 (General), AMAE; Serre to MAE, July 15, 1920, Amér. 1918–40, CA, num. 55, AMAE; chargé in Cent. Amer. to MAE, May 22, 1920, F[20] 1956, Guat., AMEF.

32. Serre to MAE, June 27, Aug. 30, Dec. 31, 1919, Min. commerce to MAE, Sept. 23, 1919, MAE to Min. commerce, Oct. 7, 1919, Amér. 1918–40, CA, num. 53, AMAE; Min. finances to Min. commerce, July 1, 1919, Serre to MAE, July 15, 1920, Amér. 1918–40, CA, num. 55, AMAE.

33. Min. finances to Min. commerce and MAE, July 1, 1919, MAE to Chayet, July 10, 1919, Serre to MAE, July 15, 1920, Amér. 1918–40, CA, num. 55, AMAE; vice-consul to MAE, May 12, 1919, Amér. 1918–40, CA, num. 63, AMAE.

34. Serre to MAE, Dec. 15, 1919, newspaper clippings from *Diario de Costa Rica*, Sept. 26 to Oct. 7, 1919, Amér. 1918–40, CA, num. 48, AMAE; Serre to MAE, Feb. 11, June 16, 1919, Aug. 2, 4, 1920, Amér. 1918–40, CA, num. 49, AMAE; Thévenot Fils to MAE, Nov. 25, 1920, Amér. 1918–40, CA, num. 50, AMAE.

35. Policarpo Bonilla to Pichon, Aug. 26, 1919, enclosing memorandum, Min. intérieur to MAE, Sept. 13, 1919, Amér. 1918–40, CA, num. 66 (Hond.), AMAE.

36. Min. C.A. to MAE, Oct. 14, 1919, Amér. 1918–40, CA, num. 40, AMAE; Aymé-Martin to MAE, Dec. 11, 1919, F^{30} 1924, Colombie, AMEF.

37. Banana du Río Grande to MAE, April 1, 1919, MAE to chargé in Guat., July 22, 1920, Perrot to MAE, July 26, 27, 1920, Amér. 1918–40, CA, num. 68, AMAE; Pierre Orenga de Gaffroy to MAE, Oct. 19, 1920, enclosing W. C. Dufour to André Lafarque, Oct. 14, 1920, Amér. 1918–40, CA, num. 50, AMAE.

38. Peralta to Andrés Venegas, Nov. 26, 1919, MRE, caja 247, leg.-Francia III, AN, CR.

39. Serre to MAE, Aug. 2, 4, 1920, MAE to chargé in Guat., Aug. 7, 1920, Amér. 1918–40, CA, num. 49 (CR), AMAE; Perrot to MAE, Sept. 20, 1920, Jan. 12, May 30, 1921, Paul Cambary to MAE, Dec. 3, 1920, and other correspondence, Amér. 1918–40, CA, num. 66 (Hond.), AMAE; Serre to MAE, July 11, 1921, Amér. 1918–40, CA, num. 50, AMAE.

40. Edmond Plauchut, "La Pénétration des États-Unis en Amérique latine," *Revue des deux mondes* 100 (Oct. 15, 1930): 840–63; Bernard, *La Fin d'un monde: 1914–1929*; Kemp, *Economic Forces in French History*, 270–75; Charles P. Kindleberger, *Economic Growth in France and Britain, 1851–1950* (Cambridge, MA, 1964), 287.

7

A Modest Revival

Trade and Investment in the 1920s

France's relations with Central America in the 1920s were influenced by its bitterness toward Germany and its desire to revive broader economic ties through cultural and financial activity. The first major step came in mid-1921, when the French government sent General Charles Mangin, a hero of colonial conflicts and World War I, and a naval lieutenant named Lecoq on a five-month mission to study French interests in Latin America and to suggest the best means of reentering that area.[1]

French officials recognized, often grudgingly, the preeminence of U.S. power in the region, and they generally intended that any cultural or economic programs developed for Central America produce the least possible friction with the United States. The U.S. political economy, having achieved hegemony in the Caribbean and Central American area during the war, continued aggressive interventionism—sending troops into Santo Domingo, Haiti, Cuba, Nicaragua, and Panama—throughout the 1920s. The weakened European powers lacked either the capacity or the will to force equal opportunity in this vital area, so they had to settle for whatever crumbs the United States allowed to fall from its table.[2]

A revival of Franco-Central American relations seemed feasible because many French citizens still resided in the region. Mangin reported about 2,000 Frenchmen on the isthmus. Panama had the largest number, followed by El Salvador and Costa Rica. The 1920 Nicaraguan census had ranked the French fourth among inhabitants from industrial powers, behind the British, the North Americans, and the Germans. During the 1920s the number of French settlers in Guatemala, Costa Rica, and

Honduras increased significantly (Table 1), which suggested a strengthening of commercial and cultural activity.

International trade data measured the success of France's effort to reestablish its prewar commercial role. French importation of Central American products grew steadily in the 1920s before leaping to 100 million francs in 1926, after which it declined to about 55 million francs in the late 1920s (Table 3). French exports to Central America also rose steadily after 1921, reaching a plateau at about 40 million francs annually for the 1926 to 1930 period. These figures reflected increasing exchange and the devalued French franc.

Despite some high expectations, the French share of Central American trade did not revive in the 1920s. On the average, the French purchased less than 1 percent of Guatemalan and Honduran exports, although the figure had risen to 2 percent by 1930. French products only made up 2 or 3 percent of Guatemalan and Honduran imports. French purchases of Salvadoran exports declined throughout the decade, yet averaged 8 percent annually. French exports to El Salvador rose slowly, reaching 6 percent near the end of the decade. Nicaraguans sold 15 percent and Costa Ricans sold 10 percent of their exports to France, but purchased only 2 or 3 percent of their imports there.[3] In sum, French commerce stagnated, preserving its modest role.

In the post-World War I years, the Central American societies faced persisting disruptions—social turmoil, coups, revolutions—that were reactions to the failures of the liberal elites to perform as advertised. During the Great War and then the postwar readjustment, Central American societies were required to contribute more, both materially and culturally, to the preservation of metropole well-being and security because reduced growth hampered economic and educational development. The comprador politicians met resistance and disfavor while enforcing these metropole demands. Recovery in the world economy allowed the Central American political economies to find some respite by the mid-1920s.[4]

As the competition for accumulation grew sharper and as fewer new sources for accumulation were uncovered, the gap between the haves and have-nots expanded. German special agent Gustav Noske commented incisively upon this in the mid-1920s. In all forms of export-oriented economic enterprise, he noted, the "ethnic" (class-race) assignment of historical occupations and economic roles were common. Culture, civilization, westernization, and modernization were used to undermine the indigenous or local culture, institutions, and value system to weaken the periphery and make it more susceptible to metropole exploitation. Metropoles used racism, education, progress, and experts to change the "periphery" societies.[5]

Mangin's mission underscored the French determination to build stronger ties in Latin America. He reported to the army and foreign ministries and described the mission in a series of articles for the *Revue des deux mondes*. Lecoq reported to the Navy Ministry. The two men visited Guatemala and Panama and reported on Nicaragua although they did not visit that country. Mangin envisioned commercial opportunity in Central America if French industrialists and financiers revised their attitude toward isthmian business. For example, the Nancy Chamber of Commerce had sent a commercial delegation to the New World at great expense only to undercut its own efforts by not recognizing the need to extend credit to potential wholesalers and retailers. In another case, Pierre Arthuys, an agent for French metal foundries, was well received in Guatemala, but he demanded large prepayments that limited his success in getting orders. The Guatemalan minister of development even showed Arthuys documents that revealed German willingness to accept an installment plan, and he suggested that the French establish a banking consortium to arrange credit. In Mangin's view, French manufacturers could build a market in Central America only if they offered longer term credit. Unless French businessmen became more aggressive, Lecoq warned, the recovery of both the domestic economy and foreign trade would be impossible.[6]

Mangin hoped to use President Carlos Herrera's desire for closer economic and political relations between Guatemala and France to obtain an advantageous commercial treaty. In contrast, Guatemalan hostility to U.S. influence had surfaced when a Guatemalan struck the U.S. legation secretary during the U.S. celebration of July 4, 1921. Still, the U.S. challenge to French influence persisted. Before the Great War, Guatemalans had most frequently learned French, but the influx of U.S. and Jamaican workers for United Fruit plantations and railroad projects had made English the most common foreign language. This shift was pragmatic and did not reflect cultural preference. Mangin and Lecoq claimed that neither North Americans nor Germans were well liked in some circles in Guatemala.[7] These circumstances opened possibilities for French interests.

Only two years after the war, about 40 percent of Guatemala's annual coffee production was again in German hands. While citizens of other countries controlled another 40 percent, Mangin wanted France to pursue the remaining 20 percent. Trade between the two countries had gradually declined since 1879 when Guatemala renounced its commercial treaty with France. Guatemalan coffee had once been a major import commodity in Le Havre and Bordeaux, but the exchange dwindled to a trickle after the duty on coffee became prohibitive. Guatemala wanted to trade entry of its coffee into France for a reduction of its import duties on French wines, silks, perfumes, and pharmaceutical products. But the French in Central America blamed the loss of the coffee market and the weak showing of French export products on the lack of adequate steamship service, not on tariffs. Without a connecting freight service, French goods, passengers, mail, and parcels were forced to use Dutch or British lines or to bear the higher costs through the port of New York. Mangin agreed that France needed direct communications if its commerce were to expand significantly. French diplomats and businessmen wanted a branch line to connect Central America with direct French lines at Vera Cruz, Mexico, or at Colón in Panama. Lecoq advised the business community interested in isthmian trade of the need for credit and direct steamer service, if it wished to compete adequately with German firms.[8]

The French encountered other competitors in Central America beside the Germans and North Americans. The Spanish government, striving to recover its influence in Latin America, frequently opposed French objectives. Spanish officials and firms had often represented German interests during the war, and French officials assumed that friendly postwar Hispanic-German relations would facilitate other cooperation. France needed to undermine Spanish policy. The Spanish minister in Guatemala recognized the importance of the Mangin mission when it arrived in two war vessels. He saw a connection between the French propaganda campaign, which used lectures and films, and the signing of a treaty favorable to French wines and oils, both chief export products of Spain. French diplomats were trying to negotiate similar commercial agreements with Costa Rica and Honduras, also to Spain's disadvantage. The Spanish minister judged that Spain's chief nemesis was not the United States, but French competition in commercial and military affairs.[9] The shared Latin culture that French officials had burnished in the mid- and late nineteenth century disappeared before the rivalry for influence and economic opportunity.

The Spanish minister criticized French "maneuvers" that threatened Spain's efforts to revitalize its position in a former colony. For example, he blamed the French military mission for Guatemala's cancellation of a contract with the Spanish army for military personnel. And the Franco-Guatemalan treaties on commerce and literary property, and similar ones under negotiation with Costa Rica and Honduras, created advantages for France at Spain's expense. He worried that France's "Latin American campaign" could impress the Central American and other Hispanic states with "its Paris and its victory [in World War I]" and undercut Spain's socioeconomic involvement in the New World. He advised vigorous measures to preserve Spain's role in Latin America, and the longer Spain waited to counteract French influence, the greater would be the burden.[10]

French officials were attracted to communications in their effort to rebuild influence in Central America. The French foreign minister granted a 10,000-franc subsidy to establish a newspaper in Guatemala that would counter the German information program, and Lecoq saw an opportunity for a French news service. French interests had had brief contact with cable schemes to the Caribbean since 1869 but had always withdrawn or sold their interests. In 1895 the French used the U.S. and Haiti Telegraph Company to link to the Brest-New York line to establish a permanent link to the Caribbean. Service to the mainland isthmus remained indirect. The lack of a direct telegraph service meant that French news arrived late and secondhand. Several Latin American governments, desiring an alternative to biased U.S. news services, solicited the French Agence Havas to connect Latin America and Europe and link the Latin American capitals with each other. After a Havas agency opened in Panama, French minister Emmanuel Léonce Neuville claimed that the local population greatly preferred receiving Havas reports to Associated Press reports. And when United Press resorted to anti-European propaganda, the Latin Americans responded with antipathy toward their powerful Anglo-Saxon neighbor and sympathy toward France.[11] The French news service did not obtain spectacular success, but it remained competitive.

The bitterness of individual Frenchmen toward Germany occasionally clouded the reputation of France. In Costa Rica in 1921, German chargé Wilhelm Erythropel and a French hotel owner in San José engaged in a dispute over protocol and manners. During the funeral commemoration for Costa Rica's bishop

Johann Kaspar Storck, a native German, Erythropel flew the German flag at half-mast out of his hotel apartment. The hotel owner protested, claiming that U.S. officers had demanded the removal of the flag. After several confrontations threatened to spoil the memorial ceremonies, Erythropel took down the flag and moved out of the hotel. The incident generated strong public reaction against the hotel owner because Storck was widely loved and respected. Erythropel avoided alienating the United States by publicly proclaiming that the hotel owner was solely responsible for the trouble.[12]

Later, the French minister to Central America, Henri Eugène Aymé-Martin, embarrassed the Guatemalan government when he tactlessly thanked it for having joined France in the Great War for "freedom and order" in the presence of German officials. The Guatemalan president also ignored his reference to a new trade treaty because France wanted a reciprocal treaty and would not welcome a most-favored-nation treaty such as the United States and Germany had negotiated.[13] Given the powerful U.S. position in the Caribbean and the inability of the weakened French economy to supply goods, capital, or technology, the French were unlikely to receive any special favors.

Some French residents in Costa Rica supported French goals only when it was convenient. In 1921, French consul Serre recommended rewarding Henri Peyroutet, a former French canal company employee, with a medal for publishing a series of articles in Costa Rica's *La tribuna* condemning the German reparations position. Later, Serre realized that Peyroutet, a shady character who had enriched himself in the ill-fated La Palma colony, was a nuisance. For no apparent reason, Peyroutet resisted the reorganization of the French Society of Benevolence, and he wrote an abusive letter to German chargé Franz von Tattenbach. On another occasion, Peyroutet, under the protection of a Costa Rican exequatur as consul, and carrying a pistol that was visible in his clothing, threatened Serre.[14] Serre held Peyroutet chiefly responsible for creating divisiveness in the French colony in Costa Rica.

In mid-1921, Nicaraguan president Diego Chamorro sent his foreign minister, Maximilio Zepeda, to France to demonstrate a special friendship. Chamorro had supported Nicaragua's adoption of July 14 as a national holiday because his brother had died in France fighting the Germans. The French Foreign Ministry considered Zepeda, a former student of the Faculty of Law and the School of Political Science of the University of Paris, to be a loyal friend of France. He headed a faction that wanted France to have the leading role in the regeneration of Nicaragua, whereas Emiliano Chamorro, a principal conservative leader and the president's nephew, and his faction looked to the United States for guidance. The Nicaraguan government wanted a commercial treaty, but the French foreign minister saw no need for one because a 1902 treaty granted to products from each country unhindered access to the other.[15]

French officials were not always in agreement with the selection or conduct of Central American agents. In 1921 the French minister in Central America, Georges Auguste Alexandre Perrot, described the Honduran minister to France, Raul Toledo López, as a man without conscience who had sold his services to Germany during the war. Some officials in Paris disagreed, indicating that Toledo López had supported the declaration of war against Germany and the choice of July 14 as a Honduran national holiday. Perrot cautioned that since the Germans had launched a propaganda campaign in Honduras to support Toledo López, a refusal to receive him would be ill-advised.[16]

The French minister in Central America, Albert Antoine Revelli, argued that the inadequate French representation in El Salvador could be corrected with the appointment of a professional consul. A Frenchman complained that there was no French response to German propaganda in the major Salvadoran journals. The French Foreign Ministry wanted the part-time consular agent in San Salvador and Revelli to respond intelligently to the German campaign. Revelli denied that France needed a diplomat in each Central American capital, but he conceded that El Salvador had more important French investment and commercial interests (coffee export) than did Guatemala.[17]

Revelli believed that some citizens and protectees of dubious character—Syrians and Palestinians resident in Central America—plotted to profit from French protection. He wanted all Frenchmen and Syrians who resided on the volatile north coast of Honduras to refrain from political activity because the contests often continued beyond the elections. For example, Syrian merchants had offered Revelli bribes to support their claims for alleged losses in the revolution that had occurred when Tiburcio Carías Andino, who had received a plurality of the votes, was denied the presidency in 1923. By May 1924, French citizens and protectees had filed $50,000 in claims against the Honduran government. Revelli expected French claims to balloon to $300,000, if U.S. insurance companies agreed to pay

$800,000. French firms inflated their claims. In Nicaragua the Banana du Río Grande blamed its losses, totaling $15,000, in the Chamorro revolt in 1926 on inadequate protection from the government. But it could document a loss of only $562.50 for requisitioned fruit.[18]

The French government faced a more serious diplomatic and financial challenge in Costa Rica when the postwar Costa Rican government took advantage of the depreciated franc. Some Costa Rican leaders proposed paying off the 1911 loan while the franc was cheap. A French bondholders' association responded by demanding better protection from their government. It complained that the Costa Rican government was forcing payment in francs, although the 1911 loan called for payment in francs in Paris, dollars in New York, or pounds in London. Consul Serre, noting that British bondholders were being paid at the prewar exchange rate in pounds, could not see why French bondholders should not be paid in the same manner. But Peralta argued that former Costa Rican presidents Ricardo Jiménez and Cleto González Víquez had convincingly refuted the case for any obligation to repay the French loan in dollars or pounds. When the Costa Rican government refused to make payments in pounds, dollars, or gold francs at par, Serre retorted in frustration that Peralta, the illegitimate child of an Indian servant, had no right to either the "de" or the title of marquis. The French finance minister considered the bondholders' demands for payment in pounds just. But many Costa Ricans considered the 1911 loan the source of Costa Rica's economic woes and believed that their country was entitled to the cheapest form of repayment.[19]

The French government wanted the French bondholders treated with the same financial equity as the British bondholders. If the British were paid in pounds sterling, it expected French bondholders to be paid in gold francs, marks, dollars, or pounds sterling. The French position was less logical than it appeared because the contracts for the loans in Paris and London in 1911 were not identical. The French contract allowed payment in several designated currencies, but the British contract specified repayment in pounds sterling. Moreover, the French contract called for exhausting all judicial avenues to resolve disputes before appealing to the diplomatic process.[20] The French bondholders had not used any judicial avenue.

Costa Rican debt problems were linked to France's commercial recovery in Central America. Costa Rica increased the duties on French wines and liqueurs to ameliorate its debt servicing, revenue, and budgetary position. In mid-1920 the French government warned that if those duties were not rescinded, the minimum French duties in effect for Costa Rican products would be quadrupled. The two governments agreed to a provisional compromise: Both countries would collect minimum tariffs until a new accord could be reached. In 1922, French minister Léonce Neuville advised bondholders not to sell below par, pending the outcome of negotiations for a U.S. loan to refinance Costa Rica's 1911 loan. He discovered that all Costa Rican custom duties were dedicated to guaranteeing the U.S. loan that paid off the 1910 British loan, but not the French loan. As the dispute over repaying the 1911 loan heated up, French officials again threatened to remove Costa Rican coffee from the minimum tariff list. In turn, the Costa Rican finance minister refused to dedicate funds from the U.S. loan to repay the 1911 debt until the French consented to maintain only a minimum tariff on Costa Rican products.[21] This U.S. loan, however, was not approved.

The loan repayment issue descended into intrigue when the bankers behind the 1911 bonds sent a coded telegram to their agent in Costa Rica. Neuville's suspicions were aroused when he was refused access to the telegram. The agent for the bankers was the nephew of the owner of the firm that was seeking a U.S. loan. Neuville feared that the agent would sacrifice French interests to secure the commission for his uncle from the U.S. loan. Frustrated, he addressed the Costa Rican government in terms that it found both erroneous and menacing. It rejected his charges and insisted on repaying the loan within the terms of the original contract.[22]

Throughout the early 1920s, the Costa Rican government labored to stabilize its domestic economy despite delays in resolving the loan issue. It wanted to resolve the loan repayment issue because it wished to borrow additional funds to bolster its ailing economy. But the issue of paper or gold francs persisted dividing the two sides. Costa Rica continued to seek a large refinancing loan in the United States, in effect, trading a French for a U.S. loan. Many Costa Ricans and Frenchmen disliked this tactic because it would make Costa Rica even more dependent on the United States. French bondholders, when their debt was excluded from the U.S.-Costa Rican loan of 1923, brought suit before the Seine Civil Court in June 1923. The suit halted the loan negotations and left Costa Rica financially strapped. In March 1925 the French bondholders and the Costa Rican government reached a repayment agreement, but its implementation was delayed when allegations arose that Costa Rican finance minister Tomás Soley Güell—a former student at a Bordeaux lycée who had always been an opponent of France—had led a group of his friends to purchase the bonds in France at a low price and stood to reap a 250 percent profit from the transaction.[23]

Implementation of the bond redemption agreement was delayed still further by disagreement over how many bondholders had to agree before the settlement was considered accepted. The bondholders' association initially said that ratification required acceptance by 75 percent of the bondholders, but it later reduced that figure to a simple majority. By 1929 the redemption agreement had won approval from all but about five thousand of the more than sixty thousand bondholders. The Foreign Ministry refused to intervene on behalf of this last group, which held out for gold, arguing that a Hague Tribunal decision had required Brazil to repay its loans of 1909, 1910, and 1911 in gold. This settlement removed the burdensome suit from the French courts, but probably did little to stabilize Costa Rica's finances.[24]

The bitter dispute over the terms for repaying the 1911 loan left a mark on Franco-Costa Rican relations. French consul Louis Desrousseaux predicted in 1923 that President-elect Ricardo Jiménez's government would not have much sympathy for France. France had lost influence, he said, because the leading members of the Franco-American committee would never forgive Neuville for opposing a commercial convention and for ruining three loan agreements by insisting upon unsatisfactory repayment terms. But Neuville charged Soley Güell with delaying the commercial convention in 1925. Desrousseaux saw some hope, however. French influence could be preserved in cultural affairs. He recommended expending the modest funds available to promote the French language and advance French culture in Costa Rica, to aid Costa Ricans who wanted to study in France, and to establish regular steamship service to Costa Rica. Although Costa Rica had approved a postal agreement that reduced the fees on books, newspapers, and magazines, the French legislature had ignored this advantageous agreement, and it was still pending in late 1927.[25] Yet, better communications and freer access for printed matter would bolster French culture in Costa Rica and ease feelings over the loan repayment dispute.

During World War I, many members of the Central American elites became apprehensive about the escalation of U.S. influence in the region. Lecoq observed that U.S. enterprises controlled all important affairs in Guatemala—the railroads, the port of Barrios, the banana plantations, and the iron mines. Still, Guatemala offered the best hope of resistance to the expanding U.S. presence, but it needed external aid. Lecoq reported on a French firm that exploited mica deposits on the isthmus, and Guatemala had other exploitable minerals, including iron ore and mercury, that French mining firms might extract.[26] The Middle American societies hoped to create opportunities for French interests as counterweights to U.S. investment and influence.

In the 1920s foreign interests on the isthmus exploited a new mineral—petroleum. Guatemala's government preferred to grant the petroleum concession to a French firm, but no enterprise applied. In another petroleum-related situation, Lecoq suspected that the United States had rejected using force to settle the Costa Rican-Panamanian border dispute so that it could make a deal favorable to U.S. petroleum interests. In 1921 the Costa Rican government seized the territory that U.S. Supreme Court Chief Justice Edward Douglas White had awarded it in a 1914 arbitration judgment of its border dispute with Panama and that Panama had refused to vacate. Serre expected that this "operetta war" or "hundred hour war" would convince the French government not to take Central American governments too seriously. When Costa Rica seized the area, Panama called upon the U.S. government to fulfill its commitment to guarantee Panamanian territorial integrity. When the U.S. government offered only to mediate, Lecoq suspected that Costa Rica had promised preference to Standard Oil over the British Amory firm for a disputed petroleum concession in return for U.S. support in the border dispute. But there was another explanation—Costa Rican control also offered advantages to the large United Fruit interests in the disputed region. Displeased with the U.S. response, Panama's government requested French intercession on its behalf. The French vice consul, Ernest Maurice de Simonin, skillfully avoided placing France in the path of U.S. policy by stating that he would gladly intervene on behalf of Panama if instructed by his government.[27] France was trapped between its desire for closer ties to Latin America and its unwillingness to oppose any determined U.S. policy.

Franco-Panamanian relations benefited from sympathy for France created during the Great War. The Panamanian reception of General Mangin was a muffled form of anti-Americanism because the orators eulogized France for protecting small, weak nations. Mangin recommended establishing a legation as a reward for Panama's loyalty during the war, and he argued that

Panama could be the distribution center for a large area in which France must develop commercial interests to achieve its objectives in the world economy. Franco-Panamanian relations were not without friction, however. The French engineer and former canal official Philippe Bunau-Varilla remained a villain in the historical recollection of Panama. The monument dedicated to the Frenchmen who had died while working on the Panama Canal project bore no mention of the John Hays–Bunau-Varilla Treaty, and the French foreign minister inquired how Panamanian authorities might respond to the suggestion to add Bunau-Varilla's name. The chargé speculated that such a request would produce ill-feelings. He assumed that Panamanians would react with hostility because they believed that Bunau-Varilla had gained 3 million francs after he signed the treaty, a treaty that was detrimental to Panamanian interests. Neuville thought the Panamanian government seemed anxious to show its goodwill toward France, if unpleasant memories of the past were not recalled. But Panama's sympathy for France eroded in the 1920s, as French diplomats struggled against Panama's immigration restrictions that discriminated against French Antilles blacks, Syrians, Lebanese, and metropolitan citizens. Neuville suspected that special pleading for Bunau-Varilla might evaporate the remaining sympathy.[28]

The shrinking demand for coffee in the United States after 1920 presented the French government with an opportunity to reduce its negative trade terms with Latin America. In early 1921 the Colombian government offered to reduce duties on French wines and spirits in return for lower duties on its coffee. The French government studied this attractive offer in light of relations with Central America. About two-thirds of French purchases in Central America were coffee, but Central America bought few French goods. This situation could be altered because the Central American states were seeking new coffee markets. They recognized the pitfalls of depending too heavily upon one outlet—the United States—for their coffee and other products. The French commerce minister believed that the duty on coffee would be the key weapon in France's trade negotiations with all Central American countries except Honduras. He advised studying the impact of lower coffee duties upon the national revenue, while not forgetting that the new trade terms would benefit French exportation.[29]

In the postwar years, the French government conceded a multitude of medals and honors as rewards for service to wartime France. In early 1922, after Serre reported that Costa Rica considered itself the only country in the world without a citizen who had received a French decoration since the Great War, the French government decorated the president, the foreign minister, and the diplomat Francisco Cabezas Gómez with the Légion d'honneur. Revelli believed that the French government needed to reward its friends. In 1922, Guatemala signed a commercial treaty with France, its first treaty with a European power in forty years. In recognition, Revelli wanted the grand officier de la Légion d'honneur for President José María Orellana, the commandant de la Légion d'honneur for Foreign Minister Adrian Recinos, and the chevalier de la Légion d'honneur for Subsecretary of the Foreign Ministry Sinforoso Aguilar. Occasionally, the "friends" were not shy about indicating their wish for decorations. In the course of negotiating treaties on commerce, printed matter, and a possible military mission, Salvadoran minister A. M. Deperetti repeatedly observed that the Salvadoran president, foreign minister, and minister of war held French honors in high esteem. The French Foreign Ministry was inclined to decorate these three politicians as a means of undermining German plans to send a military mission to El Salvador.[30]

The enduring French military mission in Guatemala exerted social and political influence. In 1921 a committee of the Pan American Union, the Permanent Group Committee for Guatemala, blamed the French military instructors for contributing to Guatemala's unfriendly attitude toward the United States. Despite persistent challenges from U.S. diplomats, the mission continued throughout the 1920s. Some discontent with the mission appeared, however. L. Cotty of Générale Transatlantique alleged that the low quality of the military mission discredited France in the region. The "radicals," opponents of the Guatemalan government, attacked the mission. A feud between Minister Revelli's predecessor and Major Contresty became a public scandal, and Revelli sent Contresty and Lieutenant Frémont home, while Captains Roche and C. Chartier remained in Guatemalan service. Revelli assumed that a new contract that specified that the French officers were technical advisors as well as military instructors would produce better results. In late 1922, Foreign Minister Recinos confided to Revelli that some Guatemalan officials intended to replace the French officers with a U.S. mission. Alerted, Revelli persuaded President Orellana to reject the U.S. officers, who would have received less pay than their French counterparts. Afterward, Revelli speculated that the U.S.

minister would be livid when Guatemala ordered French military materials with funds borrowed from the Blair Company in New York. In the 1920s other U.S. attempts to replace the French military mission were also failures. Despite the apparent French success, German diplomat Johannes Kretzschmar reported in 1926 that French influence on the Guatemalan army was greatly reduced because the mission had not created a good spirit in the Guatemalan army.[31]

French diplomats in Central America were interested in a resolution discussed at the 1923 Pan American Conference that aimed to block foreign military missions from serving in Latin America. One French diplomat speculated that Germans were behind the failed resolution. In the late 1920s the French government eagerly sought arms orders in Central America. It sold at least 48 cannons with 2,000 shells, 110 Hotchkiss machine guns, 1,000,000 rounds of Hotchkiss ammunition, and various other miscellaneous materials to El Salvador through a dummy Levant company.[32] The French sold indirectly because world and French opinion increasingly condemned arms sales and because the Versailles treaties restricted such transactions.

Although the French government hoped to supply traditional military missions and arms, it focused on military aviation in the 1920s. French officials and entrepreneurs recognized a potential for selling military and commercial aviation technology on the isthmus. Mangin recommended that French aviation firms demonstrate their planes at the centennial celebrations of Central American independence. Naturally, the demonstrations would promote sales. He expected air communications to be important in Central America's future. Revelli boasted that French nationals pioneered aviation in Central America.[33]

British, German, Italian, and U.S. agents competed with the French for air service concessions in Middle America. U.S. businessmen confronted considerable antipathy during a two-year competition with French entrepreneurs for a concession to serve Nicaragua with air transport. General Labro, a former noncommissioned officer with the French artillery, past employee of the New Panama Canal Company, military instructor for several Central American governments, and a former general in the Honduran army, received a concession for water-plane service on the major lakes and for conventional airplane service elsewhere in Nicaragua. He fronted for a company, capitalized at 3 million francs, which intended to exploit the concession with French planes and to initiate conventional air service throughout Central America and seaplane service in Guatemala between Izabal and Puerto Barrios. In late 1924 a second French aviation company contemplated a direct air connection from Guatemala City to San José. Revelli expected the success of these firms to elevate French prestige and commerce.[34]

U.S. opposition to foreign aviation in the Caribbean area exacted a toll on French military orders. In early 1925, Major General Mason M. Patrick, chief of the U.S. Air Service, concluded that although "both German and French capital are now competing for aerial contracts in Central America, the defense of the Panama Canal practically demands that the United States dominate aeronautical employment throughout Central America." In 1928 the U.S. consul forced reconsideration of a Guatemalan order for French airplanes after word of the order had been leaked to the press. He obtained for the United States half of the order for six planes. General Patrick wanted to eliminate foreign competition on the isthmus.[35]

Some Central American leaders stubbornly resisted further encroachment of U.S. influence. Despite accidents that destroyed two French Brequet aircraft, in late 1929 the Salvadoran minister of war resisted pressure to acquire U.S. Falcon-Curtiss aircraft. He pleaded with the French to offer a suitable alternative. When French Potez aircraft were unavailable, he ordered French Guacos as training planes. French consul Emile Gissot cautioned that discredited Hanriot and Brequet planes sat in hangar corners in El Salvador. Indifference after the sale and a lack of material and technical support were hurting long-term French commercial interests. But a satisfied El Salvador might influence the other Central American governments to acquire French planes.[36]

Gissot hoped to stimulate sales of other French military products. In late 1929, El Salvador considered purchasing machine guns and additional artillery in France, but the French firm, Schneider, demanded an "excessive price." Rejecting the overpriced equipment, El Salvador considered a bid from the Czechoslovakian Skoda works at an "affordable" price. Gissot hoped that the French government could persuade the Schneider firm to charge a reasonable price because German influence could return if the Salvadoran government purchased Skoda equipment.[37]

Revelli lamented that France often got advantages of form —the display of a few planes in an air demonstration or public recognition for its culture—while Germany received more substantial benefits. For example, Guatemala doubled its duties on key French exports—luxury goods and wines—while it treated German products more gently. Revelli conceded that the French firms attempted to profiteer from the exchange rate, rarely sent catalogues or samples, insisted upon advance payment, and often refused to answer correspondence or replied perfunctorily. He wanted the French businessmen to study the market conditions and the methods of their U.S. and German competitors.[38]

By 1923, Revelli believed that his labors might reverse the French commercial decline. The Guatemalan congress hoped to halt the march of a U.S. monopoly in Guatemala by approving a Franco-Belgian concession for a tramline and for electric light and power. Revelli gushed: "A new era commences from this moment for our commerce in Central America." The concession was a legitimate reward for his patient labors. He found the other metropole diplomats and businessmen to be jealous of French success in obtaining concessions. While he encouraged large investment groups, he had strong reservations about small or individual investors coming to the isthmus, particularly in agriculture, because the fincas were commonly heavily in debt and rural life was primitive and hard. He boasted that the economic benefits from his mission had just begun.[39]

While Revelli was optimistic regarding French economic activity in Guatemala, his fellow officials saw opportunity elsewhere on the isthmus. Since Latin Americans were discontented with the inferior quality of North American goods, French products could recover a preponderant place if properly presented. French officials seemed optimistic about commercial opportunities in Honduras and El Salvador. The French minister of commerce and industry submitted a list of numerous firms in a wide variety of businesses that wanted the Honduran Chamber of Commerce to help them locate ventures or business partners. In March 1929, although the Salvadoran government denounced the Franco-Salvadoran commercial treaty, Gissot described interesting commercial opportunities in El Salvador for French firms.[40]

Banking and financial institutions were vital for fulfilling developmentalist projects and for stabilizing isthmian governments. In the early postwar years, French financial penetration of Guatemala would be difficult, in Lecoq's view, because German and American banks worked together, leaving little for the weakened French finance capital. The Banco Colombiano, however, was friendly to French interests. In 1921 the French Foreign Ministry contemplated requesting a place for at least one Frenchman on the governing board of the Banco Agrícola Hipotecario de Guatemala because French investment and commerce had grown, and the private bank Lazard Frères et Compagnie owned shares in the Banco Agrícola. The Lazard firm, however, sold its shares. Revelli was flattered in 1922 when the new government—which had named Felipe Solares, a friend of France who had worked for a French firm, finance minister—consulted him regarding a proposed loan contract with Blair Company of New York. He responded with great reserve, however, because the government favored the United States, and he believed that France would find a patient course more profitable.[41]

North American bankers confided to Revelli that the U.S. government had secretly encouraged the depreciation of the pound and the franc in the early 1920s to gain a financial edge in Latin America. The bankers suggested that the entourage around President Calvin Coolidge and Secretary of State Charles Evans Hughes wished to envelop Latin America exclusively in U.S. capital. They strove to make the dollar so strong that European banks would be unable to intervene in New World capital markets, and European trade would be inhibited in the New World.[42]

U.S. policymakers had long wished to drive most foreign investment out of the Caribbean area. Yankee imperialism posed a special danger to French interests in the Caribbean region, and it distorted world commerce, which handicapped France's capacity to service its war debts. Before the Great War, British and French financial markets had supplied capital and, along with German entrepreneurs, the commercial tools to manage trade in Latin America. By 1920 the U.S. political economy had pushed all three into lesser roles, although Britain and Germany were striving to regain their positions. A French army study predicted that the competition would become sharper, especially between the United States and Germany or Britain. It assumed that French interests would have difficulty reestablishing their prewar roles.[43]

In 1923, U.S. and Spanish agents monitored French interest in the Guatemalan loan.The United States exerted influence to prevent a loan by the French banks, which offered the best terms. After the U.S. government induced the French financiers to withdraw, U.S. financial interests decided that conditions were unfavorable for a loan to Guatemala. The French were embarrassed.

The Spanish minister concluded, nevertheless, that the loan was not a good opportunity for the French because "it will be difficult for them to collect the principal." He recognized that only the North Americans could exercise the power to assure collection of the loan. A U.S. intelligence agent found the French minister's efforts to secure the loan unusual given the severe financial problems in France. He conceded, however, that "the French Minister is thoroughly cognizant of the most approved Latin business methods, consequently, any loan proposed by him should have the closest scrutiny."[44] Although the French government seldom publicly promoted private business interests, it commonly offered support behind the scenes.

Some French officials dreamed of rebuilding France's commercial role in Central America and recognized the need for banks that facilitated commerce rather than pursued long-term investment. French chargé Perrot lent moral support to the Frenchman René Keilhauer, who represented a U.S. consortium authorized to create a central emission bank in El Salvador with a maximum capital of $10 million and had an option on a $16 million loan, because Keilhauer would facilitate French commerce with El Salvador. Revelli recognized that since the 1870s, French businessmen on the isthmus had participated principally in banking, investment, and finance, not commerce. He encouraged the shift toward the latter activity because postwar France lacked the surplus capital that prewar France had had.[45]

French officials often contemplated a renewed financial role in combination with commerce. In one instance, Revelli hoped to combine a French-controlled central bank with a regular, direct steamship service to revive commerce. He accepted the idea of using some U.S. and Guatemalan capital for a central bank provided "the direction would remain essentially French," to serve France's commercial and financial penetration. The bank should allow France to dominate the Guatemalan capital market and to pry open the rest of Central America. When his project bogged down, he warned that if French interests did not act, German-American firms would undertake the bank. He projected that the bank—with enough U.S. participation to manage local disturbances or political pressure—and direct steamer service would encourage French economic penetration.[46]

Revelli's enthusiasm, however, did not persuade the French finance minister. He had grave reservations about participation in a central bank of emission. Whereas Revelli considered the high interest rates and tight credit in Guatemala a banking opportunity, the finance minister suspected that the tough lending terms reflected risky conditions. Even if a recently signed commercial treaty increased France's 3 percent share of Guatemala's trade, he suspected that the lack of direct communications would hamper commercial expansion. It was premature, in his view, to plan for a bank of emission where French banking had not operated and where the bank could place France at odds with U.S. policy. To reduce the likelihood of a clash with the U.S. government, he and Revelli agreed that France would participate in the bank's formation only if requested by the Guatemalan government. While the finance minister intended to avoid even the appearance of opposition to U.S. economic and financial activity in Guatemala, he agreed to inform private banks of the opportunities without applying any pressure on them to enter the area. He specifically recommended that the French National Bank for Foreign Commerce study whether it could enter Central America on the model Revelli projected.[47] The project was seductive.

The profit prospect for a Guatemalan state bank funded with external capital induced various groups to seek the concession. Despite the French government's reservations, Bauer, Marchal, and Company solicited the concession for French financiers. Revelli aided the Bauer, Marchal agent to submit a proposal, although he regretted that the Bauer, Marchal group was aligned with the Schroeder Bank of London, which had German origins. But the other firms competing for the concession, Schwartz and Company and the Speyer group from New York, both had German connections as well. Revelli hoped that this venture would facilitate French economic penetration of Central America.[48] The Bauer group held out a promise of material benefits and the emotional satisfaction of undermining German economic recovery on the isthmus.

French and German officials considered their economic interests in sharp competition on the isthmus. Lecoq believed that French immigrants and businessmen could learn from the Germans who "had not lost a day in their efforts to reconquer their lost role." The German recovery challenged plans to reestablish French economic interests. He compared social characteristics of the French and German residents to underscore German success in the political economy. The German colony was hierarchical and strictly disciplined, whereas the French settled as individuals. Many Germans married into the best Guatemalan families, whereas French emigrants often took Indian women as mistresses and became social outcasts. By 1922 the Germans had already made a strong economic recovery in Central America at the expense of Britain, the United States, and France.[49]

French and German officials expected politics in the host countries to affect their competition for influence. In 1923, Adrian Recinos, whom Tattenbach labeled ambitious, ruthless, and dangerous, was named Guatemalan minister to Paris. While foreign minister, Recinos had smoothed the way for French propaganda and the Franco-Guatemalan Trade Treaty of 1923, which prompted his successor, Robert Lowenthal, the son of a German Jew, "to raise a shield against French commerce." Tattenbach considered the Franco-Guatemalan Trade Treaty a great danger to German interests if it should become the model for treaties with other Middle American states. This course seemed distinctly possible when the French minister planned a trip to Costa Rica to negotiate a commercial agreement. German consul Heinrich Johannes Kroeger expected little from Franco-Costa Rican negotiations, however, because Costa Rica could not offer attractive tariff reductions on French luxury goods. Moreover, the candidate of the francophile group lost the Costa Rican presidential election.[50]

French officials pondered their nation's modest role in Nicaragua during the postwar years. A mere consular agent served in Managua. By 1923, however, French coffee merchants had recovered their prewar role as chief purchasers of Nicaraguan coffee. A French Foreign Ministry memorandum advised reopening the stymied trade negotiations in order to expand commerical ties. While U.S. sensitivity prohibited any foreign political role, the French position in Nicaragua's coffee industry offered France leverage to negotiate for a larger trade opportunity.[51]

The French government was sensitive to U.S. authority in Nicaragua. When General Emiliano Chamorro, the commander of the army, initiated a revolt in 1926, Minister Aymé-Martin argued that since it had only a small role in Nicaragua, there was no inconvenience in France's recognizing the new regime de facto. A Quai d'Orsay official rejected this ill-considered reasoning. There were indeed inconveniences in placing France in opposition to U.S. policy.[52]

U.S. special interest in Nicaragua hindered justice for Frenchmen. In 1926, Nicaraguan officials held a Compagnie Générale Transatlantique vessel responsible for damaging the Corinto wharf. Corinto officials forced the Transatlantique captain to pay damages and to promise not to mention the incident. The

Générale Transatlantique wanted the French government to protest in Central America and to raise the question in Washington since the customs receiver was a North American. But the company dropped the matter after the French consul stressed to the Nicaraguan government the need to prevent such conduct by its customs and port officials.[53]

French officials repeatedly complained that propaganda assaults upon the image and reputation of France harmed its cultural and commercial mission. In 1922, L. Cotty with Générale Transatlantique complained to the French Foreign Ministry that both the German and U.S. governments had adopted anti-French propaganda for commercial reasons. The French community protested a German-funded film, *La Garçonne, La Emancipada, La Mariposa de París,* which condemned French society. It was banned in Guatemala. Aymé-Martin alerted other French officials to guard against this movie. Captain Chartier complained that anti-French propaganda appeared regularly in the German-owned Spanish-language *Gaceta de Munich,* which had ready access to local papers while French information did not. Not all propaganda was unfriendly. *El imparcial* (Guatemala City) and *Revista de Yucatán* explained the French occupation of the Rhine in a manner friendly to France.[54] The negative propaganda disrupted the French government's campaign to preserve its cultural role in Middle America.

During the 1920s, France remained a spiritual center for Latin American intellectuals. French officials urged closer cultural ties with the isthmus states. French residents occupied many important offices in the isthmian cultural institutions, and several Central American countries called upon French expertise in administrative and educational matters. For example, El Salvador requested a specialist to organize its statistical service. And Mangin and Lecoq recommended awarding Madame Antoine Peyre, head of the girls' school and the Alliance française in Guatemala, the "palmes académiques" for excellent work in spreading French influence in the school system. Aymé-Martin noted that the modest number of French in Costa Rica were influential because they were concentrated in San José and organized to support French cultural activities in Costa Rica. He warned of the ethnic danger for Latin culture if French, Spanish, and Italians did not migrate, because then Guatemala would draw upon Germans (and Anglo-Saxons) to stimulate development.[55]

Revelli boasted that ample French economic, educational, and cultural institutions operated in Guatemala to direct French influence throughout the isthmus. He emphasized the value of the Alliance française, the French lycée, a French director heading the Institut Guatemaltèque, a military mission, numerous merchants, and a few planters. He marveled that the French lycée survived with an annual subsidy of merely 3,000 francs. Its finances were in a pitiful state, yet it reached over one hundred day students, not all of whom paid, and four hundred attending night classes. Captain Chartier encouraged the French language by offering French books as prizes to the best students in the boys' and girls' lycées in Guatemala. Revelli urged more metropole support for the institutions of French culture on the isthmus.[56]

French officials retained interest in the cultural impact of French teachers in the school systems on the isthmus outside of Guatemala. The Dames de Sion were active in education at the Collège de Sion in Costa Rica, which received an annual subsidy of 3,000 francs from the French government. When the Nicaraguan government adopted measures hostile to the Frères des Écoles Chrétiennes (Christian Brothers), the French foreign minister reminded Nicaraguan officials that 47 brothers, of whom 20 were French, taught a minimum of 6 hours of French per week to 1,900 students (1,404 without cost) in the schools in Managua, León, and Jinotega. Although a contract existed between the Christian Brothers and the Nicaraguan government, the foreign minister appealed to the good record of the brothers.[57]

In 1928 the renowned philosopher and anthropologist Lucien Lévy-Bruhl undertook a major mission to strengthen the cultural exchange between France and Central America. As a consequence of this mission, Costa Rica became interested in a teacher-exchange program and a Franco-Costa Rican Society and in "purchasing" about a half-dozen student rooms at 20,000 pesos each (50,000 francs) in the Cité Universitaire in Paris. Other agreements facilitated the studies of Guatemalans in France, contracted for the exchange of students and teachers between the University of El Salvador and the University of Paris, and planned to create Franco-Costa Rican and Franco-Salvadoran institutes for joint cultural and scientific purposes. The mission developed educational programs with Guatemala, Costa Rica, and El Salvador.[58]

The cultural and educational agreements were not implemented well. In 1929, Gissot complained that France was frittering away the influence that the Lévy-Bruhl mission had won in El Salvador. After the teacher-exchange agreement was signed, the University of El Salvador indicated preference for a "genital-urinary" specialist. The University of Paris did not even bother to explain why it was unwilling to participate in the exchange, although funding had been arranged. Gissot managed to get students, doctors, professors, and a colonel sent to France, but he needed specialists, technicians, and others coming from the opposite direction to preserve French influence.[59] The French educational impact remained effective at the elementary and secondary school level, but French institutions of higher education seemed reluctant to participate.

French cultural influence went beyond schools and language training. French religious orders had a long and varied record of service on the isthmus. In Panama, Mangin praised the de la Salle lycée, the French language books that were displayed widely in libraries and bookstores, and the impressive French House, which owed much to the labors of Minister Simonin and his wife. A French official appreciated that Panamanians had resisted English and remained Catholic. He rejoiced that French missionaries—the Frères de la Salle, Frères Eudistes, Soeurs de St. Vincent de Paul, and Soeurs Franciscaines—were valued in Panama because religious orders were allowed to teach. In 1925 the Vatican created a new bishopric in Panama with Rojas y Arrieta, a native Costa Rican, as bishop. Rojas, a longtime member of the Franco-American Committee, intended to form a national priesthood by founding a seminary under the direction of French priests. The Filles de la Charité and the Dames de Sion supplied nurses for a hospital in Costa Rica. The Catholic church in Guatemala, supported by an important French religious mission, was a strong French cultural force. Aymé-Martin welcomed the appointment of Monseigneur Duron, a native French-speaker but a U.S. citizen, as archbishop of Guatemala because Duron supported French culture. French clergy or clergy sympathetic to France often obtained high office in Middle America.[60]

While French influence bowed to U.S. preeminence in Panama, French culture still was respected. The French chargé and colony in Panama unsuccessfully resisted a move to place Theodore Roosevelt's statue in the "Plaza de Lesseps" and rename it "Plaza Roosevelt." But a broad, lovely promenade elsewhere in Panama was named after de Lesseps. Later, the French agent decided that the change was for the best because the former Plaza de Lesseps was not in a desirable area. The new promenade, however, was near the French legation, ended in the Plaza de France, and was located with other monuments of interest to

French people. The French business weekly, *L'Action industrielle et commerciale*, believed a victory for U.S. influence on the isthmus would be unfortunate because North Americans think only of weapons and money. It urged a Franco-Latin American alliance to prevent an irreparable depression of the human ideal.[61]

In the late 1920s, El Salvador's government initiated several prizes for architectural plans for buildings. French architects won two prize competitions with plans for a theater and a casino. Later, another architectural competition to design four public buildings—a Palace of Justice, the National University, a public nursery, and a police building—was opened. French architects received the $1,000 first prizes for their plans for the National University and Palace of Justice; no prizes were awarded for the other two buildings. A third French architect was awarded $600 to submit his plan for a lycée to the Ministry of Development. Gissot lamented that despite these artistic triumphs, French firms were not competing to construct the buildings.[62] Often French economic activity failed to match France's cultural, intellectual, or artistic triumphs.

Relations between France and El Salvador, elevated after the Lévy-Bruhl mission and the architectural success, deteriorated when disputes arose over several issues. El Salvador wished to place busts of German Field Marshal Helmuth von Moltke and French Marshal Ferdinand Foch in the hall of honor in its military school. The French minister in Central America responded that if von Moltke entered the hall, it would be best if he remained alone. The Salvadoran minister of war assured the French that von Moltke's bust would not enter the military school. The German Foreign Ministry believed that both the French and U.S. ministers had acted to block von Moltke's entrance into the military school.[63]

Middle American political leaders were apprehensive about the vastly increased power of the United States after World War I. This condition facilitated French efforts to rebuild economic and political influence on the isthmus. Paradoxically, the U.S. surge had displaced German interests on the isthmus and thus briefly created opportunities for any entrepreneurs or firms that could fill the gaps. The special mission of General Mangin in 1921 underscored the importance that French leaders assigned to reviving France's role on the isthmus. Mangin and others pursued the possibilities of reattracting investment, protecting merchant marine access to interoceanic transit, reestablishing purchases of coffee, and rebuilding cultural influence. The deterioration of the French franc produced a decade-long dispute with the Costa Rican government over repaying the 1911 loan, which was finally resolved in 1929 in a settlement favorable to Costa Rica. French diplomats labored diligently to recreate a significant role for France in commerce and investment, but support in the home country was erratic.

French cultural and military policies remained the high points of French relations with Central America. The French language remained widely taught. In 1928 the Lévy-Bruhl mission opened higher education to closer ties with Guatemala, Costa Rica, and El Salvador. In Guatemala the French military mission remained a source of influence and pride, and French industry benefited from arms orders. French pilots and entrepreneurs pioneered aviation in Central America, although German and U.S. aviation interests were not far behind. Whereas the French focused upon pilots and planes, the German and Austrian entrepreneurs organized SCADTA, which soon entered a partnership arrangement with Lufthansa, a large government-supported company, to obtain key concessions in Latin America, and the U.S. government used its geopolitical authority, a close relationship with Pan American Airlines, and its leadership in military aviation to become a major player on the isthmus. The desire of the Central American states for a counterweight to the preponderance of U.S. influence in their region contributed to the successes of the French military and French civil aviation. Throughout the 1920s French society had to struggle against its own internal problems as well as against metropole competition in its effort to regain financial and cultural eminence on the isthmus. But with inconsistent support, French policy achieved only a small part of its goal.

Notes

1. Caron, *An Economic History of Modern France*, 177–308; Asselain, *Histoire économique de la France*; Bernard, *La Fin d'un monde, 1914–1929*, 131–238; Jacques Crokaert, *La Méditerranée américaine: L'Expansion des États-Unis dans la mer des Antilles* (Paris, 1927); Charles Mangin to MAE, July 20, 1921, Amér. 1918–40, CA, num. 21, AMAE; "Amérique du Sud," Sept. 8, 1923, 7N3374, dossier 2, AAT; Lecoq, "Guatemala du 5 au 8 Juillet 1921: Renseignements politiques," Sept. 2, 1921, I BB3 6, dossier 1921, AAM; Charles Mangin, "Autour du continent latin avec le 'Jules Michelet.' II. Le Guatemala-Panama," *Revue des deux mondes* 92 (Oct. 1922): 559–79.

2. Williams, *The Tragedy of American Diplomacy*, 90–161; LaFeber, *Inevitable Revolutions*, 54–67; Zahniser, *Uncertain Friendship*; Duroselle, *La France et les États-Unis*, 131–56; Langley, *The United States and the Caribbean in the*

Twentieth Century, 95–136; Lloyd Gardner, *A Covenant with Power: America and the World Order from Wilson to Reagan* (New York, 1984), 3–28; Lloyd Gardner, *Safe for Democracy: The Anglo-American Response to Revolution, 1913–1923* (New York, 1987), 233–346.

3. Schoonover and Schoonover, "Statistics for the Understanding of the Foreign Intrusion into Central America," 77–119.

4. Victor Bulmer-Thomas, *The Political Economy of Central America since 1920* (Cambridge, Eng., 1987), 25–47; Cardoso, "Central America: The Liberal Era, c. 1870–1930"; Woodward, *Central America*, 182–223; Pérez Brignoli, *Breve historia de Centro-América*, 107–33; Bermann, *Under the Big Stick*, 176–217; Handy, *The Gift of the Devil*, 77–89.

5. "Reisebericht," Gustav Noske to Preußischer Min. des Innern, June 28, 1927, III, M.-Amer., Pol. 15, PAAA; Wallerstein, *Historical Capitalism*, 72, 82.

6. Mangin to MAE, July 20, 1921, Amér. 1918–40, CA, num. 21, AMAE, (copy in 7N3378, Mission Mangin, dossier 3, AAT); proposed route of cruiser *Jules Michelet*, 7N3379, Mission Mangin, dossier 1 (Divers), AAT; Etat-major de l'armée, 2eme bureau, "Renseignements politiques, militaires et économiques sur les différents pays de l'Amérique Latine que doit visiter la mission du Général Mangin," May 23, 1921, 7N3378, dossier 1, Mission Mangin, AAT; Hinam Rivas to MRE, July 25, 1923 (No. 62), H1610, Guat. correspondencia 1913–1930, AMAE, Madrid; Mangin, "Autour du continent latin," 559–79; Carlos J. Perret and Pierre Arthuys, "Rapport sur la situation économique et financière au Guatemala," July 6, 1921, Amér. 1918–40, CA, num. 38, AMAE.

7. Mangin to MAE, July 20, 1921, Amér. 1918–40, CA, num. 21, AMAE; Mangin, "Autour du continent latin," 559–79.

8. Mangin to MAE, July 20, 1921, Amér. 1918–40, CA, num. 21, AMAE; Mangin, "Autour du continent latin," 559–79; Lecoq, "Guatemala: Renseignements économiques," Sept. 2, 1921, I BB^4 6, dossier 1921, AAM; Revelli to MAE, Oct. 21, 1923, F^{30} 1956: Guat., AMEF.

9. Etat-major de l'armée, 2eme bureau, "Renseignements politiques, militaires et économiques sur les différents pays de l'Amérique Latine que doit visiter la mission du Général Mangin," May 23, 1921, 7N3378, dossier 1, Mission Mangin, AAT; Hinam Rivas to MRE, July 25, 1923 (No. 62), H1610, AMAE, Madrid.

10. Hinam Rivas to MAE, July 25, Aug. 8, 1923, H1610, AMAE, Madrid.

11. Perret and Arthuys, "Rapport sur la situation économique et financière au Guatemala," July 6, 1921, Amér. 1918–40, CA, num. 38, AMAE; Simonin to MAE, May 25, 1921, Amér. 1918–40, CA, num. 94; Emmanuel Léonce Neuville to MAE, March 20, 1926, Amér. 1918–40, num. 85, AMAE; Lecoq, "Panama: Renseignements politiques," July 1921, I, BB^4 6, dossier 1921, AAM; Daniel R. Headrick, *The Invisible Weapon: Telecommunications and International Politics, 1851–1945* (New York, 1991), 33, 35, 41–43; Raymond Betts, *Tricouleur: The French Overseas Empire* (London, 1978): 28–29.

12. Wilhelm Erythropel to AA, Jan. 26, 1921, Abt. III, CR, Pol. 10, PAAA.

13. Wilhelm von Kuhlmann to AA, Dec. 10, 1926, III, Guat., Handel 13, PAAA.

14. Serre to MAE, April 26, 1921, Amér. 1918–40, CA, num. 50, AMAE; Serre to MAE, Oct. 7, 1921, Amér. 1918–40, CA, num. 7, AMAE; Serre to

Alvarado Quiros, Nov. 11, 1921, MRE, caja 257, leg.-Francia (Consules extranjeros), AN, CR.

15. Note pour le président, June 16, 1921, Amér. 1918–40, CA, num. 69, AMAE; Nic. chargé to MAE, Aug. 25, 1922, MAE to Medina, [n.d.], F[30] 1996: Nic., AMEF.

16. George Auguste Alexandre Perrot to MAE, May 29, 1921, MAE, Note, June 16, 1921, Amér. 1918–40, CA, num. 71, AMAE.

17. Albert Antoine Revelli to MAE, July 17, 1923, Amér. 1918–40, CA, num. 1, AMAE; Louis Stirnemann to Abbé E. Wetterle, June 27, 1923, MAE to Revelli, Aug. 2, 1923, MAE to Wetterle, Aug. 2, 1923, Amér. 1918–40, CA, num. 76, AMAE; Revelli to MAE, May 23, 1924, Amér. 1918–40, CA, num. 30, AMAE.

18. Revelli to MAE, [Aug., 1923], Amér. 1918–40, CA, num. 1, AMAE; Banana du Río Grande to MAE, Feb. 11, 1927, MAE to Aymé-Martin, April 9, 1927, Aymé-Martin to MAE, July 13, 1927, Feb. 20, 1928, MAE to Tournyre, Aug. 10, 23, 1927, Amér. 1918–40, CA, num. 70, AMAE; Darío Euraque, "The Arab-Jewish Presence in the Honduran Economy, 1880s–1930s: The Case of San Pedro Sula, Cortés," in Ignacio Klich and Jeff Lesser, eds., *Arab and Jewish Immigrants in Latin America* (London, 1998).

19. Association nationale des porteurs français de valeurs mobilières to premier and MAE, Aug. 13, 1920, Min. finances to MAE, Aug. 25, 1920, MAE to Serre, Aug. 31, 1920, Serre to MAE, Oct. 4, 1920, Amér. 1918–40, CA, num. 58, AMAE; Peralta to Alejandro Alvarado Quiros, Jan. 8, 1921, MRE, caja 257, leg.-Francia (Leg. de CR), AN, CR; Serre to MAE, June 5, 1921, Amér. 1918–40, CA, num. 57, AMAE; Serre to MAE, Aug. 16, 1923, Amér. 1918–40, CA, num. 59, AMAE.

20. Perrot to Alvarado Quiros, May 6, 1921, Alvarado Quiros to Perrot, July 20, 1921, MRE, caja 257, leg.-Francia (Leg. extranjeros), AN, CR.

21. Urist to Alvarado Quiros, May 5, 1921, MRE, caja 257, leg.-Francia III, AN, CR; Peretti de la Rocca to Fr. Min. Guat., Aug. 16, 1921, Perrot to MAE, Aug. 17, 1921, Amér. 1918–40, CA, num. 55, AMAE; chargé to MAE, June 3, 1922, F[30] 1924: C.R., AMEF; Neuville to MAE, Sept. 28, Nov. 15, 29, 1922, Amér. 1918–40, CA, num. 58, AMAE.

22. Neuville to MAE, Sept. 28, Nov. 15, 29, 1922, March 18, 1923, Amér. 1918–40, CA, num. 58, AMAE; Tomás Soley Güell to MRE, Nov. 17, 1922, MRE, caja 265, leg.-Hacienda y Comercio, AN, CR; Soley Güell to MRE, Feb. 23, 1923, Peralta to Miguel Obregón, March 16, 1923, MRE, caja 269, leg.-Francia (Leg. de CR), AN, CR.

23. Louis Desrousseaux to MAE, Sept. 10, 1925, MAE to Fr. bondholders, Oct. 1922, Min. finances to MAE, Aug. 13, 1923, Amér. 1918–40, CA, 59, AMAE; AA to Germ. Leg. in Guat., June 1, 1925, Kuhlmann to AA, Sept. 16, 25, 1925, Jan. 4, 1926, III, CR, Finanzwesen 2, PAAA; Grosvenor M. Jones, "Proposed Refunding of Costa Rican-French Loan of 1911," Special Circular No. 118 (Confidential), May 11, 1925, MRE, caja 279, leg.-E.U. consules de CR, AN, CR.

24. Desrousseaux to MAE, Aug. 25, 1924, Sept. 10, 1925, MAE to French bondholders, Oct. 1922, Min. finances to MAE, Aug. 13, 1923, "Note au sujet de l'accord transactionnel intervenu avec l'Etat de Costa Rica pour l'emprunt 5% 1911," Nov. 1928, Chevrier to CR min., Nov. 17, 1929, Amér. 1918–40, CA, 59, AMAE; AA to Germ. leg. in Guat., June 1, 1925, Kuhlmann to AA, Sept. 16, 25, 1925, Jan. 4, 1926, III, CR, Finanzwesen 2, PAAA; Jones,

"Proposed Refunding of Costa Rican-French Loan of 1911," Special Circular No. 118 (Confidential), May 11, 1925, MRE, caja 279, leg.-E.U. consules de CR, AN, CR.

25. Desrousseaux to MAE, May 27, 1924, Amér. 1918–40, CA, num. 51, AMAE; Kroeger to AA, Oct. 16, 1923, III, CR, Postwesen 4, PAAA; Fritz Sauter to Min. Guat., Sept. 15, 1927, III, CR, Postwesen 3, PAAA.

26. Lecoq, "Guatemala: Renseignements économiques," Sept. 2, 1921, I BB[4] 6, dossier 1921, AAM; Serre to MAE, Feb. 28, 1921, Amér. 1918–40, CA, num. 90, AMAE.

27. Lecoq, "Panama: Renseignements politiques," July 1921, I, BB[4] 6, dossier 1921, AAM; Lecoq, "Guatemala: Renseignements économiques," Sept. 2, 1921, Lecoq, "Guatemala du 5 au 8 Juillet 1921: Renseignements politiques," Sept. 2, 1921, I BB[3] 6, dossier 1921, AAM; Serre to MAE, March 8, 15, 1921, Amér. 1918–40, CA, num. 91, AMAE; MID agent in Panama to MID, July 20, 1921, RG 165, MID, 2501–28, NA; Michel Demyk and Noëlle Demyk, "Conflits frontaliers en Amérique centrale," in *Les Phénomènes de "frontière" dans les pays tropicaux* (Paris, 1981), 401–17; Richard Salisbury, *Costa Rica y el istmo, 1900–1934* (San José, 1984).

28. Mangin to MAE, July 21, 1921, 7N3378, Mission Mangin, dossier 3, AAT; Lecoq, "Panama: Renseignements politiques," July 1921, I, BB[4] 6, dossier 1921, AAM; correspondence throughout the 1920s, for example, MAE to Louis Eugène Langlais, Jan. 11, 1927, Langlais to MAE, July 25, 1927, April 12, 14, 1928, March 9, 1929, Amér. 1918–40, CA, num. 93, AMAE; MAE to Delage, July 16, 1923, Delage to MAE, Aug. 27, 1923, Amér. 1918–40, CA, num. 87, AMAE; Neuville to MAE, Oct. 14, 1924, Amér. 1918–40, CA, num. 91, AMAE; LaFeber, *The Panama Canal*, 70–83.

29. Unsigned, "Note sur l'état des relations économiques de la France avec les républiques du Centre-Amérique, du Panama, . . . " 7N3377, dossier 1 (Amér. cent.), AAT; Min. commerce to president du conseil, MAE, Feb. 9, 1921, F[30] 1924: Colombie, AMEF.

30. Serre to MAE, Jan. 4, 1922, MAE to Revelli, March 4, 1922, Revelli to MAE, July 28, 1922, memoranda, June 5, July 5, 8, 1924, Amér. 1918–40, CA, num. 10, AMAE.

31. Leo S. Rowe to A. G. Bates, June 29, 1921, and enclosure, Pacific Mail Steamship Co. records, box 50, folder-Central American Republics, Huntington Library, San Marino, CA; L. Cotty to Dejean de la Batie, June 23, 1922, Amér. 1918–40, CA, num. 93, AMAE; Revelli to MAE, Sept. 4, 19, Dec. 22, 1922, Amér. 1918–40, CA, num. 58, AMAE; Revelli to MAE, July 31, 1924, Adrian Recinos to MAE, Dec. 3, 1924, Aymé-Martin to MAE, Dec. 10, 1926, José Matos to MAE, Jan. 5, 1929, Amér. 1918–40, CA, num. 34, AMAE; Johannes Kretzchmar Bericht, July 14, 1926, III, M.-Amer., Pol. 5, PAAA.

32. Min. Venezuela to MAE, Dec. 18, 1922, MAE to Min. guerre, Jan. 10, 1923, 7N3374, dossier 1, AAT; MAE to prime minister, Nov. 14, 1927, May 24, 1928, Min. guerre to MAE, Dec. 28, 1927, Min. finances to Min. guerre, Nov. 30, 1928, Amér. 1918–40, CA, num. 76, AMAE.

33. Etat-major de l'armée, 2eme bureau, "Renseignements politiques, militaires et économiques sur les différents pays de l'Amérique Latine que doit visiter la mission du Général Mangin," May 23, 1921, 7N3378, dossier 1, Mission Mangin, AAT; Neuville to MAE, March 20, 1926, Amér.

1918–40, num. 85, AMAE; Harry M. Gwynn to War Department (G-2), Sept. 4, 1923, RG 165, MID, 2610-P-8, NA.

34. Revelli to MAE, April 15, 1922, Amér. 1918–40, CA, num. 54, AMAE; Gaston Contresty to Min. guerre, April 17, 1922, 7N1729, dossier Guat., AAT; R. Dean to Peralta, Nov. 24, 1924, J. R. Argüello de Vars to Peralta, Dec. 20, 1924, MRE, caja 273, leg.-Francia, AN, CR; J. Menault, "La pénétration des États-Unis dans l'Amérique centrale et l'Amérique du sud par les lignes aériennes," Feb. 1, 1929, 7N3348, E.U. attaché militaire, AAT; Anthony Sampson, *Empires of the Sky: The Politics, Contests and Cartels of World Airlines* (New York, 1984), 25–26, 45.

35. Mason M. Patrick to adjutant general, Jan. 19, 1925, RG 165, MID, 183–76, NA; W. G. Peace to Gwynn, May 22, 1925, William Lassiter to adjutant general, Aug. 21, 1925, RG 165, MID, 2538-21 (8, 18), NA; C. Chartier to Min. guerre, Dec. 31, 1925, 7N3376, dossier 2 (Guat.), AAT; Aymé-Martin to MAE, Oct. 6, 1928, 7N3376, dossier CR, AAT (copy in F^{30} 1956: Guat., AMEF); Matos to MAE, April 8, 1929, Amér. 1918–40, CA, num. 34, AMAE; Crokaert, *La Méditerranée américaine*, 196–201.

36. Emile Auguste Charles Blaise Gissot to MAE, May 12 (2 items), Aug. 30, 1929, Amér. 1918–40, CA, num. 78, AMAE.

37. Gissot to MAE, Dec. 6, 1929, Amér. 1918–40, CA, num. 78, AMAE.

38. Revelli to MAE, March 23, 1922, Amér. 1918–40, CA, num. 26, AMAE; Revelli to MAE, May 2, 1922, Paris, F^{12} 9243: Guat., Haiti, AN; Revelli to MAE, Oct. 21, 1923, F^{30} 1956: Guat., AMEF.

39. Revelli to MAE, March 14, April 28, May 30, 1923, March 15, 1924, Amér. 1918–40, CA, num. 38, AMAE; Revelli to MAE, Nov. 29, 1924, MAE to Sous-préfet de Guingamp, Dec. 26, 1924, Amér. 1918–40, CA, num. 29, AMAE.

40. Lecoq, "Panama: Renseignements politiques," July 1921, Lecoq, "Guatemala: Renseignements économiques," Sept. 2, 1921, I BB^4 6, dossier 1921, AAM; list, *Boletín de la cámara de comercio de Honduras*, June–July, 1925, III, Hond., Handel 20, PAAA; Gissot to MAE, March 20, 1929, Amér. 1918–40, CA, num. 78, AMAE; Victor Meza and Héctor López, "Las inversiones extranjeras en Honduras antes del Mercado Común Centroamericano," *Economía política* (UNAH, Tegucigalpa) 6 (Sept.–Dec. 1973): 47–80.

41. Revelli to MAE, May 5 and 26, 1922, F^{30} 1956: Guat., AMEF; MAE to Revelli, June 4, 1921, Lezard to MAE, June 7, 1921, Amér. 1918–40, CA, num. 41, AMAE.

42. Revelli to MAE, Jan. 13, 1924, Amér. 1918–40, CA, num. 40, AMAE.

43. Unsigned, "Les Germes de conflit en Amérique du sud et la situation respective des puissances intéressées," Oct. 3, 1928, 7N3375, dossier 2, AAT; Langley, *The United States and the Caribbean in the Twentieth Century*, 95–136; Rippy, "French Investments in Latin America"; Eusebe, "Les Investissements français en Amérique centrale et dans l'aire des Caraïbes"; Rosenberg and Rosenberg, "From Colonialism to Professionalism"; Stalling, *Banker to the Third World*, 58–67.

44. Hinam Rivas to MRE, July 25, 1923 (No. 62), Hinam Rivas to MRE, July 25, 1923 (No. 63), H1610, MAE, Madrid; MAE to Jean-Marie Pierre Delaye, July 16, 1923, Delaye to MAE, Aug. 27, 1923, Amér. 1918–40, CA, num. 87, AMAE; MID agent to "784," Nov. 23, 1923, RG 165, MID, 2347-P-

27, NA; Blankenburg, "Der französische Kapitalexport," 72–75, 106–07; Crokaert, *La Méditerranée américaine*, 121–27.

45. Perrot to MAE, July 2, 1921, Amér. 1918–40, CA, num. 75, AMAE; Revelli to MAE, June 15, 1923, MAE to Min. finances, July 2, 1923, Min. finances to MAE, July 24, 1923, F[30] 1956: Guat., AMEF; MAE to Delaye, July 16, 1923, Delaye to MAE, Aug. 27, 1923, Amér. 1918–40, CA, num. 87, AMAE.

46. Revelli to MAE, Aug. 10, 1922, June 15, Sept. 12, 1923, F[30] 1956: Guat., AMEF.

47. MAE to Min. finances, July 2, 1923, Min. finances to MAE, July 24, 1923, F[30] 1956: Guat., AMEF; MAE to Delaye, July 16, 1923, Delaye to MAE, Aug. 27, 1923, Amér. 1918–40, CA, num. 87, AMAE; Jules Cambon, "La Doctrine de Monroe," *Revue des deux mondes* 98 (Sept. 1, 1928): 90–101; Donald Castillo Rivas, *Acumulación de capital y empresas transnacionales en Centroamérica* (Mexico, 1980).

48. Revelli to MAE, Dec. 3, 1923, Feb. 10, April 9, May 5, 1924, F[30] 1956: Guat., AMEF.

49. Lecoq, "Guatemala du 5 au 8 Juillet 1921: Renseignements politiques," Sept. 2, 1921, I BB[3] 6, dossier 1921, AAM; Hinam Rivas to MRE, July 25, 1923 (No. 62), H1610, MAE, Madrid; Lecoq, "Guatemala: Renseignements économiques," Sept. 2, 1921, I BB[4] 6, dossier 1921, AAM; "Amérique du Sud," Sept. 8, 1923, 7N3374, dossier 2, AAT; Revelli to MAE, May 23, 1924, Amér. 1918–40, CA, num. 30, AMAE.

50. Tattenbach to AA, Aug. 13, 1923, III, Guat., Pol. 8, PAAA; Revelli to MAE, May 11, 1924, Amér. 1918–40, CA, num. 5, AMAE; Revelli to MAE, March 15, 1924, Amér. 1918–40, CA, num. 38, AMAE; Tattenbach to AA, Sept. 1, 1923, III, Guat., Handel 13, PAAA; Kroeger to AA, Sept. 9, 1923, III, Wirtschaft-Frankreich/CR, Handel 12, PAAA.

51. Henri Pourverelle, "Economie du Nicaragua," Oct. 23, 1923, "Note sur le Nicaragua," March 25, 1924, Amér. 1918–40, CA, num. 1, AMAE.

52. Aymé-Martin to MAE, Jan. 26, April 30, 1926, Amér. 1918–40, CA, num. 70, AMAE.

53. Aymé-Martin to MAE, June 30, July 29, Nov. 12, 1926, Amér. 1918–40, CA, num. 46, AMAE.

54. L. Cotty to Dejean de la Batie, June 23, 1922, Amér. 1918–40, CA, num. 93, AMAE; Revelli to MAE, March 9, 1924, Aymé-Martin to MAE, June 11, 1925, Amér. 1918–40, CA, num. 30, AMAE; Chartier to Min. guerre, Dec. 31, 1925, Chartier to MAE, Dec. 12, 1926, 7N3376, dossier 2 (Guat.), AAT; Aymé-Martin to MAE, Jan. 29, 1928, Amér. 1918–40, CA, num. 35, AMAE.

55. Matheu to MAE, Feb. 9, 1921, Amér. 1918–40, CA, num. 75, AMAE; "Guatemala," [1921?], N3376, Mission Mangin, Amér. cent., dossier Guat., AAT; Serre to MAE, May 17, 1921, Amér. 1918–40, CA, num. 69, AMAE; Lecoq, "Guatemala du 5 au 8 Juillet 1921: Renseignements politiques," Sept. 2, 1921, I BB[3] 6, dossier 1921, AAM; MAE to Desrousseaux, Aug. 6, 1924, Amér. 1918–40, CA, num. 63, AMAE.

56. Revelli to MAE, Sept. 22, 1921, Amér. 1918–40, CA, num. 71, AMAE; Min. CA to MAE, March 6, 1922, Amér. 1918–40, CA, num. 30, AMAE; Chartier to MAE, Dec. 12, 1926, 7N3376, AAT.

57. Lecoq, "Guatemala du 5 au 8 Juillet 1921: Renseignements politiques," Sept. 2, 1921, I BB[3] 6, dossier 1921, AAM; Charles Courbin to

Min. CA, Aug. 16, 1929, and supporting documents, Amér. 1918–40, CA, num. 71, AMAE.

58. Aymé-Martin to MAE, Oct. 26, 1928, Amér. 1918–40, CA, num. 7, AMAE; Fernand Pila to Sébastian Charlety, Nov. 3, 1928, and enclosures, Amér. 1918–40, CA, num. 30, AMAE; Aymé-Martin to MAE, Nov. 8, 1928, Amér. 1918–40, CA, num. 45, AMAE; J. A. Aguila Machado to Peralta, April 19, 1929, MRE, l.c. #128, p. 288, AN, CR.

59. Gissot to MAE, Aug. 30, 1929, Amér. 1918–40, CA, num. 78, AMAE.

60. Aymé-Martin to MAE, Nov. 19, 1928, Amér. 1918–40, CA, num. 21, AMAE; Mangin to MAE, July 20, 21, 1921, 7N3378, Mission Mangin, dossier 3, AAT; Delage to MAE, Nov. 26, 1923, Neuville to MAE, April 30, 1926, Amér. 1918–40, CA, num. 91, AMAE.

61. Langlais to MAE, Dec. 18, 1928, Amér. 1918–40, CA, num. 3, AMAE; Langlais to MAE, March 12, 1929, Amér. 1918–40, CA, num. 15, AMAE; "La Diplomacía del dolar: La Tragédie de Panama," *L'Action industrielle et commerciale,* Dec. 1, 1927, 7N3361, dossier Canal du Panama, AAT.

62. Gissot to MAE, Feb. 18, 23, Aug. 24, 1929, Amér. 1918–40, CA, num. 78, AMAE.

63. Aymé-Martin to MAE, April 26, 1929, Gissot to MAE, Aug. 2, 1929, Amér. 1918–40, CA, num. 8, AMAE; Kuhlmann to AA, Sept. 9, 1929, Memo of conversation with El Salvador's minister, Nov. 29, 1929, III, San Salv., Pol. 2, PAAA.

Conclusion and Epilogue

France matured into a metropole state with strands of political, economic, financial, social, and strategic interests binding it to regions on the periphery and semiperiphery. French entrepreneurs sought a tapline to the accumulation of surplus value from the isthmian region and especially from the transit that would connect the Atlantic and Pacific half-worlds. France's foreign relations experienced major shifts by altering its exploitation of the factors of production, expanding its distribution system, developing different consumption patterns, and acquiring new security needs. Developments in Central American societies and the competition with other metropole states for access to Central American raw materials, consumer markets, and investment opportunities influenced France's quest for well-being and security.

France's relationship with Central America varied considerably over the years. In the early decades after Central American independence in 1823, French trade remained appreciable; French ideas, language, and culture were highly valued on the isthmus; and French promoters acquired concessions near the interoceanic transit routes at Panama and Nicaragua. The political instability of the restoration and July monarchies in France, however, temporarily diverted attention from international affairs, especially from areas as distant as Latin America. Once in power, Napoleon III's government nurtured interest in a revived French empire and acted aggressively in the Caribbean-Central American region. In response to domestic economic problems, French entrepreneurs and promoters pursued two policies in Central America. They encouraged interoceanic transit schemes that would exchange French goods for foodstuffs and raw materials and help maintain higher production and employment levels; and they pursued colonization schemes, such as those of Félix Belly and Gabriel Lafond, to exploit the surplus domestic labor. On the international level, the fear of restricted access to raw materials, labor, or capital drove domestic businesses into pools, trusts, larger corporations, holding companies, cartels, and transnational (or multinational) corporations. The Franco-British Commerce Treaty of 1860 and the decline in France's population growth just after mid-nineteenth century contributed to a thirty-five year stagnation in the French economy. A more aggressive relationship to the periphery and semiperiphery was expected to alleviate the stagnation and related domestic social, economic, and political tensions.

In the 1860s and 1870s the mixed results from Napoleon III's expansionism, the economic consequences of the Franco-Prussian War, long-standing French economic and trade policies, plus the decline in foreign trade, contributed to a stagnating domestic market. Although France sought outlets first in the Mediterranean, African, Asian, and Caribbean areas, it later attempted to secure a position in Central America. It opposed unobtrusively the Monroe Doctrine and the U.S. vision of pan-americanism, which rejected an open door policy for Latin America in favor of a privileged position for U.S. power. From 1868 to 1884, French merchants exported to Central America in monetary values that were not surpassed until the 1920s. The French presence in Central America shifted direction in the 1880s when a French company under Ferdinand de Lesseps undertook to build a canal at Panama. Beginning about 1880, consistently large purchases of raw materials from the isthmus strengthened the French economy's interests in this part of the periphery. French business circles recognized that to protect their maritime interests in any interoceanic route, France would have to improve its relations with the isthmian nations. At the turn of the century, French trade began a slow retreat from Central America in response to mismanagement of the Panama Canal project, the general economic slump in France, and U.S. opposition.

Nevertheless, the impulse of French financiers to invest in Central America did not abate in the decades after the Universal Interoceanic Canal Company went bankrupt. French officials and intellectuals argued that the nation's human and financial sacrifices for the project gave it the right to exert a major influence in the region and to recover some of the capital that had been lost. From 1880 until 1903, French financiers were the largest foreign investors on the isthmus. When the tension between France and Germany rose in the first years of the twentieth century, French leaders retreated slowly from their policy of financial and technological expansion. French investors on the isthmus surrendered hesitantly in the years between 1903 and 1914. The French government approved a large loan to Nicaragua in 1909, but withdrew it in the face of extraordinary pressure from Washington. French financiers made major loans to El Salvador in 1910 and to Costa Rica in 1911. A second large Salvadoran loan approved in 1911 collapsed under official U.S. objections. Except for U.S. opposition, covert as well as overt, French financiers would have remained the largest foreign investors on the isthmus until World War I.

From the turn of the century until the Great Depression, French military missions were common on the isthmus, despite the U.S. policy of limiting foreign influence where it affected strategic defense of the transit area. Prewar competition among the French, German, British, and U.S. interests remains the key to understanding metropole intrusions in Middle America. The disruption of war facilitated metropole manipulations to control access and accumulation on the isthmus. During World War I, the United States secured formal political and strategic and informal economic hegemony in the Caribbean and Central American area by using its economic and political power to displace foreign, including French, interests on the isthmus. During the war, French participation in Central America's political economy declined more sharply than even the larger German share. Although ostensibly a victor nation, France bore heavy demographic and economic losses in its homeland and suffered a great deterioration in its commercial and financial position around the world.

In the small nations of the isthmus, the rise of U.S. power after 1898 and through the 1920s stimulated much rancor; but French officials and businessmen usually lacked the means to undertake projects that would take advantage of the anti-Americanism. Although entrepreneurs from Germany (the vanquished nation) recovered well in the 1920s, victorious France struggled to retain its cultural influence, and its efforts to regain a strong economic and financial role in Central America proved unsuccessful. An unstable currency and a slow domestic economic recovery handicapped the efforts of French businesses to revive commercial activity. Without the political capacity to demand equal opportunity in the region, the French government had to settle for whatever modest opportunities the United States chose to allow.

Metropole rivalry had a profound, lasting, and transforming impact on the Central American states, which struggled to find a secure role in the revised world order. In general, metropole initiatives and expansion generated the ongoing difficulties between metropole powers, such as France, and states on the periphery, such as the five Central American republics. When Central American leaders, upon occasion, sent agents to the United States or Europe to obtain capital, colonists, or technologies, they usually sought advantageous alternatives to foreign groups or schemes that had proposed development projects. The isthmian states formulated policies and undertook specific activities in an effort to accomplish their desired objectives, but they lacked any means to assure respect or fair treatment for their proposals. The huge power imbalances between the periphery and the metropoles largely determined the success of the metropole state.

When liberal, industrial states such as France confronted domestic economic crisis, they often decided that escape from their socioeconomic problems could be achieved by expanding the area of competition and accumulation within the world system. Other metropole and some semiperiphery states pursued similar courses. By the late nineteenth century, the Central American states were swamped with hordes of metropole agents pushing development schemes. Up and down the isthmus, domestic comprador leaders, convinced that positivist programs meant material progress, readily agreed to development projects. Soon these states gave foreign interests control or significant influence over their internal communications, public utilities, national debt, currency, state revenue, judiciary, and other economic and political activities, which collectively represented the national production and distribution of wealth. These states had participated in restricting their own sovereignty, and they were incorporated by bits and pieces—often through enclaves—into the broadening exploitation and accumulation system of the metropoles.

The consequence was rampant metropole competition (encouraged because the sovereign resistance of the periphery was weakened), the excesses of which were largely unchecked by the traditionally weak institutions of international law. This competition intimidated the host Central American states not only because they were pressured to take sides in major metropole conflicts, such as World War I, but also because they were forced to make similar choices on concessions for canals, steamship lines, loans, and so forth. Until 1914 the French had appreciable success in obtaining access to opportunities on the isthmus.

Thereafter, the efforts of French entrepreneurs and financiers were generally less well rewarded. Central American leaders complained that their nations' economies were largely ignored during and immediately after World War I as the metropoles decided alone on the priorities of the world economy.

The depression of the 1930s destroyed economic recovery on the isthmus and facilitated the rise of harsh, dictatorial leaders (commonly compradors) in every Central American nation. Costa Rica under its president and kingmaker Rafael Angel Calderón Guardia from 1940 to 1948 (until displaced by José Figueres in the 1949 revolution), and Honduras under President Tiburcio Carías Andino from 1932 to 1948 were governed only slightly less callously than Nicaragua (under Anastasio Somoza Debayle), El Salvador (under Maximiliano Hernández Martínez), and Guatemala (under Jorge Ubico). The dictators established order and assured the continuation of foreign exploitation of the land and labor, a step that satisfied both the multinational firms and the domestic comprador groups that benefited from this exploitation, thus reaffirming the alliance supporting dictatorial rule.

U.S. hegemony in Central America seemed secure in the 1930s, but the contradictory and unstable nature of transnational, corporate capitalism allowed little room for self-confidence in a highly competitive world system. Investment data indicate that French capital had recovered from the early twentieth-century sale of the Panama Canal Company and the losses of World War I. French investors had placed 217 million francs in Middle America in 1938, and this figure increased to about 635 million francs in 1943. In 1943, French capital was largely in Guatemala (400 million francs, much of that possibly in Vichy French dummy firms that acquired German property) and in Costa Rica (120 million francs). Panama (59.24 million francs) and El Salvador (53.8 million francs) were secondary places of French investment. Nicaragua and Honduras possessed insignificant amounts of French capital (Table 6).

The Great Depression and World War II shattered the remnants of French economic and cultural influence in Central America. After World War II, French entrepreneurs and government officials followed a course of modest economic and political activity in Central America. One period of exception, the 1960s, was related to President Charles de Gaulle's persistent attempt to resurrect a pan-Latin movement, recalling in some ways Napoleon III's pan-Latin vision of the 1850s and 1860s.

In the early nineteenth century, France was one of the world's major commercial powers. By the late nineteenth century, it had become the second most important capital-exporting nation. Its well-being, economic growth, and accumulation rates were intertwined with the world economy. Many of its policies and programs, both private and public, were responses to disturbances in its domestic social order. When its social order failed to adjust well to industrialization, France crafted imperial and colonial policies that were aimed at alleviating the material, emotional, and cultural shortcomings of French society. It was not exceptional in this regard. Almost every nation or entrepreneurial group around the world dreamed of benefiting from better integration into the world economy.

Social imperialism—responses to home-country internal disorders that are implemented on a worldwide economic and strategic battlefield—guided French leaders through the nineteenth century. Between 1820 and 1870 it led them to resolve dysfunctions in production, labor, and the social order, with colonization schemes, commercial initiatives, and efforts to rebuild French prestige and influence through isthmian promotions. After the 1870s, France sought transit projects and related enterprises in Central America to utilize its technology, engineering, and capital in a form that could benefit specific domestic classes, the nation's emotional state, and national material objectives. It fostered private and public cultural and social programs that were intended to solidify its self-proclaimed cultural mission and more than incidentally facilitate its commercial and financial penetration of the isthmus. The Great War seriously disrupted France's worldwide efforts, but French leaders saw good opportunities in Middle America for reviving its commerce and its cultural influence and for strengthening its security by hindering German recovery and placating U.S. aspirations.

In sum, France's relations with Central America, both public and private, reflected the economic, cultural, and security aspirations of a western European metropole state. France turned to Central America as one of two transit systems (the other being Suez) capable of joining two half-worlds into a unified whole that would facilitate world-scale capital accumulation. The cultural and economic policies that guided French relations with Central American states were intended to fulfill the objectives of the various elites, factions, and enterprises that participated in the decision making, implementation, and administration of governmental policies. French officials and businessmen used diplomacy to assist technology and engineering, investment, and cultural programs that aimed to promote French civilization on the isthmus. The historical record shows that these policies did not always serve French interests well, in part because French subordinates in Central America often failed to implement them with sympathy and intelligence and in part because metropole competition within the world system commonly limited the success of any metropole. It also shows—the other side of the coin—how Central American societies responded to this crippling process.

Appendix: French Economic Ties with Central America, 1827–1943

Table 1. French Settlers in Central America, 1827–1927

Year	*Guatemala*	*Nicaragua*	*El Salvador*	*Costa Rica*	*Honduras*	*Panama*	*Central America*
1827	100[a]						
1844	30[b]						
1850						400[c]	
1852			22[d]				
1859				215–265[e]			
1861		12–15[f]	50[f]	20–25[f]	12–15[f]		
1864				64[g]			
1876		40[h]		60[h]			
1883	85[i]			198[i]			
1885	50[j]	12[j]	2[j]		15–20[j]		200[j]
1886					50[k]		
1887					72[l]		
1888				233[g]			
1890				233[m]			
1892			40[n]	189[g]	50[n]		
1892/4	200–400[o]	54[p]	65[p]	325[p]	58[p]	1,925[p]	4,000[p]
1897				400[f]			
1899		100[q]					
1902					48[f]		
1904		200[f]			50[f]		
1906				500[r]			
1907		112[r]			200[r]	200[r]	
1910	1,100[s]	100	1,250	300	300	3,050	
1920		200[t]					
1921	130[u]	60[u]	250[u]	150[u]	50[u]	450[u]	1,090[u]
1923	150[v]			200[w]			

1924	350[x]		250[w]
1927		327[g]	

[a]F. L. Voidet de Beaufort to MAE, June 20, 1827, CP 1871, Amér. cent., v. 1, AMAE.
[b]Men only, R. Baradère to MAE, Feb. 20, 1844, CP 1871, Amér. cent., v. 4, AMAE.
[c]A. Vanvert de Méan, "Note sur l'isthme et de ville de Panama," July 22, 1850, A.E.B. ^{III} 455, Fonds des affaires étrangères, AN.
[d]Lapelin to Odet-Pellion, March 26, 1852, Marine BB^4 1596, AAM.
[e]Also est. 200–250, Nugent de Majoureaux, renseignements, *Constantine*, July 1859, Marine BB^4 1023, AN.
[f]Eusèbe, "Les Investissements français en Amérique centrale et dans l'aire des caraïbes," 12.
[g]Chester Jones, *Costa Rica and Civilization in the Caribbean* (Madison, 1935).
[h]Seignlay to Périgot, June 24, 1876, BB^4 1075, AAM.
[i]Forty-two men, Marie Emile LeBrun to MAE, July 30, 31, 1883, Affaires divers commerciales, carton 258, AMAE.
[j]Descamps to admiral, March 2, 1885, BB^4 1596, AAM. About two hundred French in Central America. Only La Libertad in Salvador.
[k]Cochet to Min. marine, June 5, 1886, BB^4 1193, AAM.
[l]Charles A. Brand, "The Background of Capitalistic Underdevelopment: Honduras to 1913" (Ph.D. diss., University of Pittsburgh, 1972), 57, quoting Honduras, *Censo de 1887*.
[m]French vice-consul list, Oct. 25, 1890, CCC, San José, CR, v. 1, AMAE.
[n]J. Gourdoy to Min. marine, March 15, 1892, BB^4 1596, AAM.
[o]Ninety-eight names in the French commercial registry, Alfred Charpentier to MAE, March 8, 1894, Affaires divers commerciales, carton 258, AMAE.
[p]Estimates based on men only figures, lists in Commerce, F^{127414}, AN. Total of four thousand French in Central America.
[q]R. Duval to Min. marine, Feb. 11, 1899, BB^4 1319, AAM.
[r]Pector, *Les Richesses de l'Amérique centrale*, 291–92, men, women, and children.
[s]Ernst B. Filsinger [consul of Costa Rica and Ecuador], "Immigration—A Central American Problem," *Annals of the American Academy of Political and Social Science* 37:3 (May 1911): 167.
[t]1920 Nicaraguan census, Paul Adolphe Serre to MAE, May 17, 1921, Amér. 1918–40, CA, num. 69, AMAE. Nicaragua had 10,375 foreign residents.
[u]Men, Mission Mangin, "Guatemala," [1921?], N3376, Amér. cent., dossier Guat., AAT. Total of 1,090 French in Central America.
[v]Men, unsigned, "Guatemala," Oct. 2, 1923, Amér. 1918–40, CA, num. 72, AMAE.
[w]Désiré Pector, *Régions isthmiques de l'Amérique tropicale* (Paris, 1925), 44, 93.
[x]Hugo Grothe, *Die Deutschen in Übersee* (Berlin, 1932), 70.

Table 2. French Imports from and Exports to Central America, 1840–1906*

Year	French imports from Central America (in francs)	Central America (% total French imports)	Total French imports (in francs)	French exports to Central America (in francs)	Central America (% total French exports)	Total French exports (in francs)
1840	—	—	—	11,865	0.00	695,000,000
1841	—	—	—	106,325	0.01	760,700,000
1850	296,552	0.03	790,700,000	—	—	—
1851	215,761	0.03	765,100,000	561,703	0.05	1,158,100,000
1852	562,661	0.06	980,400,000	884,977	0.07	1,256,900,000
1853	199,349	0.02	1,195,100,000	1,025,962	0.07	1,541,900,000
1854	420,202	0.03	1,291,600,000	916,957	0.06	1,413,700,000
1855	1,215,311	0.08	1,594,100,000	1,498,585	0.10	1,557,900,000
1856	1,064,595	0.05	1,989,500,000	640,533	0.03	1,893,000,000
1857	2,196,244	0.12	1,872,900,000	689,807	0.04	1,865,800,000
1858	2,866,520	0.17	1,640,700,000	791,812	0.04	1,887,300,000
1859	2,370,149	0.15	1,640,700,000	1,207,054	0.05	2,266,400,000
1860	927,157	0.05	1,897,300,000	850,802	0.04	2,277,000,000
1861	1,081,853	0.05	2,442,300,000	837,690	0.04	1,926,300,000
1862	680,475	0.03	2,193,600,000	371,363	0.02	2,242,700,000
1863	787,778	0.03	2,426,400,000	38,208	0.00	2,612,600,000
1864	1,010,097	0.04	2,528,200,000	668,888	0.03	2,924,200,000
1865	892,500	0.03	2,641,800,000	138,419	0.00	3,088,400,000
1866	541,123	0.02	2,793,500,000	801,227	0.03	3,180,600,000
1867	972,463	0.03	3,026,500,000	871,702	0.03	2,825,900,000
1868	832,318	0.03	3,303,700,000	1,359,611	0.05	2,789,900,000
1869	1,629,702	0.05	3,153,100,000	1,374,855	0.05	3,074,900,000
1870	3,500,604	0.12	2,867,400,000	2,548,022	0.10	2,802,100.000

1871	1,443,076	0.04	3,566,700,000	3,837,482	0.13	2,872,500,000
1872	778,335	0.02	3,570,300,000	4,697,395	0.13	3,761,600,000
1873	495,493	0.01	3,554,800,000	3,675,196	0.10	3,787,300,000
1874	1,100,026	0.03	3,507,700,000	2,042,632	0.06	3,701,100,000
1875	896,600	0.03	3,536,700,000	2,297,860	0.06	3,872,600,000
1876	1,402,748	0.04	3,988,700,000	2,841,032	0.08	3,575,600,000
1877	1,057,547	0.03	3,679,800,000	2,615,197	0.08	3,436,300,000
1878	2,308,243	0.06	4,176,200,000	2,893,486	0.09	3,179,700,000
1879	2,575,441	0.06	4,595,200,000	3,173,111	0.10	3,231,300,000
1880	2,553,370	0.05	5,033,200,000	2,625,092	0.08	3,467,900,000
1881	2,767,934	0.06	4,863,400,000*	4,123,630	0.12	3,561,500,000
1882	2,781,644	0.06	4,821,800,000	2,284,480	0.06	3,574,400,000
1883	4,358,891	0.09	4,804,300,000	1,336,532	0.04	3,451,900,000
1884	3,851,231	0.09	4,343,500,000	1,387,796	0.04	3,232,500,000
1885	4,604,168	0.11	4,088,400,000	623,942	0.02	3,088,100,000
1886	2,215,658	0.05	4,208,100,000	784,615	0.02	3,248,800,000
1887	5,224,230	0.13	4,026,000,000	994,364	0.03	3,246,500,000
1888	4,182,512	0.10	4,107,000,000	966,623	0.03	3,246,700,000
1889	3,786,152	0.09	4,316,800,000	947,041	0.03	3,703,900,000
1890	7,404,761	0.17	4,436,900,000	1,080,130	0.03	3,753,400,000
1891	3,733,305	0.08	4,767,900,000	933,246	0.03	3,569,700,000
1892	2,838,237	0.07	4,188,100,000	462,663	0.01	3,460,700,000
1893	2,233,554	0.06	3,853,700,000	496,173	0.02	3,236,400,000
1894	2,786,236	0.07	3,850,400,000	574,391	0.02	3,078,100,000
1895	2,764,092	0.07	3,719,600,000	634,836	0.02	3,373,800,000
1896	3,142,157	0.08	3,798,600,000	1,477,365	0.04	3,400,900,000
1897	2,344,168	0.06	3,956,000,000	954,552	0.03	3,598,000,000
1898	1,544,008	0.03	4,472,500,000	369,482	0.01	3,510,900,000
1899	1,860,427	0.04	4,518,300,000	311,292	0.01	4,152,600,000
1900	1,981,006	0.04	4,697,800,000	528,000	0.01	4,108,700,000
1901	2,451,018	0.06	4,369,200,000	497,000	0.01	4,012,900,000

Year	French imports from Central America (in francs)	Central America (% total French imports)	Total French imports (in francs)	French exports to Central America (in francs)	Central America (% total French exports)	Total French exports (in francs)
1902	2,605,000	0.06	4,394,000,000	413,000	0.01	4,252,200,000
1903	3,469,421	0.07	4,801,300,000	676,000	0.02	4,252,200,000
1904	2,183,205	0.05	4,502,300,000	695,000	0.02	4,451,000,000
1905	3,533,099	0.07	4,778,900,000	1,003,000	0.02	4,866,900,000
1906	4,901,070	0.09	5,627,200,000	1,816,000	0.03	5,265,500,000

Sources: France, Statistique générale de la France, *Annuaire statistique de la France, 1926, 1930, 1939* (Paris, 1927, 1931, 1941), 94–95, 100–101, 55; Roses-Alvarado, "Les Échanges commerciaux entre la France et l'Amérique centrale: 1850–1930," 134–39.
*Commerce special.

Table 3. French Imports from Central America, 1907–1930* (in thousands of French francs)

Year	From Guatemala	From El Salvador	From Honduras	From Nicaragua	From Costa Rica	Total from Central America	Central America (as % of French imports)	Total French imports from the World
1907	151	1,908	7	2,475	585	5,126	0.08	6,223,000
1908	19	1,241	122	1,873	169	3,424	0.06	5,640,500
1909	42	1,056	—	2,220	241	3,559	0.06	6,216,100
1910	73	1,109	59	1,658	410	3,309	0.05	7,173,300
1911	182	1,043	87	2,893	490	4,695	0.06	8,065,800
1912	11	1,235	—	2,674	685	4,605	0.06	8,230,800
1913	102	1,600	136	1,522	439	3,799	0.05	8,421,300

1914	—	—	—	—	—	3,006	0.05	6,402,200
1915	—	647	11	3,624	640	4,922	0.04	11,035,800
1916	3	1,030	42	1,994	519	3,588	0.02	20,640,400
1917	—	4,036	157	4,637	613	9,443	0.03	27,554,000
1918	—	9,778	582	4,522	462	15,344	0.07	22,306,400
1919	321	23,981	880	12,291	284	37,757	0.11	35,799,300
1920	3,427	24,876	766	25,264	4,748	59,081	0.12	49,904,900
1921	121	9,582	4	10,106	334	20,147	0.09	22,755,200
1922	198	17,964	124	18,218	1,322	37,826	0.16	24,275,100
1923	813	17,401	110	23,445	1,539	43,308	0.13	32,859,500
1924	2,290	12,256	412	34,216	3,557	52,731	0.13	40,162,800
1925	1,474	16,849	510	36,710	4,534	60,077	0.14	44,095,300
1926	728	9,679	1,681	81,093	12,806	105,987	0.18	59,598,300
1927	2,948	12,318	1,787	48,614	13,317	78,984	0.15	53,049,900
1928	4,583	8,711	4,849	33,429	4,054	55,626	0.10	53,435,600
1929	4,832	9,417	3,713	31,605	1,584	51,151	0.09	58,220,600
1930	2,645	13,154	10,293	27,552	2,251	55,895	0.11	52,344,400

Sources: France, Statistique générale de la France, *Annuaire statistique de la France* (Paris, [1947]), 55; Roses-Alvarado, "Les Échanges commerciaux entre la France et l'Amérique centrale: 1850–1930," 134–39.

*Commerce special; current francs.

Table 4. French Exports to Central America, 1907–1930* (in thousands of French francs)

Year	To Guatemala	To El Salvador	To Honduras	To Nicaragua	To Costa Rica	Total exports to Central America	Central America (as % of French exports)	Total French exports to the World
1907	838	209	61	197	800	2,105	0.04	5,596,100
1908	405	269	78	65	754	1,571	0.03	5,050,700
1909	131	329	38	139	541	1,178	0.02	5,718,100
1910	175	332	61	96	620	1,284	0.02	6,232,800
1911	200	476	50	235	828	1,789	0.03	6,078,900
1912	157	364	87	95	862	1,479	0.02	6,712,600
1913	344	351	65	465	884	2,109	0.03	6,880,200
1914	—	—	—	—	—	1,292	0.03	4,868,800
1915	89	630	66	92	112	989	0.03	3,937,400
1916	349	1,191	89	468	299	2,396	0.04	6,214,500
1917	641	1,069	200	586	310	2,806	0.05	6,012,700
1918	372	1,001	113	266	143	1,895	0.04	4,722,700
1919	1,782	1,452	190	305	509	4,238	0.04	11,879,600
1920	2,455	4,567	397	2,114	1,082	10,615	0.04	26,894,900
1921	1,044	3,270	601	1,381	731	7,027	0.04	19,772,500
1922	6,231	1,935	501	633	1,104	10,404	0.05	21,378,900
1923	6,231	5,354	2,109	1,451	3,158	18,303	0.06	30,866,800
1924	8,510	6,440	1,661	3,764	4,961	25,336	0.06	42,368,900
1925	5,456	9,507	1,616	3,665	6,927	23,871	0.05	45,754,900
1926	14,357	20,452	3,246	4,446	6,426	48,927	0.08	59,677,900
1927	8,914	13,350	2,180	6,776	7,083	38,303	0.07	54,924,800
1928	9,587	15,573	2,744	6,095	6,484	40,483	0.08	51,374,700

1929	13,928	15,463	4,676	6,461	7,486	48,014	0.10	50,139,200
1930	7,731	10,721	5,228	3,924	3,534	31,138	0.07	42,829,700

Sources: France, Statistique générale de la France, *Annuaire statistique de la France*; Roses-Alvarado, "Les Échanges commerciaux entre la France et l'Amérique centrale: 1850–1930," 134–39.
[*]Commerce special; current francs.

Table 5. French Firms in Central America, 1852–1907

Year	*Guatemala*	*Nicaragua*	*El Salvador*	*Costa Rica*	*Honduras*
1852	2[a]	1[a]	2–3[a]		0[a]
1861	2[b]				
1871				1	
1874				8[c]	
1876				3[d]	
1879	9[e]				
1882					2[f]
1885	6[g]	2[g]	4[g]	1[g]	1[g]
1889				4[h]	
1890					15[i]
1907	9[j]				

[a]T. de Lapelin to Marie-Joseph A. Odet-Pellion, March 26, 1852, Marine BB[4] 1596, AAM.
[b]One joint German-British, René Louis Adolphe de Botmilian to MAE, Feb. 1, 1861, CCC, Guat., v. 6, AMAE.
[c]Commander Miet, renseignements, *Hermitte*, Jan.–April 1874, Marine BB[4] 1396, AAM.
[d]"Solid firms," du Seignlay to Perigot, June 24, 1876, BB[4] 1075, AAM.
[e]Firms signing complaint against augmented Guatemalan customs duties, CCC, Guat., v. 9, AMAE.
[f]In Amapala, Chateaumincis to admiral, Jan. 7, 1883, BB[4] 1596, AAM.
[g]Descamps to admiral, March 2, 1885, BB[4] 1596, AAM. Only La Unión and San Salvador in El Salvador, León in Nicaragua.

[h]Eduardo Hernández Alcarón, "Comercio y dependencia en Costa Rica durante los años 1880–1890," *Anuario de estudios centroamericanos* 3 (1977): 258.

[i]French vice-consul list, Oct. 25, 1890, CCC, San José, CR, v. 1., AMAE.

[j]Involved in Franco-Guatemalan commerce, Charles H. Stephan, *Le Guatemala économique* (Paris, 1907).

Table 6. French Investment in Central America, 1896–1943[*]

Year	*Guatemala*	*Nicaragua*	*El Salvador*	*Costa Rica*	*Honduras*	*Panama*	*Central America*
1896						220mF	350mF[a]
1902	8.62mF	6.15mF	10.45mF	10mF	6.5mF	220mF	267mF
1906	3.75mF[b]						
1913	9mF	6mF	12mF	38mF	7mF	0.5mF	88mF
1918		25mF[c]	20mF				
1919		2.5mF[d]	10m$[e]				
1938							217mF
1943	400mF	1.8mF	53.8mF	120mF	0.28mF	59.24mF	

Sources: [a]United Nations, *El financiamiento externo de América Latina* (New York, 1964); Organization of American States, *Foreign Investment in Latin America* (Washington, DC, 1955); "La Fortune française à l'étranger," 476–77; R.-G. Levy, "Les Capitaux français à l'étranger," 477; Poidevin, *Les Relations économiques et financières entre la France et l'Allemagne de 1898 à 1914*, 36–40; Frédéric Mauro, "Les Investissements français en Amérique latine xixe–xxe siècles," in Maurice Lévy-Leboyer, ed., *La Position internationale de la France: Aspects éconómiques et financières xixe–xxe siècles* (Paris, 1974), 193–202; Rippy, "French Investments in Latin America."

[*]m = million; b = billion; M = German marks; F = French francs; $ = U.S. dollars.

[a]Includes about 220mF invested in the Panama Canal and 80mF in the Honduran Railroad.

[b]Stephan, *Le Guatemala économique*.

[c]Banana du Río Grande to MAE, April 1, 1919, Amér 1918–40, CA, num. 68, AMAE.

[d]Chayet to MAE, Nov. 9, 1919, Amér. 1918–40, CA, num. 75, AMAE.

[e]Chayet to MAE, Jan. 21, 1919, Amér. 1918–40, CA, num. 68 (Nic.), AMAE.

Table 7. Foreign Investment in Central America, 1839–1939*

Year	*French*	*German*	*British*	*United States*
1839			0.0679m£[a]	
1880			7.5m£	
1890			11.7m£	
1896	350mF			
1897				11.5m$
1899		67.12m$[b]		
1900		250mM[c]		
1902	267mF[d]			
1906		300mF[c]		
1908				31.8m$
1909				50.0m$[f]
1912				47.5m$[f]
1913	88mF		118.6m$	
1914			21m£	82m$
1919				96.3m$
1923				67.3m$[f]
1924				119m$
1929				201.7m$
1930			126.3m$	227.1m$
1938	217mF			
1939			13m£	

Sources:United Nations, *El financiamiento externo de América Latina*; Organization of American States, *Foreign Investment in Latin America*; "La Fortune française à l'étranger," 476–77; R.-G. Levy, "Les Capitaux français à l'étranger," 477; Poidevin, *Les Relations économiques et financières entre la France et l'Allemagne de 1898 à 1914*, 36–40; Mauro, "Les Investissements français en Amérique latine xixe–xxe siècles," 193–202; Rippy, "French Investments in Latin America," 52–71.

*m = million; b = billion; M = German marks; F = French francs; $ = U.S. dollars; £ = British pound

[a]Central American Federation external debt upon dissolving, Victor Quintana Díaz, *Inversiones extranjeras en Guatemala* (Guatemala, 1973), 34.
[b]U.S. Manufacturer's Bureau, *Monthly Consular and Trade Report* (Washington, DC, 1900), v. 63, no. 239, pp. 460–61, in José Francisco Guevara-Escudero, "Nineteenth Century Honduras: A Regional Approach to the Economic History of Central America, 1839–1914," 419.
[c]Henri Monod to MAE, June 28, 1900, Affaires divers commerciales, carton 280—Missions commerciales (1896–1901), AMAE.
[d]Includes 220mF invested in the Panama Canal, but excludes 80mF invested in the Honduran Railroad.
[e]Pector, *Les Richesses de l'Amérique centrale*, 298–99.
[f]Grosvenor M. Jones to Emmet, March 28, 1926, RG 151, 620-Lt. Amer., NA.

Bibliography

In addition to the extensive holdings of the Archive du ministère des affaires étrangères, Paris offers the researcher many other sources of material on French relations with Central America. The Archive de l'armée de la mer, Château de Vincennes, is a mine of information for the nineteenth century. Reports of naval officers describe the role of other competitive powers as well as the role of the French in investment and firm operation and as colonists. The Archive de l'armée de la terre, Château de Vincennes, holds little on the nineteenth century but contains interesting material for the years after the French established military missions on the isthmus. Useful materials are also found in the Archive du ministère de l'économie et des finances and the Archives nationales. Guides to archives for the study of French-Central American relations include France, Archives nationales, *Guide des sources de l'histoire de l'Amérique latine et des Antilles dans les archives françaises* (Paris: Archives nationales, 1984); Kenneth J. Grieb et al., eds., *Research Guide to Central America and the Caribbean* (Madison: University of Wisconsin Press, 1985); Thomas Schoonover, "European Primary Research Materials on Nineteenth Century Relations with Central America," *The Americas* 31 (April 1975): 514–17; and Thomas Schoonover, "The Guatemalan Foreign Ministry Archives at the Archivo General de Centro América," *Society for Historians of American Foreign Relations Newsletter* 23 (June 1992): 10–24.

Outside of France the records of other nations allow different insights into French activity on the isthmus. In the United States, National Archives, Record Groups 59 and 165 describe French activity. The holdings of two German archives—the Politisches Archiv des Auswärtigen Amts (Bonn) and the former Deutsches Zentrales Staatsarchiv, now the Bundesarchiv, Merseburg—illuminate German perspectives on French activity. The Costa Rican Archivos Nacionales and the Guatemalan Archivo General de Centro América shed light on the cultural closeness that developed between the French and the Costa Ricans and Guatemalans in the nineteenth and twentieth centuries.

Archival Sources

Costa Rica

Archivos Nacionales, San José
  Relaciones exteriores
    cajas numbered 1–233
    libros copiadores

Federal Republic of Germany

Bundesarchiv, Merseburg (formerly Deutsches Zentrales Staatsarchiv)
  Abteilung II, Auswärtiges Amt
Industrie- und Handelskammer, Dortmund
Politisches Archiv des Auswärtigen Amts, Bonn
  Abteilung IA: Columbien; Galápagos Inseln; Handel; Panama; San Salvador
  Abteilung II: Wirtschaft—Frankreich / Costa Rica
  Politische Abteilung III: Costa Rica; Guatemala; Honduras; Mittel-Amerika; San Salvador

France

Archive de l'armée de la mer, Paris
  Series: BB^4, BB^7, and BB^8
Archive de l'armée de la terre, Paris
  2ème Bureau, Attachés militaires
Archive du ministère de l'économie et des finances, Paris
  Series: B and F^{30}
Archive du ministère des affaires étrangères, Paris
  Affaires divers, commerciales
  Affaires divers, politiques
  Correspondance commerciale et consulaire (CCC), 1793–1901: Colón; Guatemala; Panama; San José de Costa Rica; San Salvador
  Correspondance politique (CP) à 1871: Amérique centrale
  Correspondance politique (CP), 1871 à 1896; Amérique centrale; Amérique latine; Costa Rica; Guatemala; Honduras; Nicaragua; Panama; San Salvador

Correspondance politique et commerciale (CP), 1897–1918 (Nouvelle série): Amérique centrale; Amérique latine; Costa Rica; Guatemala; Honduras; Nicaragua; Panama; San Salvador
Internationale-Y, 1918–40
Mémoires et documents (MD): Amérique; Espagne; États-Unis; Mexique
Négociations commerciales: Centre-Amérique
Papiers d'agents (PA): Delcassé; Jusserand; Lanen
Série A. Paix, 1914–1928
Série B. Amérique, 1918–1940: Centre Amérique; Dossiers généraux; États-Unis
Série C. Administratives, 1876–1907
Série Z. Europe, 1918–1929
Archives nationales, Paris
Archives d'entreprises: 6 AQ, 7 AQ
Fonds de la marine, série moderne: BB^3, BB^4, GG^{242}
Fonds du ministère de commerce: F^7, F^{12}, F^{23}

Great Britain

Public Record Office (PRO), London
Foreign Office (FO): FO 15 (Costa Rica); FO 21 (Central America / Guatemala); FO 39 (Honduras); FO 53 (Miskito Coast); FO 56 (Nicaragua); FO 66 (San Salvador)

Guatemala

Archivo General de Centro América, Guatemala City
Ministerio de Relaciones Exteriores

Spain

Archivo del Ministerio de Asuntos Exteriores, Madrid

United States

Olin Library, Cornell University, Ithaca, New York
John M. Dow
Huntington Library, San Marino, California
Pacific Mail Steamship Company

Louisiana State University, Baton Rouge
Edward A. Burke
National Archives, Washington, DC
RG 59, Department of State
Country Series, 1776–1906
Despatches from U.S. Consuls: Guatemala (T-337)
Diplomatic Despatches: Central America (M-219)
Diplomatic Instructions (M-77): France
Notes to Foreign Legations (M-99): Central America; France
RG 165, Military Intelligence Division (MID)

Primary Sources

Central America

Costa Rica. *Informe de secretario de relaciones exteriores, 1862*. San José, CR: Nacional, 1863.

Guzmán, Gustavo. *Canal de Nicaragua*. Paris: L'étoile de France, 1887.

Herrán, Victor. *Notice sur les cinq états du Centre-Amérique*. Bordeaux: A. Pechade, 1853.

Irisarri, Antonio José de. *Epistolario inédito de A. J. de Irisarri*. Ed. Enrique del Cid Fernández. Guatemala: Editorial del ejército, 1966.

Medina, Crisanto. *Le Nicaragua en 1900*. Paris: Kugelmann, 1900.

Paredes, Juan E. *The Morgan-Honduras Loan, 1908–1911*. New Orleans: L. Graham, 1911.

Solis, Ignacio. *Sobre el fomento de la inmigración y colonización extranjeras*. Guatemala: Augusto M. Chamba, 1889.

Tible Machado, J. Le Guatémala en 1896. *L'Exposition Centre-Américaine de 1897. Quelques notes*. Bordeaux: G. Delmas, 1896.

France

Airiau, Athanase. *L'Achèvement du canal de Panama*. Paris: A. Airiau, 1894.

———. *Canal interocéanique par l'isthme du Darien Nouvelle-Grenade. Canalisation par la colonisation*. Paris: France librairie, 1860.

D'Arlach, H. de T. *Souvenirs de l'isthme de Panama par le canal de Nicaragua*. Paris: Librairie nouvelle, 1858.

Belly, Félix. *Percement de l'isthme de Panama par le canal de Nicaragua*. Paris: Librairie nouvelle, 1858.

———. "La Question de l'isthme américain." *Revue des deux mondes* 30 (July 15, 1860): 328–68; 30 (Aug. 1, 1860): 597–633; 30 (Aug. 15, 1860): 865–902.

Belot, Gustave de. *La République du Salvador*. Paris: Dentu, 1865.

———. *Utilité pour Bordeaux d'un dock de marchandises au Centre-Amérique*. Bordeaux: Imprimerie générale de Mme Grugy, 1862.

Belot, Gustave de, and Charles Lindemann. *Amérique centrale. La République du Honduras et son chemin interocéanique*. Paris: Dentu, 1867.

Bionne, Henry. *Le Percement de l'isthme de Panama*. Paris: Eugène La Croix, [1875].

Bizemont, Henri Louis Gabriel de. *L'Amérique centrale et le canal de Panama*. Paris: La Société bibliographique, 1881.

Blanchet, Aristide-Paul. *La Lumière sur Panama. Analyse et critique du rapport lu par M. Ferdinand de Lesseps*. Paris: Jules Lecuir, 1882.

Botmilian, René L. M. A. de. "Notice sur les états de l'Amérique centrale." *Bulletin de la société géographie* 44 (Nov. 1865): 465–85.

Bourgeois, Henry, and Manuel Lemus. *Breve noticia sobre Honduras*. Tegucigalpa: Nacional, 1897.

Bourgeot, Alexander. *Le Honduras: Son passé et son avenir*. Paris: L'oeuvre de Saint-Paul, 1878.

Bunau-Varilla, Philippe. *The Great Adventure of Panama: The German Conspiracies against France and the United States*. New York: Doubleday, 1920.

———. *Panama, the Creation, Destruction, and Resurrection*. London: Constable, 1913.

———. *Panama: Le Trafic. Annexe de l'ouvrage Panama: Le Passé-le présent-l'avenir*. Paris: G. Masson, 1892.

Caille, Alexis. *Au Pays du printemps éternel. Le Guatémala et son avenir économique*. Paris: Louis Conrad, 1914.

Cambon, Jules. "La Doctrine de Monroe." *Revue des deux mondes* 98 (Sept. 1, 1928): 90–101.

Chevalier, Michel. "L'Isthme de Panama; l'isthme de Suez." *Revue des deux mondes* 14 (Jan. 1, 1844): 5–74.

———. "Le Renouvellement des traités de commerce." *Revue des deux mondes* 46 (June 15, 1876): 721–56.

Comité national du centenaire de 1848. *Documents diplomatiques du gouvernement provisoire et de la commission du pouvoir exécutif. Tome 2, mai-juin 1848*. Paris: Nationale, 1954.

Compagnie de l'isthme de Panama: *Jonction des deux océans, chemin de fer, canal maritime*. Paris: 1844.

"Correspondencia de los Consules Franceses Deloffre y Bonhenry." *Lotería* 330–31 (Sept.–Oct. 1983): 157–71.

Cravéri, Marie-Jean-Joseph. *La République de Costa-Rica. Ses besoins et ses ressources*. Paris: Schiller, 1895.

Denain, Adolphe. *Considérations sur les intérêts politiques et commerciaux qui se rattachent à l'isthme de Panama et aux différents isthmes de l'Amérique centrale; relation directe de ces isthmes avec celui de Suez*. Paris: Tous les marchands de nouveautés, 1845.

———. *Ensayo sobre los intereses políticos y comerciales del istmo de Panama considerándolos bajo el punto de vista de la Nueva Grenada.* Panama: J. M. Bermudez, 1844.
Ebray, Alcide. "Une réconciliation, l'Espagne et l'Amérique latine." *Revue des deux mondes* 71 (Nov. 15, 1901): 427–53.
"La Fortune française à l'étranger." *Bulletin de statistique et de législation comparée* 26 (Oct. 1902): 450–83.
Gamond, Thome de. "Note extraite de l'avant-projet pour la construction du canal de Nicaragua." In *Carte d'étude pour le tracé et le profil du canal de Nicaragua.* Ed. Thome de Gamond. Paris: Dalmont et Dunod, 1858, pp. 64–90.
Laferrière, Joseph. *De Paris à Guatémala. Notes de voyages au Centre-Amérique.* Paris: Garnier frères, 1877.
Lafond de Lurcy, Gabriel. *Fragments de voyages autour du monde.* Paris: Bureau du siècle, 1863.
———. *Notice sur le Golfo Dulce dans l'état de Costa-Rica (Amérique centrale) et sur un nouveau passage entre les deux océans.* Paris: Chez Fontaine, 1856.
———. *Nouvelle route pour la Californie.* Paris: Paul Dupont, 1850.
Laugel, Auguste. "Les Communications interocéaniques dans l'Amérique centrale." *Revue des deux mondes* 27 (Jan. 15, 1857): 436–65.
Lesseps, Ferdinand de. "The Interoceanic Canal." *North American Review* 130 (Jan. 1880): 1–15.
———. *Recollections of Forty Years.* 2 vols. New York: D. Appleton, 1888.
Levy, Paul. "Amérique centrale de Panama à Managua." *Société de géographie bulletin* 18 (1869): 177–91.
Levy, Raphael-Georges. "Les Capitaux français à l'étranger." *Revue des deux mondes* 67 (March 15, 1897): 415–45.
Lewandowski, Maurice. "La Puissance financière des États-Unis et son expansion mondiale." *Revue des deux mondes* 88 (Feb. 1, 1918): 662–91.
Mangin, Charles. "Autour du continent latin avec le 'Jules Michelet.' II, Le Guatémala-Panama." *Revue des deux mondes* 92 (Oct. 1922): 559–79.
Molinari, Gustave de. *A Panama. L'Isthme de Panama-la Martinique-Haïti.* Paris: Guillaumin, [1887].
Napoléon Bonaparte, Louis. "Le Canal de Nicaragua." In *Carte d'étude pour le tracé et le profil du canal de Nicaragua.* Ed. Thome de Gamond. Paris: Dalmont et Dunod, 1858, pp. 36–45.
Neymarck, Alfred. *Le Honduras. Son chemin de fer. Son avenir industriel et commercial.* Paris: E. Dentu, 1872.
Pector, Désiré. *Artículos sobre la Mosquitia.* Tegucigalpa: Tipografía Nacional, 1908.
———. *Régions isthmiques de l'Amérique tropicale.* Paris: Société d'éditions géographiques, maritimes et coloniales, 1925.

———. *Les Richesses de l'Amérique centrale.* Paris: E. Guilmoto, [1912].

Périgny, Maurice de. *Les Cinq Républiques de l'Amérique centrale.* Paris: Pierre Roger, 1911.

———. *La République de Costa Rica: Son avenir économique et le canal de Panama.* Paris: Félix Alcan, 1918.

Plauchut, Edmond. "Le Futur Canal interocéanique de l'Amérique centrale." *Revue des deux mondes* 49 (Aug. 1, 1879): 668–97.

Pougin, Edouard. *L'État de Costa-Rica.* Anvers, Belg.: Kornicker, 1863.

Reclus, Elisée. "Les Républiques de l'isthme américain." *Revue des deux mondes* 38 (March 15, 1868): 479–98.

Roger, Paul-André. *De l'intérêt qu'a la marine française à l'ouverture de l'isthme américain par le canal du Darien.* Paris: Ernest Meyer, 1861.

Stephan, Charles-H. *Le Guatémala économique.* Paris: Chevalier et Rivière, 1907.

Vaneechout, Edouard. "Les côtes de l'Amérique centrale et la Société Hispano-Américaine." *Revue des deux mondes* 27 (May 15, 1857): 444–65.

Varigny, Charles de. "Un homme d'état américain: James G. Blaine et le congrès des trois amériques." *Revue des deux mondes* 60 (Jan. 15, 1890): 433–62.

Vergrugghe, Louis, and George Vergrugghe. *Forêts vierges: Voyage dans l'Amérique du sud et l'Amérique centrale.* Paris: Michel Lévy frères, 1880.

Other

Ammen, Daniel. *The American Inter-oceanic Ship Canal Question.* Philadelphia: L. R. Hammersly, 1880.

———. *American Isthmian Canal Routes.* Philadelphia: Franklin Institute, 1889.

Bülow, Alexander von. *Die Verbindungswege des Welthandels durch Central-America.* Berlin: Deckersche Geheime Ober-Hofbuchdruckerei, 1850.

Loomis, Francis B. "Attitude of the United States toward Other American Powers." *Annals of the American Academy of Political and Social Sciences* 26 (July 1905): 21–24.

———. "The Position of the United States on the American Continent—Some Phases of the Monroe Doctrine." *Annals of the American Academy of Political and Social Sciences* 22 (July 1903): 1–19.

Squier, Ephraim George. *Nicaragua: Its People, Scenery, Monuments, Resources, Condition, and Proposed Canal.* New York: Harper and Brothers, 1860.

———. *Notes on Central America.* New York: Harper, 1855.

"Suez and Panama Kanäle." *Westermanns Jahrbuch der illustrierten deutschen Monatshefte* 2 (July 1857): 478–80.

Statistical Sources

Albarracin, Priscilla, and Héctor Pérez Brignoli. *Estadísticas del comercio exterior de Costa Rica (1907–1946)*. Avances de investigación, 5. San José: Universidad de Costa Rica, 1977.

Bosch Spencer, Guillaume Henri. *Commerce de la côte occidentale de l'amérique du sud*. Bruxelles: D. Raes, 1848.

France. *Annales du commerce extérieur, [year]*. Paris: various, 1845–1867.

———. *Annuaire statistique de la France, [year]*. Paris: Nationale, [1872–1948].

———. Direction générale des douanes. *Tableau général du commerce et de la navigation, [year]*. Paris: [Royale or nationale], 1821–1907.

Gille, Bertrand. *Les Sources statistiques de l'histoire de France des enquêtes du xviie siècle à 1870*. Paris: Minard, 1964.

Organization of American States. Interamerican Economic and Social Council. *Foreign Investment in Latin America*. Washington, DC: Pan American Union, 1955.

Pan American Union. *Foreign Trade of Latin America, 1910–1929*. Washington, DC: Pan American Union, 1930.

———. *Foreign Trade Series* for Costa Rica, El Salvador, Guatemala, Honduras, and Nicaragua, [Nos. 1–214]. Washington, DC: Pan American Union, 1918–1950.

United Nations. *El financiamiento externo de América Latina*. New York: United Nations, 1964.

U.S. Department of Commerce. *Trade and Investment in Central America*. Washington, DC: GPO, 1965.

Secondary Sources

Books and Articles

Acker, Alison. *Honduras: The Making of a Banana Republic*. Boston: South End, 1988.

Acuña Ortega, Victor H., and Iván Molina Jiménez. *El desarrollo económico y social de Costa Rica: De la colonia a la crisis de 1930*. San José, CR: Alma Mater, 1986.

Agulhon, Maurice. *1848 ou l'apprentissage de la république: 1848–1852*. Paris: Seuil, 1973.

Aldrich, Robert. *Greater France: A History of French Overseas Expansion*. New York: St. Martin's, 1996.

Allen, Cyril. *France in Central America: Felix Belly and the Nicaraguan Canal*. New York: Pageant Press, 1966.

Ameringer, Charles. "Bunau-Varilla, Russia, and the Panama Canal." *Journal of Inter-American Studies and World Affairs* 12 (July 1970): 328–38.

———. "Philippe Bunau-Varilla: New Light on the Panama Canal Treaty." *Hispanic American Historical Review* 46 (Feb. 1966): 28–52.

Andrew, Christopher, and A. S. Kanya-Forstner. *France Overseas. The Great War and the Climax of French Imperial Expansion*. London: Thames and Hudson, 1981.

———. "French Business and the French Colonialists." *Historical Journal* 19:4 (1976): 981–1000.

———. "The French 'Colonial Party': Its Composition, Aims and Influence, 1885–1914." *Historical Journal* 14:1 (1971): 99–128.

Anguizola, Gustave. *Philippe Bunau-Varilla*. Chicago: Nelson-Hall, 1980.

Argueta, Mario, and Eduardo Quiñós. *Historia de Honduras*. Tegucigalpa: Escuela superior del profesorado 'Francisco Morazán,' 1978.

Ariès, Philippe. *Histoire des populations françaises et de leurs attitudes devant la vie depuis le xviii*[e] *siècle*. Paris: Seuil, 1971.

Asselain, Jean-Charles. *Histoire économique de la France du xviii*[e] *siècle à nos jours*. 2 vols. Paris: Seuil, 1984.

Aubrun, Charles V. *L'Amérique centrale*. Paris: Presses universitaires de France, 1968.

Azéma, Jean-Pierre, and Michel Winock. *La troisième République*. Paris: Calmann-Lévy, 1976.

Bailleu, G. "L'Europe et le canal interocéanique. Un conflit possible entre les États-Unis et l'Angleterre." *Revue politique et parlementaire* 7 (Jan. 10, 1901): 129–39.

Bairoch, Paul. *Commerce extérieur et développement économique de l'Europe au xix*[e] *siècle*. Paris: Mouton, 1976.

———. *Révolution industrielle et sous-développement*. 4th ed. Paris: Mouton, 1974.

Barak, Michel. "Intérêts régionaux, haute banque parisienne et pouvoir d'état: (à propos d'un projet marseillais de navigation à vapeur transatlantique en 1840)." *Revue historique* 251 (April–June 1974): 331–72.

Barbier, Frédéric. "Le commerce international de la librairie française au xixe siècle (1815–1913)." *Revue d'histoire moderne et contemporaine* 28 (Jan.–March 1981): 94–117.

Baumgart, Winfried. "Das größere Frankreich. Neue Forschungen über den französischen Imperialismus, 1880–1914." *Vierteljahrschrift für Sozial- und Wirtschaftsgeschichte* 61 (1974): 185–98.

Bergeron, Louis. *Les Capitalistes en France (1780–1914)*. Paris: Gallimard, 1978.

Bernard, Philippe. *La Fin d'un monde: 1914–1929*. Paris: Seuil, 1975.

Betts, Raymond F. *The False Dawn: European Imperialism in the Nineteenth Century*. Minneapolis: University of Minnesota Press, 1976.

———. *Tricouleur: The French Overseas Empire*. London: Gordon and Gremonesi, 1978.
Blumenthal, Henry. *France and the United States: Their Diplomatic Relations, 1789–1914*. Chapel Hill: University of North Carolina Press, 1970.
Bolaños Alvarez, Pío. "Napoleon III y el diplomático nicaraguënse Francisco Castellón." *Revista conservadora de pensamiento centroamericano* 16 (Feb. 1967): 42–45.
Bouvier, Jean. "Encore sur l'impérialisme: Des rapports entre banque et industrie dans l'expansion française au dehors (1880–1914)." *Revue française d'histoire d'outre-mer* 67 (1980): 217–26.
Bouvier, Jean, François Furet, and Marcel Gillet. *Le Mouvement du profit en France au xixe siècle. Matériaux et études*. Paris: Mouton, 1965.
Bouvier, Jean, and René Girault, eds. *Impérialisme français d'avant 1914: Recueil de textes*. Paris: Mouton, 1976.
Braudel, Fernand. *Civilisation matérielle, économie et capitalisme, xve-xviiie siècle*. 3 vols. Paris: Armand Colin, 1979. [Translated as *The Structures of Everyday Life, The Wheels of Commerce*, and *The Perspective of the World*. New York: Harper, 1984.]
Brunschwig, Henri. *La Colonisation française du pacte colonial à l'union française*. Paris: Calmann Lévy, 1949.
———. *Mythes et réalités de l'impérialisme colonial français, 1871–1914*. Paris: Armand Colin, 1960.
———. *Vom Kolonialimperialismus zur Kolonialpolitik der Gegenwart*. Wiesbaden: Franz Steiner, 1957.
Bulmer-Thomas, Victor. *The Political Economy of Central America since 1920*. Cambridge, Eng.: Cambridge University Press, 1987.
Burns, E. Bradford. *Progress and Poverty: Latin America in the Nineteenth Century*. Berkeley: University of California Press, 1980.
Bury, J. P. T. *France, 1814–1940*. New York: A. S. Barnes, 1962.
Cambiaire, Célestin-Pierre. *Le Rôle de la France dans l'expansion des États-Unis*. Paris: Albert Messein, 1935.
Cameron, Rondo E. "Economic Growth and Stagnation in France, 1815–1914." *Journal of Modern History* 30 (March 1958): 1–13.
———. "L'Exportation des capitaux français, 1850–1880." *Revue d'histoire économique et sociale* 33 (1955): 347–53.
———. *France and the Economic Development of Europe, 1800–1914*. Princeton: Princeton University Press, 1961.
———. "Die französische Wirtschaft—Vergangenheit, Gegenwart, Zukunft." In *Wirtschaft und Gesellschaft in Frankreich seit 1789*. Ed. Gilbert Ziebura. Cologne: Kiepenheuer und Witsch, 1975, 149–65.
"Le Canal de Panama, la documentation française." *Notes et études documentaires* (March 10, 1950): 1–44.
Cardoso, Ciro F. S. "Central America: The Liberal Era, c. 1870–1930." In *The Cambridge History of Latin America*. Ed. Leslie Bethell. 8 vols.

Cambridge, Eng.: Cambridge University Press, 1982–1993, 5: 197–227.

Cardoso, Ciro F. S., and Héctor Pérez Brignoli. *Centro América y la economía occidental (1520–1930)*. San José, CR: EDUCA, 1977.

Caron, François. *An Economic History of Modern France*. Translated by Barbara Bray. New York: Columbia University Press, 1979.

———. "La Stratégie des investissements en France aux xixe et xxe siècles." *Revue d'histoire économique et sociale* 54 (1976): 64–117.

Carré, Jean-Jacques, P. Dubois, and E. Malinvaud. *French Economic Growth*. Stanford, CA: Stanford University Press, 1975.

Carroll, E. Malcolm. *French Public Opinion and Foreign Affairs, 1870–1914*. London: Frank Cass, 1965.

Chinchilla Aguilar, Ernesto. "El positivismo y la reforma en Guatemala." *Antropología e historia de Guatemala* 12 (June 1960): 35–43.

Cobban, Alfred. *A History of Modern France*. 2 vols. Harmondsworth, Eng.: Penguin, 1961.

Cooke, James J. *New French Imperialism, 1880–1910: The Third Republic and Colonial Expansion*. Hamden, CT: Archon Books, 1973.

Crafts, N. F. R. "Economic Growth in France and Britain, 1830–1910: A Review of the Evidence." *Journal of Economic History* 44 (March 1984): 49–67.

Crouzet, François. "Encore la croissance économique française au xixe siècle." *Revue du nord* 54 (July–Sept. 1972): 3–20.

———. "Recherches sur la production d'armements en France (1815–1913)." *Revue historique* 251 (Jan.–March 1974): 45–84.

Cruz, Vladimir de la. *Las luchas sociales en Costa Rica, 1870–1930*. San José, CR: Editorial universitaria de Costa Rica, 1980.

Daumard, Adeline. "L'Évolution des structures sociales en France à l'époque de l'industrialisation (1815–1914)." *Revue historique* 247 (April-June 1972): 325–46.

———. *Les Fortunes françaises au xixe siècle*. Paris: Mouton, 1973.

———. "Les Placements à l'étranger dans les patrimoines des français au xixe siècle (1815–1914)." *Revue d'histoire économique et sociale* 52 (1974): 526–46.

Demyk, Michel, and Noëlle Demyk. "Conflits frontaliers en Amérique centrale." In *Les Phénomènes de "frontière" dans les pays tropicaux*. Paris: Centre national de la recherche scientifique, 1981, pp. 401–17.

Deschanel, Paul. *La Politique française en Océanie. Apropos du canal de Panama*. Paris: Berger-Levrault, 1884.

Desmarest, Jacques. *La France de 1870*. 3 vols. Paris: Hachette, 1970–77.

"La diplomacía del dolar! La Tragédie de Panama." *L'Action industrielle et commerciale* (Dec. 1, 1927): 1–4.

Dosal, Paul. *Doing Business with the Dictators: A Political History of United Fruit in Guatemala, 1899–1944*. Wilmington, DE: Scholarly Resources, 1993.

Dunham, Arthur Lewis. *The Industrial Revolution in France, 1815–1848*. New York: Exposition Press, 1955.
Durham, William H. *Scarcity and Survival in Central America*. Stanford, CA: Stanford University Press, 1979.
Duroselle, Jean-Baptiste. *La France et les États-Unis. Des origines à nos jours*. Paris: Seuil, 1976.
———. "La Politique extérieure de la IIIe République—ses traits originaux." *Centenaire de la Troisième République. Actes du colloque de Rennes, 15–17 mai 1975*. Paris: Jean-Pierre DeLarge, 1975, pp. 130–40.
Ellerich, Lee. "France in Latin America." *Current History* 28 (March 1955): 160–67.
Enjalbert, Henri. "Les Capitales de l'Amérique centrale, sites anciens et essor récent." *Caravelle* 3 (1964): 303–19.
Euraque, Darío A. *Reinterpreting the Banana Republic: Region and State in Honduras, 1870–1972*. Chapel Hill: University of North Carolina Press, 1996.
Figueroa Navarro, Alfredo. "Visión de Panamá durante la época del canal francés." *Lotería* 292 (July 1980): 17–25.
Flores Macal, Mario. *Orígenes de las formas de dominación en El Salvador*. Avances de investigación, No. 29. San José: Universidad de Costa Rica, 1978.
Ganiage, Jean. *L'Expansion coloniale et les rivalités internationales*. 2 vols. Paris: Centre de documentation universitaire, 1973.
———. *Les Relations internationales de 1890 à 1914*. 2 vols. Paris: n.p., 1971–72.
García Laguardia, Jorge Mario. *La reforma liberal en Guatemala: Vida política y orden constitucional*. Guatemala: EDUCA, 1972.
Girault, René. "Le Milieu bancaire français face aux relations internationales avant 1914." *Relations internationales* 1 (May 1974): 27–37.
———. "Ein neues Bild des französischen Unternehmers um 1914." In *Wirtschaft und Gesellschaft in Frankreich seit 1789*. Ed. Gilbert Ziebura. Cologne: Kiepenheuer und Witsch, 1975, pp. 202–29.
———. "Place et rôle des échanges extérieurs." In *Histoire économique et sociale de la France*. Eds. Fernand Braudel and Ernest Labrousse. 4 vols. Paris: Presses universitaires de France, 1980, vol. 4, pt. 1.
Golob, Eugene O. *The Meline Tariff: French Agriculture and Nationalist Economic Policy*. New York: Columbia University Press, 1944.
Gonjo, Yasuo. "Le 'Plan Freycinet,' 1878–1882: Un aspect de la 'grande dépression' économique en France." *Revue historique* 247 (July–Sept. 1972): 49–86.
González Casanova, Pablo. *Imperialismo y liberación: Una introducción a la historia contemporánea de América Latina*. 4th ed. Mexico: Siglo XXI, 1983.

González Flores, Luis Felipe. *Historia de la influencia extranjera en el desenvolvimiento educacional y científico de Costa Rica*. San José, CR: Nacional, 1921.

Gorostiaga, Xavier. *Los banqueros del imperio. El papel de los centros financieros internacionales en los países subdesarrollados*. San José, CR: EDUCA, 1978.

Griffith, William J. "Attitudes toward Foreign Colonization: The Evolution of Nineteenth-Century Guatemalan Immigration Policy." In *Applied Enlightenment: Nineteenth Century Liberalism*. New Orleans: Middle American Institute, 1972, pp. 73–110.

———. *Empires in the Wilderness: Foreign Colonization and Development in Guatemala, 1834–1844*. Chapel Hill: University of North Carolina Press, 1965.

Guillen, Pierre. "Opinion publique et politique étrangère en France, 1871–1914: Orientation des études menées en France depuis 1945." In *Opinion publique et politique extérieure*. Rome: École française de Rome, 1981, pp. 49–62.

Handy, Jim. *The Gift of the Devil: A History of Guatemala*. Boston: South End, 1984.

Hartmann, Jean. *Die Wirtschaftspolitik Napoleons III*. Bottrop: Wilhelm Postberg, 1938.

Hauser, Henri. *Frankreichs Handel und Industrie und die Konkurrenz des Auslands*. Jena: Gustav Fischer, 1919.

Headrick, Daniel R. *The Tentacles of Progress: Technology Transfer in the Age of Imperialism, 1850–1940*. New York: Oxford University Press, 1988.

Hernández Alcarón, Eduardo. "Comercio y dependencia en Costa Rica durante los años 1880–1890." *Anuario de estudios centroamericanos* 3 (1977): 258.

Hilton, Stanley E. "Latin America and Western Europe, 1880–1945: The Political Dimension." In *Latin America, Western Europe, and the United States*. Eds. Wolf Grabendorff and Riordan Roett. New York: Praeger, 1985.

Jacob, Léon. "Le Canal de Panama et les colonies françaises." *Questions diplomatiques et coloniales* 33 (Feb. 1912): 193–208.

Jaen Suárez, Omar. "La presencia francesa en Panamá durante el Siglo XIX." *Lotería* 330–31 (Sept.–Oct. 1983): 173–77.

Jardin, André, and André-Jean Tudesq. *La France des notables: 1815–1848*. 2 vols. Paris: Seuil, 1973.

Jones, Chester. *Costa Rica and Civilization in the Caribbean*. Madison: University of Wisconsin Press, 1935.

Kemp, Tom. *Economic Forces in French History*. London: Dennis Dobson, 1971.

———. *The French Economy, 1913–1939: The History of Decline*. London: Longman, 1972.

———. "Structural Factors in the Retardation of French Economic Growth." *Kykos* 15 (1962): 325–52.

Kennedy, Paul M. *The Rise and Fall of the Great Powers: Economic Change and Military Conflict from 1500 to 2000*. New York: Random House, 1987.
Kindleberger, Charles P. *Economic Growth in France and Britain, 1851–1950*. Cambridge: Harvard University Press, 1964.
Klein, Wolfgang. "Ein zweitrangiger Imperialismus? Zur Herausbildung des französischen Imperialismus vor 1914." *Neue Studien zum Imperialismus vor 1914*. Ed. Fritz Klein. Berlin: Akademie, 1980, pp. 165–95.
Kühn, Joachim. "Napoleon III. und der Nicaraguakanal." *Historische Zeitschrift* 208 (1969): 295–319.
LaFeber, Walter. *The American Age: United States Foreign Policy at Home and Abroad since 1750*. New York: W. W. Norton, 1989.
———. *The American Search for Opportunity, 1865–1913*. Vol. 2; *The Cambridge History of American Foreign Relations*. 4 vols. New York: Cambridge University Press, 1993.
———. *Inevitable Revolutions: The United States in Central America*. New York: W. W. Norton, 1983.
———. *The Panama Canal: The Crisis in Historical Perspective*. Rev. ed. New York: Oxford University Press, 1989.
Laffey, John F. "Municipal Imperialism: The Lyon Chamber of Commerce, 1914–1925." *Journal of European Economic History* 4 (Spring 1975): 95–120.
———. "Municipal Imperialism in France: The Lyon Chamber of Commerce, 1900–1914." *Proceedings of the American Philosophical Society* 19 (1975): 8–23.
———. "Municipal Imperialism in Nineteenth Century France." *Historical Reflections* 1 (June 1974): 81–113.
Lafond, Georges. *L'Effort français en Amérique latine*. Paris: Payot, 1917.
———. *La France en Amérique latine*. Paris: Plon, 1922.
Lalance, Auguste. "Les Intérêts respectifs du commerce français et du commerce américain dans le canal de Panama." *L'Économiste français* (July 3, 1886): 10–11.
Lambert, Jacques. *Amérique latine: Structures sociales et institutions politiques*. Paris: Presses universitaires de France, 1963.
Landes, David S. "French Entrepreneurship and Industrial Growth in the Nineteenth Century." *Journal of Economic History* 9 (1949): 45–61.
Langley, Lester D. *The Struggle for the American Mediterranean, 1776–1904: United States-European Rivalry in the Gulf-Caribbean*. Athens: University of Georgia Press, 1976.
———. *The United States and the Caribbean in the Twentieth Century*. Athens: University of Georgia Press, 1982.
Lanuza, Alberto, Juan Luis Vázquez, Amaru Barahona, and Amalia Chamorro. *Economía y sociedad en la construcción del estado en Nica-*

ragua. San José, CR: Instituto centroamericano de administración pública, 1983.

Lasserre, Guy. *Les Amériques du centre*. Paris: Presses universitaires de France, 1974.

Lefébure, Paul. "A la conquête d'un isthme. Les États-Unis et l'Europe." *Annales de sciences politiques* 16 (Sept. 1901): 600–619.

Léon, Pierre. *Economies et sociétés de l'Amérique latine. Essais sur les problèmes du développement à l'époque contemporaine, 1815–1967*. Paris: SEDES, 1969.

———. *Histoire économique et sociale du monde*. 6 vols. Paris: Armand Colin, 1977–78.

Leonard, Thomas. *Central America and the United States: The Search for Stability*. Athens: University of Georgia Press, 1991.

Lévy, Maurice. *Histoire économique et sociale de la France depuis 1848*. Paris: Les Cours de droit, 1952.

Levy, Pablo. "Notas geográficas y económicas de Nicaragua." *Revista conservadora del pensamiento centroamericano* 62 (Nov. 1962): 9–121.

Lévy-Leboyer, Maurice. *Les Banques européennes et l'industrialisation internationale dans la première moitié du xixe siècle*. Paris: Presses universitaires de France, 1964.

———. "La Croissance économique en France au xixe siècle." *Annales: Economies, sociétés, civilisations* 23 (July–Aug. 1968): 788–807.

———. "La Décélération de l'économie française dans la seconde moitié du xixe siècle (1)." *Revue d'histoire économique et sociale* 49 (1971): 485–508.

———. "Les Processus d'industrialisation: Le Cas de l'Angleterre et de la France." *Revue historique* 239 (1968): 281–98.

Lévy-Leboyer, Maurice, and François Bourguignon. *The French Economy in the Nineteenth Century: An Essay in Econometric Analysis*. Cambridge, Eng.: Cambridge University Press, 1990.

Leysbeth, Nicolas. *Historique de la colonisation Belge à Santo Tomás de Guatemala*. Bruxelles: n. p., 1938.

Lhomme, Jean. *La Grande Bourgeoisie au pouvoir (1830–1880)*. Paris: Presses universitaires de France, 1960.

Lindo-Fuentes, Héctor. *Weak Foundations: The Economy of El Salvador in the Nineteenth Century, 1821–1890*. Berkeley: University of California Press, 1991.

López Vallecillos, Italo. *Gerardo Barrios y su tiempo*. 2 vols. San Salvador: EDUCA, 1967.

Lough, John, and Muriel Lough. *An Introduction to Nineteenth Century France*. London: Longmans, 1978.

McCormick, Thomas J. *America's Half-Century: United States Foreign Policy in the Cold War*. Baltimore: Johns Hopkins University Press, 1989.

———. *China Market: America's Quest for Informal Empire, 1893–1901.* Chicago: Quadrangle, 1967.

McCreery, David. "Coffee and Class: The Structure of the Development in Liberal Guatemala, 1871–1885." *Hispanic American Historical Review* 61 (Aug. 1976): 438–60.

———. "Debt Servitude in Rural Guatemala, 1876–1936." *Hispanic American Historical Review* 63 (1983): 735–59.

———. *Development and the State in Reforma Guatemala, 1871–1885.* Monographs in Latin America Series, vol. 10. Athens: Ohio University Press, 1983.

———. " 'An Odious Feudalism': *Mandamiento* Labor and Commercial Agriculture in Guatemala, 1858–1920." *Latin American Perspectives* 13:1 (Winter 1986): 99–117.

McCullough, David. *The Path between the Seas: The Creation of the Panama Canal, 1870–1914.* New York: Simon and Schuster, 1977.

Magraw, Roger. *France, 1815–1914: The Bourgeois Century.* New York: Oxford University Press, 1986.

Marczewski, Jan. "Le Produit physique de l'économie française de 1789 à 1913, comparaison avec la Grande Bretagne." *Cahiers de l'Institut de science économique appliquée* 148 (July 1965): vii–cliv.

———. "Some Aspects of the Economic Growth of France, 1660–1958." *Economic Development and Cultural Change* 9 (1961): 369–86.

Markovitch, Tihomir. "Les Cycles industriels en France." *Le Mouvement social* 63 (April–June 1968): 11–39.

———. "The Dominant Sectors of French Industry." In *Essays in French Economic History.* Ed. Rondo Cameron. Homewood, IL: Richard D. Irwin, 1970, pp. 226–44.

———. "L'Industrie française de 1789 à 1964—sources et méthodes." *Cahiers de l'Institut de science économique appliquée,* AF 4, Nr. 163 (July 1965): 1–231.

Marseille, Jacques. "L'Investissement français dans l'empire colonial: L'Enquête du gouvernement de Vichy (1943)." *Revue historique* 252 (July–Dec. 1974): 409–32.

Martinière, Guy. *Les Amériques latines: Une histoire économique.* Grenoble: Presses universitaires de Grenoble, 1978.

Mauro, Frédéric. "Conjoncture économique et structure sociale en Amérique latine depuis l'époque coloniale." *Conjoncture économique, structures sociales: Hommage à Ernest Labrousse.* Paris: Mouton, 1974, pp. 237–51.

———. "Les Investissements français en Amérique latine xixe–xxe siècles." In *La Position internationale de la France: Aspects économiques et financiers xixe–xxe siècles.* Ed. Maurice Lévy-Leboyer. Paris: Écoles des hautes études en sciences sociales, 1977, pp. 193–202.

———. "Les Investissements français en Amérique latine dès origines à 1973." *Revue d'histoire économique et sociale* 55 (1977): 234–62.

———. "Tensions and the Transmission of Tensions in the European Expansion to America (1500–1900)." *Plantation Society* 1 (June 1979): 149–59.

Mayeur, Jean-Marie. *Les Débuts de la IIIe République: 1871–1898*. Paris: Seuil, 1973.

———. *La Vie politique sous la Troisième République, 1870–1940*. Paris: Seuil, 1984.

Meléndez Chaverri, Carlos. "Intereses extranjeros en Centro América durante la primera mitad del siglo XIX." In *Memoria del primer congreso de historia Centro América-Panamá*. San José, CR: Nacional, 1956.

Menjívar, Rafael. *Acumulación originaria y desarrollo del capitalismo en El Salvador*. San José, CR: EDUCA, 1980.

Meza, Victor. *Historia del movimiento obrero hondureño*. Tegucigalpa, Hond.: Guaymuras, 1980.

Meza, Victor, and Héctor López. "Las inversiones extranjeras en Honduras antes del Mercado Común Centroamericano." *Economía política* (UNAH, Tegucigalpa) 6 (Sept.–Dec. 1973): 47–80.

Milner, Susan. *The Dilemmas of Internationalism: French Syndicalism and the International Labour Movement, 1900–1914*. New York: Berg, 1990.

Milward, Alan S., and S. B. Saul. *The Development of the Economies of Continental Europe, 1850–1914*. London: George Allen and Unwin, 1977.

Molina, Felipe. *Bosquejo de la república de Costa Rica*. New York: S. W. Benedict, 1851.

Molina Chocano, Guillermo. *Estado liberal y desarrollo capitalista en Honduras*. Tegucigalpa: Banco Central de Honduras, 1976.

Morgan, Iwan. "French Policy in Spanish America: 1830–1848." *Journal of Latin America Studies* 10 (Nov. 1978): 309–28.

Murphy, Agnes. *The Ideology of French Imperialism, 1871–1881*. New York: Howard Fertig, 1968.

Newbury, Colin W. "Aspects of French Policy in the Pacific, 1853–1906." *Pacific Historical Review* 27:1 (Feb. 1958): 45–56.

Newell, William H. "The Agricultural Revolution in Nineteenth-Century France." *Journal of Economic History* 33 (Dec. 1973): 697–730.

Palmade, Guy P. *Capitalisme et capitalistes français au xixe siècle*. Paris: Armand Colin, 1961.

Pérez Brignoli, Héctor. *Breve historia de Centro-América*. Madrid: Alianza, 1985.

———. "La reforma liberal en Honduras." *Ciencias sociales* 2 (1973): 2–19.

Pernoud, Régine. *Histoire de la bourgeoisie en France*. 2. *Les Temps modernes*. Paris: Seuil, 1981.

Persell, Stuart M. *The French Colonial Lobby, 1889–1938*. Stanford, CA: Stanford University Press, 1983.

Pincetl, Stanley J., Jr. "France and the Clayton-Bulwer Treaty of 1850." *Annales* 45 (1968): 167–94.
Pizzurno-Gelos, Patricia. "Presentación de los documentos de los cónsules franceses sobre la guerra civil en Panamá." *Lotería* 330–31 (Sept.–Oct. 1983): 146–56.
Plessis, Alain. *De la fête impériale au mur des fédérés: 1852–1871*. Paris: Seuil, 1973.
Poidevin, Raymond. "Aspects du nationalisme économique et financier français et allemand au début du xxe siècle." *Memoires* [Académie National, Metz] 15 (1973): 53–68.
———. "Fabricants d'armes et relations internationales au début du xxe siècle." *Relations internationales* 1 (May 1974): 39–56.
———. *Les Relations économiques et financières entre la France et l'Allemagne de 1898 à 1914*. Paris: Armand Colin, 1969.
Posas, Mario. *Luchas del movimiento obrero hondureño*. San José, CR: Guaymuras, 1981.
Price, Roger. *An Economic History of Modern France, 1730–1914*. New York: St. Martin's, 1981.
———. *The Modernization of Rural France: Communications Networks and Agricultural Market Structures in Nineteenth Century France*. New York: St. Martin's, 1983.
———. *Revolution and Reaction: 1848 and the Second French Republic*. New York: Barnes and Noble, 1975.
Puhle, Hans-Jürgen. *Politische Agrarbewegungen in kapitalistischen Industriegesellschaften. Deutschland, USA und Frankreich im 20. Jahrhundert*. Göttingen: Vandenhoeck und Ruprecht, 1975.
Quintana Díaz, Victor. *Inversiones extranjeras en Guatemala*. Guatemala: Instituto de investigaciones económicas y sociales, 1973.
Rebérioux, Madeleine. *La République radicale? 1898–1914*. Paris: Seuil, 1975.
Rémond, René. *Introduction à l'histoire de notre temps*. 2. *Le xixe siècle, 1815–1914*. Paris: Seuil, 1974.
Renouvin, Pierre. *Histoire des relations internationales*. 8 vols. Paris: Hachette, 1970.
Richards, Edward W. "Louis Napoleon and Central America." *Journal of Modern History* 34 (June 1962): 178–84.
Rioux, Jean-Pierre. *La Révolution industrielle, 1780–1880*. Paris: Seuil, 1971.
Rippy, J. Fred. "French Investments in Latin America." *Inter-American Economic Affairs* 2 (Autumn 1948): 52–71.
Rist, Marcel. "A French Experiment with Free Trade: The Treaty of 1860." In *Essays in French Economic History*. Ed. Rondo Cameron. Homewood, IL: Richard D. Irwin, 1970, pp. 286–314.
Rojas Bolaños, Manuel. "El desarrollo del movimiento obrero en Costa Rica: Un Intento de periodización." In *Desarrollo del movimiento sindical en Costa Rica*. San José: Universidad de Costa Rica, 1981, pp. 13–21.

Rowley, Anthony. *Évolution économique de la France au milieu du xixe siècle à 1914*. Paris: SEDES, 1982.

Salem, Daniel. "Sur quelques conséquences du retour de la France au protectionnisme à la fin du xixe siècle." *Revue d'histoire économique et sociale* 45 (1967): 326–80.

Salgó, L. *Du rôle des facteurs économiques et politiques de la politique coloniale française dans la période d'après 1871*. Budapest: Akadémiai Kiadó, 1975.

Salisbury, Richard. *Anti-Americanism and International Cooperation in Central America, 1920–1929*. Wilmington, DE: Scholarly Resources, 1989.

———. *Costa Rica y el istmo, 1900–1934*. San José: Editorial Costa Rica, 1984.

Sauvy, Alfred. *Histoire économique de la France entre les deux guerres*. 4 vols. Paris: Fayard, 1965–75.

———. "Le Revenu des français au xixe siècle." *Population* 20 (May 1965): 517–18.

Scheips, Paul J. "Gabriel Lafond and Ambrose W. Thompson: Neglected Isthmian Promoters." *Hispanic American Historical Review* 34 (May 1956): 211–28.

Schneider, Jürgen. *Frankreich und die Unabhängigkeit Spanisch-Amerikas*. 2 vols. Stuttgart: Klett-Cotta, 1981.

———. "Terms of Trade between France and Latin America, 1825–1856: Causes of Increasing Economic Disparities?" *Disparities in Economic Development since the Industrial Revolution*. Eds. Paul Bairoch and Maurice Lévy-Leboyer. New York: St. Martin's, 1981, pp. 110–19.

Schneider, William H. "Geographical Reform and Municipal Imperialism in France, 1870–1880." In *Imperialism and the Natural World*. Ed. John M. McKenzie. Manchester: Manchester University Press, 1990, pp. 90–117.

Schoonover, Thomas D. *Dollars over Dominion: The Triumph of Liberalism in Mexican-United States Relations, 1861–1867*. Baton Rouge: Louisiana State University Press, 1978.

———. "France in Central America, 1820s to 1930: An Overview." *Revue française d'histoire d'outre mer* 79 (1992): 161–97.

———. *Germany in Central America: Competive Imperialism, 1821–1929*. Tuscaloosa: University of Alabama Press, 1998.

———. "Imperialism in Middle America: United States Competition with Britain, Germany and France in Middle America, 1820s–1920s." In *Eagle against Empire: American Opposition to European Imperialism, 1914–1982*. Ed. Rhodri Jeffreys-Jones. Aix-en-Provence, France: Université de Provence, 1983, pp. 41–58.

———. "Metropole Rivalry in Central America, 1820s to 1929: An Overview." *Central America: Historical Perspectives on the Contemporary Crises*. Ed. Ralph Lee Woodward, Jr. Westport, CT: Greenwood, 1988, pp. 21–46.

———. *The United States in Central America, 1860–1911: Episodes of Social Imperialism and Imperial Rivalry in the World System*. Durham, NC: Duke University Press, 1991.
Schoonover, Thomas D., and Ebba Schoonover. "Statistics for the Understanding of the Foreign Intrusion into Central America from the 1820s to 1930." *Revista anuario de estudios centroamericanos* 15 (1989): 93–117, 16 (1990): 135–56, 17 (1991): 77–119.
Siegfried, André. *Suez, Panama et les routes maritimes mondiales*. Paris: Armand Colin, 1945.
Skinner, James W. *France and Panama: The Unknown Years, 1894–1908*. New York: Peter Lang, 1989.
Smith, Cecil O., Jr. "The Longest Run: Public Engineers and Planning in France." *American Historical Review* 95 (June 1990): 657–92.
Smith, Michael S. "Free Trade Versus Protection in the Early Third Republic: Economic Interests, Tariff Policy, and the Making of the Republican Synthesis." *French Historical Studies* 10 (Spring 1977): 293–314.
———. *Tariff Reform in France, 1860–1900: The Politics of Economic Interest*. Ithaca, NY: Cornell University Press, 1980.
Smith, Robert Freeman. "Latin America, the United States and the European Powers, 1830–1930." *Cambridge History of Latin America*. Ed. Leslie Bethell. 8 vols. Cambridge, Eng.: Cambridge University Press, 1982–93, 4: 83–119.
Sorre, Max. *Mexique. Amérique centrale*. Paris: Armand Colin, 1928.
Stoltz Chinchilla, Norma. "Class Struggle in Central America: Background and Overview." *Latin American Perspectives* 7 (Spring and Summer 1980): 2–23.
Thompson, J. M. *Louis Napoleon and the Second Empire*. New York: Norton, 1955.
Torres-Rivas, Edelberto. *Elementos para la caracterización de la estructura agraria de Costa Rica*. San José: Facultad de ciencias sociales, Universidad de Costa Rica, 1978.
———. "Poder nacional y sociedad dependiente." In *Financiamiento extranjero en América Central*. Ed. Edelberto Torres-Rivas. San José, CR: Centro de estudios CEDAL, 1974, pp. 15–42.
Torres-Rivas, Edelberto, and Julio César Pinto. *Problemas en la formación del estado nacional en Centroamérica*. San José, CR: ICAP, 1983.
Vega Carballo, José Luis. *Orden y progeso: La Formación del estado nacional en Costa Rica*. San José, CR: Instituto centroamericano de administración pública, 1981.
Viallate, Achille. *L'Impérialisme économique et les relations internationales pendant le dernier demi-siècle (1870–1920)*. Paris: Armand Colin, 1923.
Wallerstein, Immanuel. *Historical Capitalism*. London: Verso, 1983.
———. *The Modern World-System*. 3 vols. New York: Academic Press, 1974–88.

Walton, Whitney. *France at the Crystal Palace: Bourgeois Taste and Artisan Manufacture in the Nineteenth Century*. Berkeley: University of California Press, 1992.

Weber, Eugen. *France: Fin de siècle*. Cambridge, MA: Harvard University Press, 1986.

Wehler, Hans-Ulrich. *Der Aufstieg des amerikanischen Imperialismus*. Göttingen: Vandenhoeck und Ruprecht, 1974.

Weiller, Jean S. *Echanges et politique commerciale de la France*. Séries economies et societés, Cahiers de l'Institut de science économique appliquée, vol. 3. Geneva: Droz, 1969, pp. 1745–1878.

———. "Long-run Tendencies in Foreign Trade: With a Statistical Study of French Trade Structure, 1871–1939." *Journal of Economic History* 31 (Dec. 1971): 804–21.

Williams, William Appleman. *The Contours of American History*. Chicago: Quadrangle, 1961.

———. *The Tragedy of American Diplomacy*. New York: Dell, 1972.

Wolf, Eric R. *Europe and the People without History*. Berkeley: University of California Press, 1982.

Woodward, Ralph Lee, Jr. *Central America: A Nation Divided*. 2d ed. New York: Oxford University Press, 1985.

———. "Central America from Independence to c. 1870." *The Cambridge History of Latin America*. Ed. Leslie Bethell. 8 vols. Cambridge, Eng.: Cambridge University Press, 1982–93, 3: 471–506.

———. "Economic Development and Dependency in Nineteenth-Century Guatemala." *Crises in the Caribbean Basin*. Ed. Richard Tardanico. Newberry Park, CA: Sage, 1987, pp. 59–78.

———. "Pensamiento científico y desarrollo económico en Centroamérica, 1860–1920." *Revista del pensamiento centroamericano* 172–73 (July-Dec. 1981): 73–86.

———. "Political Economy in Guatemala." *University of Wichita Bulletin* 37 (Aug. 1962): 3–15.

———. *Rafael Carrera and the Emergence of the Republic of Guatemala, 1821–1871*. Athens: University of Georgia Press, 1993.

Zahniser, Marvin R. *Uncertain Friendship: American-French Diplomatic Relations through the Cold War*. New York: Wiley, 1975.

Zeledón Cambronero, Mario. "Un francés en Costa Rica, 1848–1856." *Revista de la Universidad de Costa Rica* 32 (Dec. 1971): 45–94.

Ziebura, Gilbert. "Interne Faktoren des französischen Hochimperialismus, 1871–1914." In *Der moderne Imperialismus*. Ed. Wolfgang Mommsen. Stuttgart: W. Kohlhammer, 1971, pp. 85–139.

Theses, Dissertations, and Unpublished Manuscripts

Blankenburg, Jürgen. "Der französische Kapitalexport und seine Rolle als Instrument der Außenpolitik." Ph.D. diss. Universität Köln, 1966.

Bresson, Claude. "L'Image économique de l'Amérique latine dans *L'Economiste français* devant la 1ère Guerre Mondiale, 1914–1918." Maîtrise. Université de Paris X (Nanterre), 1978.

Damble, Otto. "Die Wandlungen des französischen Außenhandels in der Nachkriegszeit." Ph.D. diss. Universität Köln, 1932.

Eusèbe, Christine. "Les Investissements français en Amérique centrale et dans l'aire des caraïbes." Maîtrise. Université de Paris X (Nanterre), 1972.

Gomez de León, Aristides Isaac. "Le Commerce international et le sous-développement de l'Amérique centrale." Ph.D. diss., 3e cycle. Université Pasteur de Strasbourg, 1978.

Göroll, Wolfgang. "Die Auseinandersetzung um Freihandel und Protektionismus im Frankreich des 19. Jahrhunderts (1815–1892)." Ph.D. diss. Universität Erlangen-Nürnberg, 1977.

Lanuza Matamoros, Alberto. "Estructuras socioeconómicas, poder y estado en Nicaragua (1821–1875)." Tesis de grado. Universidad de Costa Rica, 1976.

Lowrie, Walter Edward. "France, the United States, and the de Lesseps Panama Canal: Renewed Rivalry in the Western Hemisphere, 1879–1889." Ph.D. diss. Syracuse University, 1975.

Roses-Alvarado, Carlos. "Les Échanges commerciaux entre la France et l'Amérique centrale: 1850–1930." Ph.D. diss. Université de Paris III (Sorbonne Nouvelle), 1979.

Thompson, Stanley Joseph. "The Impact of the French 'Challenge' in the Isthmus of Panama on the United States' Expansionism in the Caribbean, 1867–1881." Ph.D. diss. American University, 1974.

Index

Latin American Silhouettes
Studies in History and Culture

William H. Beezley and
Judith Ewell
Editors

Volumes Published

Silvia Marina Arrom and Servando Ortoll, eds., *Riots in the Cities: Popular Politics and the Urban Poor in Latin America, 1765–1910* (1996). Cloth ISBN 0-8420-2580-4 Paper ISBN 0-8420-2581-2

Roderic Ai Camp, ed., *Polling for Democracy: Public Opinion and Political Liberalization in Mexico* (1996). ISBN 0-8420-2583-9

Brian Loveman and Thomas M. Davies, Jr., eds., *The Politics of Antipolitics: The Military in Latin America*, 3d ed., revised and updated (1996). Cloth ISBN 0-8420-2609-6 Paper ISBN 0-8420-2611-8

Joseph S. Tulchin, Andrés Serbín, and Rafael Hernández, eds., *Cuba and the Caribbean: Regional Issues and Trends in the Post-Cold War Era* (1997). ISBN 0-8420-2652-5

Thomas W. Walker, ed., *Nicaragua without Illusions: Regime Transition and Structural Adjustment in the 1990s* (1997). Cloth ISBN 0-8420-2578-2 Paper ISBN 0-8420-2579-0

Dianne Walta Hart, *Undocumented in L.A.: An Immigrant's Story* (1997). Cloth ISBN 0-8420-2648-7 Paper ISBN 0-8420-2649-5

Jaime E. Rodríguez O. and Kathryn Vincent, eds., *Myths, Misdeeds, and Misunderstandings: The Roots of Conflict in U.S.-Mexican Relations* (1997). ISBN 0-8420-2662-2

Jaime E. Rodríguez O. and Kathryn Vincent, eds., *Common Border, Uncommon Paths: Race, Culture, and National Identity in U.S.-Mexican Relations* (1997). ISBN 0-8420-2673-8

William H. Beezley and Judith Ewell, eds., *The Human Tradition in Modern Latin America* (1997). Cloth ISBN 0-8420-2612-6 Paper ISBN 0-8420-2613-4

Donald F. Stevens, ed., *Based on a True Story: Latin American History at the Movies* (1997). Cloth ISBN 0-8420-2582-0 Paper ISBN 0-8420-2781-5

Jaime E. Rodríguez O., ed., *The Origins of Mexican National Politics, 1808–1847* (1997). Paper ISBN 0-8420-2723-8

Che Guevara, *Guerrilla Warfare*, with revised and updated introduction and case studies by Brian Loveman and Thomas M. Davies, Jr., 3d ed. (1997). Cloth ISBN 0-8420-2677-0 Paper ISBN 0-8420-2678-9

Adrian A. Bantjes, *As If Jesus Walked on Earth: Cardenismo, Sonora, and the Mexican Revolution* (1998). ISBN 0-8420-2653-3

Henry A. Dietz and Gil Shidlo, eds., *Urban Elections in Democratic Latin America* (1998). Cloth ISBN 0-8420-2627-4 Paper ISBN 0-8420-2628-2

A. Kim Clark, *The Redemptive Work: Railway and Nation in Ecuador, 1895–1930* (1998). ISBN 0-8420-2674-6

Joseph S. Tulchin, ed., with Allison M. Garland, *Argentina: The Challenges of Modernization* (1998). ISBN 0-8420-2721-1

Louis A. Pérez, Jr., ed., *Impressions of Cuba in the Nineteenth Century: The Travel Diary of Joseph J. Dimock* (1998). Cloth ISBN 0-8420-2657-6 Paper ISBN 0-8420-2658-4

June E. Hahner, ed., *Women through Women's Eyes: Latin American Women in Nineteenth-Century Travel Accounts* (1998). Cloth ISBN 0-8420-2633-9 Paper ISBN 0-8420-2634-7

James P. Brennan, ed., *Peronism and Argentina* (1998). ISBN 0-8420-2706-8

John Mason Hart, ed., *Border Crossings: Mexican and Mexican-American Workers* (1998). Cloth ISBN 0-8420-2716-5 Paper ISBN 0-8420-2717-3

Brian Loveman, *For* la Patria: *Politics and the Armed Forces in Latin America* (1999). Cloth ISBN 0-8420-2772-6 Paper ISBN 0-8420-2773-4

Guy P. C. Thomson, with David G. LaFrance, *Patriotism, Politics, and Popular Liberalism in Nineteenth-Century Mexico: Juan Francisco Lucas and the Puebla Sierra* (1999). ISBN 0-8420-2683-5

Robert Woodmansee Herr, in collaboration with Richard Herr, *An American Family in the Mexican Revolution* (1999). ISBN 0-8420-2724-6

Juan Pedro Viqueira Albán, trans. Sonya Lipsett-Rivera and Sergio Rivera Ayala, *Propriety and Permissiveness in Bourbon Mexico* (1999). Cloth ISBN 0-8420-2466-2 Paper ISBN 0-8420-2467-0

Stephen R. Niblo, *Mexico in the 1940s: Modernity, Politics, and Corruption* (1999). ISBN 0-8420-2794-7

David E. Lorey, *The U.S.-Mexican Border in the Twentieth Century* (1999). Cloth ISBN 0-8420-2755-6 Paper ISBN 0-8420-2756-4

Joanne Hershfield and David R. Maciel, eds., *Mexico's Cinema: A Century of Films and Filmmakers* (2000). Cloth ISBN 0-8420-2681-9 Paper ISBN 0-8420-2682-7

Peter V. N. Henderson, *In the Absence of Don Porfirio: Francisco León de la Barra and the Mexican Revolution* (2000). ISBN 0-8420-2774-2

Mark T. Gilderhus, *The Second Century: U.S.-Latin American Relations since 1889* (2000). Cloth ISBN 0-8420-2413-1 Paper ISBN 0-8420-2414-X

Catherine Moses, *Real Life in Castro's Cuba* (2000). Cloth ISBN 0-8420-2836-6 Paper ISBN 0-8420-2837-4

K. Lynn Stoner, ed./comp., with Luis Hipólito Serrano Pérez, *Cuban and Cuban-American Women: An Annotated Bibliography* (2000). ISBN 0-8420-2643-6

Thomas D. Schoonover, *The French in Central America: Culture and Commerce, 1820–1930* (2000). ISBN 0-8420-2792-0